GENE VINCENT AND EDDIE COCHRAN

Rock'n'Roll Revolutionaries

GENE VINCENT
AND
EDDIE COCHRAN
Rock'n'Roll Revolutionaries

John Collis

First published in Great Britain in 2004 by
Virgin Books Ltd
Thames Wharf Studios
Rainville Road
London
W6 9HA

A catalogue record for this book is available from the British
Library.

ISBN 1 85227 193 0

Typeset by TW Typesetting, Plymouth, Devon
Printed and bound in Great Britain by CPD Wales

CONTENTS

ACKNOWLEDGEMENTS AND AUTHOR'S NOTES

At the core of this book is an attempt to build up the most complete account to date of the tour that put rock'n'roll on the map of Britain. I have drawn on accounts from musicians and others involved in the tour, members of the audiences around the country, local newspapers, the national press, pop weeklies and monthlies, fanzines, disc transcriptions and previously published work.

My biggest vote of thanks for the fact that the tour section contains 'live' material from every venue goes to Bill Beard, who together with fellow enthusiast Trevor Turner publishes a biannual newsletter, *The Eddie Cochran Connection*. This is effectively an ongoing research project, dependent on feedback, attempting to ferret out every available morsel of information about Cochran's tragically brief career, and hence of his involvement with Gene Vincent.

Bill kindly gave me permission to make use of material published in the newsletter, fleshing out the information gained from my own interviews and conversations, my days in the British Library and the Colindale Newspaper Library, and earlier writings. All sources are gratefully acknowledged elsewhere in the book. Thanks go in particular to all the fans who shared their memories, prompted by advertisements placed in local papers serving all the towns visited on the tour, by contacting the *Connection*.

In return, I recommend that anyone interested in rock'n'roll should contact Bill and subscribe to the *Connection*. Do it sooner rather than later – he is never sure how much more information will come to light. He can be contacted on email at bbillbeard@aol.com (yes, two 'b's at the start) or by post at 15 St Clements Court, Mardyke Park, Purfleet, Essex RM19 1GL.

Other references, gratefully acknowledged, include the pioneering research on Vincent's early career by Rob Finnis and Bob Dunham, Rob Finnis's detailed booklet to accompany the 1988 *Eddie Cochran Box Set*, Lenny Kaye's essay to the Cochran album in United Artists' Legendary Masters series, my own 1981 Eddie Cochran songbook for Wise Publications, the tour chapter of Spencer Leigh's *Baby, That Is Rock'n'roll*, Vincent biographies by the late Britt Hagarty and Susan Van Hecke, Steve Mandich's *Sweet Gene Vincent*, and recent books on Cochran by

Julie Mundy and Darrel Higham in the UK, and by Bobby Cochran and Susan Van Hecke in the US. Tony Barrett and Derek Glenister of Rockstar Records were also very helpful, as was Steve Aynsley, president of the Gene Vincent Fan Club.

I also made use of earlier research carried out by myself and theatre director John Turner for our musical *Race with the Devil: the Legend of Eddie Cochran and Gene Vincent*, a success on the London fringe that still awaits an 'angel' – before our Eddie and Gene get too old!

Vincent's English daughter Sherri was very helpful and sympathetic to the project, and kindly allowed me access to her files on her father. I am also most grateful to her mother Margie for granting me an interview. Gene's confidant Adrian Owlett and the 1960 tour manager Hal Carter were generous with their time and gave me many useful leads. Among the musicians who helped were Terry Clemson of the Hellraisers, Bill Kingston of the Wild Angels, Sounds Incorporated's Dick Thomas and Alan Holmes, Jeff Beck, Graham Fenton, Mel Wright, David John of David John and the Mood, Jim Whittle of the Puppets, and Vincent's original drummer Dickie Harrell. Thanks also to Roger St Pierre and David Lands. Adrian Owlett and Rob Finnis also kindly helped with picture identification.

The book also covers Vincent and Cochran's life and career up to their arrival in the UK, together with the story of Cochran's lasting legacy and of Vincent's last eleven years. Inevitably, given that many of the recollections published here are more than forty years after the event, there are sometimes conflicting accounts. In such cases I have presented both, or all, and wherever possible tried to unravel the truth or make an educated guess. However, it is perfectly possible for two people to have honest but different memories of the same incident. In the case of Gene Vincent, though, I regard him as one of the greatest of all rock'n'roll stars but a wholly unreliable witness!

John Collis, February 2004

INTRODUCTION

Eddie Cochran caught up with the Gene Vincent tour of the UK on 24 January 1960, at the Ipswich Granada. It was the first-ever tour in Britain to offer wall-to-wall pop music, billed by impresario Larry Parnes as 'A Fast Moving Beat Show'. Previous exotic visitors like Bill Haley, Buddy Holly and Jerry Lee Lewis had starred on variety bills with comics and crooners – or with Des O'Connor, who claimed to be both – but Vincent and Cochran were hardcore. Although the bill varied, particularly between one-night stands and week-long residencies, compere Billy Raymond introduced such artists as the Tony Sheridan Trio and Dean Webb, who featured on Jack Good's mould-breaking television show *Oh Boy!*, the 'new singing pianist' Georgie Fame and 'the new golden voice' of Peter Wynne.

The timing of the tour had a potent symbolism. It marked the end of the monochrome 1950s, as the nation slowly recovered from the privations of war, and it launched the Swinging Sixties. It educated the first generation of British rock'n'roll guitarists like Big Jim Sullivan and Joe Brown, it inspired the Beatles when they saw the show at the Liverpool Empire, and it was the spark that ignited the rock'n'roll revolution. This was the pivotal moment, as a drunken Vincent and Cochran thrashed around the country.

Rock'n'roll would always be an American music, based on strong folk roots in black R&B and white hillbilly with an essential added measure of hype, but Vincent and Cochran provided a living seminar to eager students in the UK. They planted an enthusiasm for unadorned rock music that survived its apparent demise as yet another fad – just as the records of Buddy Holly were hits in Britain when he was little more than a fading memory at home, the same would prove true of Cochran. And, in the last ten years of his often sad and chaotic life, Vincent even found words like 'chaps' slipping naturally into his language, as his Virginia drawl moved one step away from its homeland.

During the 1950s a new species, the teenager, evolved from a spongy, spotty, lower life form known to doctors as the adolescent, seen but rarely heard except when asking politely for a second helping at the family dinner table. The teenager was new because he or she was above all an economic animal, something not possible before as the effects of war lingered on, and by the end of the decade there were five million of us in Britain. It has been calculated, God knows how, that in 1959 we had £800 million to spend.

My share, if Christmas and birthday banknotes and postal orders were added to the weekly half-crown, was probably no more than £20, lamentably short of the fabulous £160 per head that the equation implies. But with seven-inch records at 6s. 8d. (you could buy three for a pound) and a front seat at the Gaiety in Station Road, Taunton, costing ninepence, a modest cultural life was possible.

Without the deadening responsibility of paying the mortgage and putting bread on the table, teenagers gave their money to the record companies, to the Gaumonts and the Odeons. The cyclical con trick of the fashion industry was yet to grease itself into action – jeans were jeans, shirts were shirts and pullovers were sensible. There were no computer games, and amusement arcades were found only at the seaside, where one could watch a papier-mâché execution for a penny. But the distinctive smell of warm plastic that arose from the valve-glowing record player in the corner of the room lured us towards rock'n'roll heaven.

Teenage eyes always gazed enviously across the Atlantic, where youthful access to cars was seemingly commonplace if Chuck Berry was to be believed and where, in the words of Willie Dixon and Muddy Waters, 'the blues had a baby and they called it rock and roll'. In those years before the Beatles, pop music, not just rock'n'roll, remained almost exclusively American. This was in spite of the fact that British artists like Marty Wilde would briskly cover American hits and, thanks to their availability for promotion, the bias of disc jockeys and geared-up distribution, would often enjoy hits that many fans thought were theirs alone. If we take 1959 and 1960 together, only seven British records were accorded million-selling status, however, and they do not make a groovy bunch.

Chris Barber and his Jazz Band, with clarinettist Monty Sunshine to the fore, revived Sidney Bechet's 1952 Parisian reverie, the haunting 'Petite Fleur'. Grinning pianist Russ Conway honky-tonked his way through 'Side Saddle'. The king of skiffle, Lonnie Donegan, abandoned his love affair with American folk-blues, the seed of British rock'n'roll, in favour of the fag end of music hall, with 'Does Your Chewing Gum Lose Its Flavour on the Bedpost Overnight?' and 'My Old Man's a Dustman'. Emile Ford turned to a ballad written in 1916 to ask 'What Do You Want To Make Those Eyes At Me For?', top of the charts at Christmas 1959 when Vincent arrived, Cliff Richard rejected the rock'n'roll verve of 'Move It' and 'High Class Baby' for the sing-along croon tune 'Living Doll', and children's television entertainer Rolf Harris arrived from Australia with the injunction 'Tie Me Kangaroo Down,

Sport'. Yes, Britain was ready for Vincent and Cochran. Desperate for them, indeed.

In fact, in 1960 American music was somewhat in the doldrums as well. Tin Pan Alley was regaining control from the rebellious rock'n'rollers, and as the new decade dawned Frankie Avalon – clean-living, polite and respectful to his seniors – was at the top of the American charts with a three-minute shot of sickly saccharine called 'Why', soon to be replaced by Mark Dinning's death ballad 'Teen Angel'. Dinning was an improvement in that at least his song was actually *accused* of being 'sick', but in truth it was almost as sugary.

There were admittedly some delightful one-offs – Johnny Preston's Big Bopper chant 'Running Bear', Marty Robbins creating a cowboy film in song with 'El Paso', the Hollywood Argyles drawling 'Alley-Oop' and a handful of raw hits from New Orleans – but unadulterated rock'n'roll had gone the way of bobbysox and hula hoops. 'I told you,' the cigar-chomping record moguls said, 'it was just a passing craze. Now let's get back to some *real* music.'

Gene Vincent had not had a hit of any kind since late 1957, when 'Dance to the Bop' just made the American Top 50, and it was 18 months since Cochran's 'Summertime Blues'. But in Britain no one told us we were meant to prefer Frankie Avalon. Or Fabian with his atrocious 'Hound Dog Man', or Bobby Rydell with 'Wild One', two titles that surely transgressed the Trades Descriptions Act. What next – Ken Dodd? Well, yes, actually – 'Love Is Like a Violin' was to make the Top 10 in the summer. What we renegade rockers desperately needed in the face of Radio Naff was some black-leather grease, some real heroes. Cue Gene and Eddie.

At its purest, rock'n'roll was always a synthesis of sound and image, equally weighted. Sun Records boss Sam Phillips may have thought that he had found the holy grail of mid-50s pop music with a white boy who sounded black, but without Elvis Presley's dangerous, heavy-lidded sexuality as well, the grail would have been severely tarnished.

Carl Perkins had two immense talents denied to Presley – as a jaw-droppingly nimble guitarist he laid down the blueprint for clean, incisive rockabilly picking, whereas Presley was no more than a half-decent strummer, and as a songwriter Perkins brought both wit and social observation to the music in a way perhaps only surpassed by Chuck Berry and Jerry Leiber, while Presley wrote nothing. Sure, he may have seemingly coauthored some of his songs, particularly when the actual writer was as black and hungry as Otis Blackwell, but of course the undeserved co-credit was just part of 'Colonel' Tom Parker's pension portfolio.

As a sixteen-year-old Eddie Cochran, with his country-and-western partner Hank Cochran (no relation), travelled to Memphis and happened upon a performance by Presley. This experience must have been the first step towards their friendly parting a year or so later. Cochran wanted everything that Presley seemed to represent – rock'n'roll flash, wild and urgent music, screaming girls. He noted the way that Presley moved, and how a twitch here or a pelvic thrust there cued the screams like turning on a tap. Hank, on the other hand, was a dyed-in-the-wool country purist, wanting none of this vulgarity.

His younger partner was soon to develop his own distinctive but Presley-inspired mannerisms – the piston motion of his guitar, the shaking shoulders, the cunning build-up of hysteria by starting his act in darkness, back to the audience. Cochran's stage persona was also clearly – and unusually for the time – influenced by the black artists he admired, notably Little Richard.

Cochran's appearance was a curious amalgam of blond god and boy next door, a combination that could hardly fail. Although we all know that the camera lies, particularly when taking passport pictures, photographs do seem to suggest that he found it difficult to control his weight, with the puppy-fat jaws and pimples of an 'ordinary' teenager in one shot, the clean, chiselled lines of James Dean in the next. But this simply added to the dynamic contrast between the platonic, slightly jowly schoolmate and the untouchable pop star. And when he wielded his guitar, it is clear that he needed no latter-day Sigmund Freud to point out the phallic symbolism of his Gretsch. He ground it at his hip in that trademark circular motion, imitating the motion of a steam train's wheels, but the girls in the audience did not immediately think of train spotting as they watched him.

If a genetic computer had taken the narcissistic, curled-lip beauty of teenage idol Ricky Nelson and blended it with Elvis Presley's unwholesome raunchiness, it would have invented Eddie Cochran. In appearance, then, he was the perfect pop star for the age, evoking healthy jealousy in boys, moistness in girls. But the former was no bar to his popularity among half the population because his prodigious skill on the guitar was defining masculinity on *behalf* of the boys in the audience, not creating a barrier between him and them. A star like Cochran sang *to* the girls but *for* the boys, and it was ever thus.

And just to cap this image made in heaven, he suddenly upped and went there. As has been pointed out many times – and Elvis is richer now than he ever was alive – premature death is a smart rock'n'roll career move. But when it takes away a pretty boy so cruelly young, before the booze that he enjoyed with such enthusiasm could give middle-aged permanence to that puppy fat, it also adds a perfect polish to the image. Suddenly Cochran shone as brightly as Buddy Holly, and was better looking with it.

And then there was Gene Vincent. Was ever sound and image so intriguingly blended? We are talking here, of course, partly of the image imposed on him by British pop producer and all-round genius Jack Good – except that to an extent Good was only tarting up what already existed. Vincent could be wild, debauched and destructive to himself and those around him. He could also be polite in the extreme, with a kind of resigned patience, and he spoke softly, like a real Southern gentleman. So far so good – or Good, who spotted the potential in Vincent's tortured contradictions.

For a start he had the purest, most beautiful voice in rock'n'roll. Listen to 'Over the Rainbow'. What would otherwise be remembered as a schmaltzy torch song oversold by Judy Garland, as subtle as a lump hammer, is revealed as an aching meditation on mortality. Vincent, his left leg screaming in pain as a lasting legacy of his 1955 motorcycle crash, lived that song every day.

And so we must add to the lovely voice the bruised body – the useless, clanking, stinking, suppurating leg, the big, wide eyes gazing beseechingly upwards. Pathetic? OK, so put him in black leather and massage him in lard so that his jet-black hair dangles greasily over his sweating forehead. Make him abuse the microphone – lean on it like a crutch, fellate it, kick it, strangle it, turn it upside down, swing it around as if to decapitate the guitarist. The Southern gentleman with the angelic voice becomes a devil. Pure rock'n'roll, pure sound and image. Gene and Eddie, ready to take on the staid old United Kingdom.

And it is there that their legend lives on, far more than in their home country – fanzines, projects like *The Eddie Cochran Connection*, musicals, biographies, reissues. Rock'n'roll was never seen as a passing craze in the UK; it was always clearly and rightly recognised as the bedrock of popular music, resistant to fashion. Everything that has happened in pop music since owes something to the collision of rhythm and blues and hillbilly that gave birth to the music of Elvis Presley, Carl Perkins, Buddy Holly, Gene Vincent and Eddie Cochran.

Rock'n'roll guitarist Terry Clemson sums it up like this: 'There has always been a rock'n'roll scene in Britain. In America they seemed to have no idea of how it shaped the music. Rock'n'roll to them could mean the Beach Boys – just another name for popular music. The real rock'n'roll only lasted for a couple of years over there, but here it has just carried on. If Gene Vincent hadn't come to the UK his career would have been dead by the early sixties. He'd have been a truck driver or something.' Or, somehow, he may have achieved his oft-expressed dream of becoming a farmer. His last years were not prestigious, and the gigs were, in Clemson's word, 'shabby'. But at least he kept on rocking.

1. THE MARCH OF THE TEDDY BOYS

For any form of social rebellion to take root in modern-day western society, even one as straightforward as drainpipe trousers, economic health seems to be a prerequisite. After all, those trousers have to be paid for. This health breeds complacency, which in turn encourages protest. In the United Kingdom, after the bombings, bereavements and upheavals of the Second World War, such a situation had developed by the mid-1950s. Post-war reconstruction was completed in 1954, and unemployment was at its lowest since the Industrial Revolution – apart from periods of war, of course, when alas there is work for everyone. It remained below 2% until the mid-1960s.

This brought about what came to be tagged 'the affluent society', indulging in unprecedented consumption. 'Most of our people have never had it so good,' boasted Prime Minister Harold Macmillan in 1957. Industrial production increased by 80% in the 20 years from 1950, and the economy was growing faster than at any time since those boom years of Victorian industrialisation. Thanks to the establishment of the welfare state under the post-war Labour government, in particular its central glory the National Health Service, the country was healthier than ever before, nurtured on free orange juice and foul-tasting but wholesome cod-liver oil.

Food, after the fourteen long years of rationing that continued until July 1954, was now more plentiful, varied and exotic. There were lemons, bananas, oranges. It was also cheaper, with the proportion of the household budget spent on food actually declining, in spite of the temptations of extra choice. It seems strange to recall that, in these pre-battery days of non-intensive farming, chicken was an Easter treat and beef was the regular Sunday staple – though an ingenious home economist would ensure that it did manage to reappear under various guises until midweek.

The growth areas absorbing the new money were private housing – owner-occupancy doubled in the two decades from 1950 – and leisure. In the 1950s television, with a second, commercial channel symbolising the new affluence when it was launched in September 1955, was steadily transformed from rare novelty into part of the furniture. The taking of holidays abroad quadrupled in twenty years, even though the era of the cheap package deal was yet to arrive. And more and more families enjoyed the ultimate symbol of domestic prosperity and freedom, the motorcar. At the end of the war there were 1.5 million in the UK. By 1960 the figure was 5.5 million, and this doubled in the following decade. Further education was taken up by increasing numbers of teenagers: there were 50,000 university students in 1939, more than double that figure by 1960, and double again by 1970.

A new moral climate developed in the 1950s as many old barriers and beliefs began to crumble. People were no longer willing to accept the rigidly imposed puritanical standards that had governed the nation since Victorian times. The sanctity of the monarchy, the church, the law and British imperial superiority were beginning to be questioned. On radio *The Goon Show*, running from 1952 until 1960, lampooned the Establishment, representing them as cowardly army officers, suave confidence tricksters and braindead Lords. This process continued triumphantly when *That Was The Week That Was* first appeared on BBC television in November 1962. This was a topical show of unprecedented irreverence, protected from protesting politicians by a liberal-minded director-general, Hugh Carlton-Greene. On the streets *Private Eye* magazine – little changed over the years – continued the mood of impertinent questioning, as did the ex-Footlights revue *Beyond the Fringe* on stage, in what came to be known as the 'satire boom'. *Fringe* performer Peter Cook, financial fairy godmother to *Private Eye*, opened the Establishment Club in Soho, its name defining its target rather than its audience.

The outmoded concept of an all-powerful British Empire finally died in the autumn of 1956, in humiliation. President Nasser of Egypt provocatively announced that he had nationalised the vital trade route of the Suez Canal, which linked the Mediterranean to the Red Sea and saved the long, expensive and often dangerous voyage around the Cape. In spite of huge opposition within the UK, Prime Minister Anthony Eden sent troops in support of an effort to seize back control of the canal. But in the face of disapproval and lack of support from both superpowers, the USA and the Soviet Union, the exercise was doomed, the troops withdrew and Eden, in failing health, resigned.

And so the conditions were ripe for protest – economic stability, moral questioning and a collapse of the proud assumption of national superiority. Added to this was the irritating fact that the old class system seemed to remain intact, even if the occasional duke was forced to allow the hoi polloi to trample over his gardens and his carpets in an attempt to make ends meet. The Establishment may have lost the automatic right to respect, and may have been forced to grapple with death duties, but it was still in power.

In 1956 John Osborne's play *Look Back in Anger* was first performed at the Royal Court Theatre, a radical alternative to the staid, evening-dressed West End. It was largely a vehicle for the leading character Jimmy Porter to sound off against that Establishment, and though much of it sounds today like an unfocused rant its effect was powerful at the time. It marked the rude arrival of 'kitchen sink drama', with Osborne as the first of the 'angry young men'. The actual sink appeared above all in the slice-of-life plays by East Ender Arnold Wesker such as *Chicken Soup with Barley* (1958), *Roots* (1959) and *The Kitchen* (1959).

The mysterious minimalist humour and coded blasphemy of Samuel Beckett's *Waiting for Godot* (first produced in English translation in 1955), the Goonish 'Theatre of the Absurd' exemplified by N.F. Simpson's *A Resounding Tinkle* (1957) and *One-Way Pendulum* (1959) together with Eugene Ionesco's *The Rhinoceros* (1960), and the strange comic menace of Harold Pinter's *The Birthday Party* (1957) added to the heady sense of creative liberation. Perhaps their inscrutability was all that saved these subversive pioneers from the easily offended eye and twitching blue pencil of Her Majesty's theatrical censor, the Lord Chamberlain. Whatever, drama no longer took place exclusively in the middle-class drawing room so waspishly observed by Noel Coward and Terence Rattigan.

Novels like John Wain's *Hurry On Down* (1953), Kingsley Amis's *Lucky Jim* (1954), Iris Murdoch's *Under the Net* (1954), and John Braine's *Room at the Top* (1957) shared the youthful anger, if often conveyed with humour. It is ironic that Osborne, Amis and Braine moved steadily to the right in their political and social beliefs, finishing up as angry *old* men, never to be satisfied. But in their youth they spoke to a new, liberated generation, questioning authority, seeking a moral and intellectual freedom that formerly was simply not available outside the Bohemian other-world of Soho, which had always behaved just as it wished.

In November 1960, following a prosecution under the spanking new Obscene Publications Act, D.H. Lawrence's 1928 last novel *Lady Chatterley's Lover*, originally printed privately in Florence but outlawed in its unexpurgated version in the UK, was deemed to be not obscene on the grounds of overriding literary merit. Penguin's 3s. 6d. edition was soon being thumbed beneath every school desk, and we learned about a rather unusual approach to flower arranging as well as gazing at words in sober print that had previously been restricted to the walls of public lavatories at the rougher end of town.

The Campaign for Nuclear Disarmament, provoked by guilt at the awful effects of the atom bombs on Japan, and stimulated by the continuing fear of a nuclear winter as the Cold War lingered on, reached its peak in 1960. This unlikely alliance of left-wing activists, radical churchmen and free thinkers like crusty philosopher Bertrand Russell was the most significant crusade since so many of the previous generation had travelled to Spain to confront fascism. The World War that separated these two movements was a compulsory national effort, whereas these were exercises of individual moral conviction, appealing in particular to the young.

And now that the concept of the teenager was economically viable, gang culture arrived in 1953 with the rise of the teddy boys. Originating in working-class south London, the Teds chose a style of dress that was a deliberate caricature of that worn by Edwardian dandies – drainpipe trousers, long 'drape' jackets and embroidered waistcoats, to which were added western-style bootlace neckties and suede shoes with thick rubber soles, 'brothel creepers'. The new fad for hissing, clattering coffee bars gave the Teds their natural home, while the jukebox supplied the soundtrack.

In 1955 the film *Blackboard Jungle* was released and Bill Haley's crisp syncopation 'Rock Around the Clock', initially put out unsuccessfully as a B side a year earlier, was used behind the credits. The Teds were in their element, jiving in the aisles and in some cases attacking the seats. In February 1957 Haley and his Comets became the first rock'n'roll artists to tour Britain, and the Teds came out in force to greet his ship at Southampton Docks, to join the train that steamed triumphantly into Victoria Station and to block the pavements outside every concert venue.

A year later Jerry Lee Lewis arrived and left abruptly, his proposed six-week tour cancelled after three dates. He was harried out of the country by a press outraged that his third wife Myra was his thirteen-year-old cousin. 'Don't know what all the fuss was about,' said Lewis later. 'Hell, everyone knew she was only twelve.' Former fan Joyce Stevens said outside the stage door of the Tooting Granada: 'It's disgusting. He's finished as far as I'm concerned.' Her friend Barbara Morden agreed. 'We don't like him now . . . One of my friends has even smashed all the records she had of him.' Buddy Holly fared far better on his 1958 tour and, though he was still billed as a variety act, he and his band the Crickets were the noisiest, most exciting thing we had ever heard.

From the Teds to mods and rockers, to hippies and skinheads, and on to the punk rockers of the late 1970s, youth culture continued to spawn rebellious peer groups until the 1980s, when greed was installed as the national religion by Margaret Thatcher and unemployment soared. There was now no time nor inclination among the winners to join a tribe, since Thatcherism was based on the grasping individual rather than the collective good, and there was nothing left for the losers but drugs and despair. But in a more innocent age, in the years before Gene Vincent and Eddie Cochran arrived, the Teds laid the foundation for rock'n'roll culture.

To put our heroes into context, we need to consider what else the world was up to in 1960. It was a year of upheaval in Africa, a time when the death sentence was finally passed on colonialism. Prime Minister Macmillan, although a High Tory of the old school, offended his racist hosts when he addressed the South African government in Cape Town on 20 January. In a memorable and prophetic speech he observed: 'The wind of change is blowing through this continent and, whether we like it or not, this growth of national consciousness is a political fact.'

Macmillan advocated moves towards greater racial equality, advice that naturally went unheeded in bull-necked Afrikaner circles. His philosophy may not have been entirely altruistic – he saw that change, sooner or later, would be inevitable, but could not be sure whether the emerging black independent states would turn towards the West or to Soviet Russia. He recognised the need to woo them.

The process had begun in 1952 when in the British colony of Kenya the Mau Mau movement, members of the Kikuyu tribe, rose up against the white landowners. British troops were sent to Nairobi as the violence got worse, but reforms put hastily into place to improve the lot of the indigenous population were too late to halt the inevitable. In 1957 Ghana, a new nation created from two former British colonies, the Gold Coast and British Togoland, achieved independence under Prime Minister Kwame Nkrumah. 'Our task is not done until the last vestiges of colonialism have been swept from Africa,' proclaimed Nkrumah.

Just how perceptive Macmillan's acceptance of necessary change turned out to be was soon demonstrated. On the day of his South African speech a conference began in Brussels with the aim of moving the Belgian Congo towards independence. Elections were held on 11 May 1960 and Patrice Lumumba became prime minister, though without an outright majority. On 14 July the Katanga province, led by Moise Tshombe, declared its own independence from Lumumba's government, and so a day later United Nations troops moved in to secure the capital Leopoldville. Two months later Lumumba was deposed and imprisoned by troops led by Joseph Mobutu. He escaped and sought UN protection, which was refused. In desperation Lumumba went on the run but was captured, tortured and executed by Mobutu's men. African independence had made a bloody start, and more than four decades later blood is still being spilled.

On 21 February 1960, in London, agreement was reached at last on the parliamentary system that would lead to black majority rule in Kenya, and on 1 April the 'dangerous agitator' Dr Hastings Banda was released from prison. Independence for Sierra Leone was agreed, followed by British Somaliland and Nigeria.

Meanwhile France was shedding its African possessions like confetti – Madagascar, Niger, Dahomey, Ivory Coast, Upper Volta, Chad, the Central African Republic, Congo-Brazzaville and Mauritania. Algeria, where guerrillas had been fighting for independence since 1954, proved a more intractable problem, as French settlers there rose in revolt against President Charles De Gaulle's proposals for self-determination. Terrorists on both sides, Christian and Muslim, took their toll and when, in December 1960, De Gaulle visited the country, he somehow survived four assassination attempts. The police reaction cost 123 lives, mostly Muslim. At last, in January 1961, a French public tired of the violence gave majority approval in a referendum to independence for France's troublesome African neighbour.

In the face of this 'wind of change', the whites in southern Africa dug in their heels. Rhodesia gave the police even greater powers to stifle dissent, and they were enthusiastically employed. And in South Africa, on 21 March 1960, came the darkest day of all, the Sharpeville massacre. In this black township in Transvaal a campaign of civil disobedience in protest at the hated pass laws, which required blacks to carry identity cards in designated 'white' areas, gathered force, and many ignored their leaders' appeals for peaceful demonstrations.

A crowd of 15,000, boisterous but not violent, made their way to the police station in Sharpeville, where they were confronted by a rank of 75 armed officers. Stones were thrown, the crowd surged forward, and the police opened fire indiscriminately. The scene was soon like a First World War battlefield, with 56 bodies lying where they fell, and 162 injured, many of whom later died of their wounds.. A later enquiry established that 70% of the dead were shot in the back, fleeing the guns. 'If they do these things they must learn their lesson the hard way,' sneered unrepentant police chief Colonel D.H. Pienaar. A state of emergency was declared on 30 March.

Two weeks after Sharpeville Africans protested against apartheid in a township outside Durban. Police opened fire and one protestor died. The mob then headed for the city and three more died. In the township of Nyanga outside Cape Town an African policeman was hacked to death. The area was cordoned off, and an African woman asked for permission to drive through to take her sick child to hospital. She was refused, and as her car reversed a soldier fired, killing the baby.

Two days later, on 9 April, South African Prime Minister Dr Hendrik Verwoerd gave a speech at Johannesburg Agricultural Show. A 52-year-old white farmer, David Pratt, stepped forward as Verwoerd completed his speech and fired two shots from a .22 pistol, injuring Verwoerd.

Meanwhile neo-Fascist supporters of Sir Oswald Mosley attacked an anti-apartheid rally in London, and in America there were violent reactions to black and white integration. Following the desegregation in 1957 of Little Rock Central High School in Arkansas, when the National Guard had to escort black children through an angry white barricade, a bomb was now detonated at the home of one of the first black pupils to attend. In April there was a riot when blacks gathered on a segregated beach in Mississippi, and ten were shot. Martin Luther King was arrested in February on a trumped-up charge of perjury in relation to income tax affairs, only to be acquitted in May. In early 1960 the world was changing slowly, but white racists in Africa, America and Britain were not going to give up without a fight. Meanwhile, to the eternal glory of rock'n'roll, the late Buddy Holly had formed a deep and genuine friendship with Little Richard, and now Eddie Cochran was promoting the work of the little-known Ray Charles.

At the outset of the year the tension between the United States and Russia was increasing, and on 1 May it reached dangerous levels when an American spy plane, a Lockheed U-2, was shot down by a ground-to-air missile while pilot Gary Powers was taking photographs of Russian military installations. Powers was captured unhurt and Soviet president Nikita Khrushchev, seizing the propaganda moment, demanded an apology from Washington. This coincided with a scheduled summit meeting in Paris, due to be attended both by Khrushchev and his American counterpart, Dwight D. Eisenhower.

America initially denied that Powers was on a spying mission, claiming that he had simply lost his way. This was easily refuted by the Russians, who produced cameras, photographs and maps salvaged from the wreckage of the U-2. Eisenhower would still not apologise, however, citing the number of Russian spies known to be active, and the summit conference collapsed. Powers was tried in August, sentenced to ten years imprisonment, and released after two years in exchange for a Russian spy.

Eisenhower moved on to a ticker-tape welcome in Rio de Janeiro, part of the USA's strategy of improving links with South America as a bulwark against communism. Khrushchev, meanwhile, returned to France on an official state visit, and was presented with a live pig, which he graciously accepted. Relations between the UK and Russia thawed when a twice-weekly Comet service was inaugurated between London and Moscow. In November the Democratic candidate, John F. Kennedy, was elected to the White House, where he inherited Eisenhower's Cold War problems.

On 1 March the city of Agadir in Morocco was flattened in seconds, destroyed by an earthquake and the subsequent tidal wave and fires. It was reckoned to be the worst natural disaster of modern times. Once 2,000 bodies had been dug from the rubble and an estimated 3,000 remained buried, the entire city was bulldozed and sealed off to prevent the spread of disease. On 25 April the town of Lar in Iran was similarly devastated by earthquake.

With their relationship with Russia under such strain, and feeling newly threatened by 1959's revolution in Cuba when guerrilla troops led by Fidel Castro removed the government of the dictator General Batista, the US put on a symbolic show of strength. Off the Florida coast, the nearest point to Cuba, the submarine *Washington* fired two Polaris missiles, which found their practice targets 1,100 miles away in the ocean.

In September, though, Castro was in New York for talks, but any hope of accommodation between the government of the United States and Castro's communist revolutionaries was to be finally destroyed in the following April, when the CIA bungled an attempt to foment a right-wing coup in Cuba. Anti-Castro exiles were landed at the Bay of Pigs on the island but Castro's troops were ready for them, presumably as a result of leaky security. Eighteen months further on and the world came the closest it has ever been to nuclear war, when American reconnaissance activity confirmed that Russian missiles had been supplied to Cuba. After a tense period of brinkmanship, including an American naval blockade of Cuban supply lines, Khrushchev agreed to remove the weapons.

In 1960 there were two nuclear-age landmarks in Britain: in June the Windscale (now Sellafield) nuclear reactor came on stream, and in October the Queen visited the shipyard at Barrow-in-Furness to launch the UK's first nuclear-powered submarine, the *Dreadnought*, named after the first British battleship of the modern era.

Although Africa's wind of change, Cold War posturing and Jack Kennedy's presidential campaign dominated world news in 1960, there were lighter items in the news. Doctor Martens boots, claiming to bring a 'walking on air' sensation to the working man, arrived in the UK, Princess Margaret married Antony Armstrong-Jones in Westminster Abbey, while Tommy Steele arrived at St Patrick's in Soho Square for his own wedding. A Bolton couple won £100 in the Rock'n'roll Championships of Great Britain at the Lyceum Ballroom in the Strand and a Hull carpenter, Stanley Wilson, did rather better. His penny stake on the football pools netted him £100,000.

Traffic wardens took to the streets of London to 'assist' motorists with their parking problems and Elvis Presley – his hair already restored to civilian luxuriance – left Frankfurt after seventeen months in the service of Uncle Sam, stopping off briefly at Prestwick Airport near Glasgow while his plane refuelled. On his arrival on American soil a breathless press corps wanted to know if being in the army had changed his mind about rock'n'roll. After a moment's thought Elvis replied: 'No, it's not. I was in tanks for a long time and they rock and roll quite a bit.'

Britain's women tennis players regained the Wightman Cup from America, seemingly in slow motion on the evidence of newsreel footage, and on the salt flats of Bonneville, Utah, Donald Campbell climbed unhurt from the wreckage of his 40-ton, £1 million car Bluebird, capsized by a side wind during his attempt on the world land-speed record. He was within the measured mile of the course, accelerating towards success, when the accident happened, and owed his life to his safety belt.

Although the Derby was filmed in Technicolor for the first time in 1960 (Lester Piggott triumphant) most of these events, both world-threatening and trivial, were reflections of a monochrome world. Buildings, cars, films and clothes were in muted tones. But to the Teds, living rock'n'roll colour had already arrived in the shape of Gene Vincent and Eddie Cochran.

2. ON THE ROAD

At the time of Gene Vincent's arrival in the UK for his first tour, the British music industry was in one of its periodic agonies over alleged corrupt practices. On 28 November 1959 the *Melody Maker* led with 'Payola Probe Sensation: Split in Tin Pan Alley', reflecting questions that had been raised in the national press and had even reached the floor of the House of Commons. But hard facts were thin on the ground, merely musings as to whether 'deejays, music publishers and record A&R managers were involved in an American-styled "payola scandal" concerning plug-money payments and record-pushing rackets'. Surely not. It was also suggested that it was unfair that artists and recording managers should have interests in publishing, since inevitably they would favour material they had a financial interest in, regardless of quality.

There was logic in this. In America the disc jockey and all-powerful television presenter Dick Clark emerged from the payola investigation smelling of roses, in spite of extensive publishing interests involving artists he ceaselessly plugged on *American Bandstand*.

Disc jockey Pete Murray reacted haughtily to the controversy. 'I have been offered a bribe only once,' he said loftily. 'A character in a club offered me ten pounds to plug an American singer he was interested in. I told him what he could do with his money.' And the producer of *Juke Box Jury*, Russell Turner, claimed that 'you get so that you can brush off an approach before it has even been made'.

The controversy rumbled on as the tour proceeded around the country. On 16 April 1960 – a fateful day for rock'n'roll as Vincent and Cochran took to the stage together for the last time in Bristol – the *MM*'s parliamentary correspondent, Reg Robinson (holder of a post most readers were no doubt unaware of until then), wrote: 'Disc jockeys emerged victorious in the House of Commons last week despite a slashing payola attack on them by Mr Roy Mason, Labour MP for Barnsley. All his allegations were shot down by Postmaster General Reginald Bevin, who spoke of disc jockeys as "men of honour".' With this bizarre endorsement the matter slid from the headlines.

Meanwhile, plans had been announced for a VIP dawn greeting to be laid on when Vincent's plane landed at London Airport North on Saturday 5 December 1959. At this stage he was principally flying in to star on Jack Good's ABC-TV show *Boy Meets Girls* on 12, 19 and 26

December, a visit coinciding with the release of his latest single 'Wild Cat', coupled with 'Right Here On Earth', and he was to be met by the show's residents Marty Wilde and the Vernons Girls. 'Other TV and possible concert dates were being lined up at press time,' said the *MM*. Rival *New Musical Express* added the detail that Vincent would also be entertaining American servicemen in Germany over Christmas – the second and third *Boy Meets Girls* appearances would be tele-recorded.

The *NME* writer Ifor Griffiths pointed out that, unlike other recent visitors such as Jerry Keller and the Browns, Vincent had not had a hit for about three years – accurate indeed, with 'Bluejean Bop' in autumn 1956 his most recent UK success. But reference was made to his loyal following, and while the tour did revive his chart career in Britain this would remain true for the rest of his career – Vincent became the first artist of the rock'n'roll generation to transcend the need for a current hit, although naturally his appeal dwindled among those influenced only by the latest chart heart-throbs. Among true rockers, his charismatic image remained potent until his death. As he arrived *Disc* went to town with a front-page story greeting 'The Rock'n'roll Idol of Millions'.

Griffiths was more analytical. 'His powerful rocking style has a pronounced country-and-western flavour to it,' he said, 'no doubt due to Gene's interest in folk music during his youth. When he was a mere twelve-year-old, he used to delight in listening to the Negro folk songs he heard on visits to a Virginia backwoods store.' Vincent was said to own a farm in California ready for his eventual retirement from the music business – over the years, the location of this fantasy farm was to vary.

In 1959 he said: 'I intend to settle down one of these days and farm . . . after all, this business cannot go on the way it is for ever . . . Just outside of Norfolk I bought me some acres, and one of these days I intend to start a farm going.'

A week before he was due to arrive, a single concert date was confirmed for 6 December, when he would be guest star on *The Marty Wilde Show*, featuring various artists from the 'stable' of management impresario Larry Parnes, at the Granada, Tooting, and he was also booked for an interview on Brian Mathews' *Saturday Club* on the Light Programme. Tooting was where Jerry Lee Lewis's tour had been abruptly aborted. At the time that the concert date was announced, incidentally, a feature headline in the *Melody Maker* screamed: ' "Biscuits? I Dunk Them!" says hit singer Adam Faith.' Gritty, no-holds-barred stuff.

As Vincent's plane crossed Ireland a huge reception committee assembled in the arrivals building at the airport. His record company had been active in papering the house, laying on buses to take fans from central London to greet him, and alerting the press to this 'spontaneous' demonstration of support. Meanwhile *Boy Meets Girls* was represented not just by Wilde and backing group the Vernons Girls as announced, but by Good himself and Italian rocker Little Tony. At Jack Good's suggestion Joe Brown and his band were also there and had set up their equipment in the corner, desperately trying to keep their fingers warm and supple in the dark December chill. Brown and the band, the Firing Squad, said the *NME*, would later be rehearsing with Vincent for his Tooting date.

In 1998 Brown recalled his first impressions of Vincent. 'We went down to Heathrow and played him off the plane . . . We were a little bit in awe of him . . . He was very, very polite, called everybody sir, but he had this glint in his eye . . . He was a bit of a strange bloke but we put this down to artistic temperament, really.' Brown later observed: 'He had this great presence on stage, and he looked ominous . . . He had this evil eye he used to fix on you.'

Vincent came in off the tarmac to be greeted with 'Be Bop a Lula', and of course was moved and delighted by the reception. Among the fans present was Alan Vince. 'When I first came face to face with Gene . . . I couldn't have been more thrilled or excited had it been Elvis Presley. In fact I doubt if Elvis could have meant as much to us all . . . Gene must have been tired but he still managed to keep smiling and sign autographs.'

There was a busy day ahead – a live appearance on *Saturday Club*, a recorded interview for Radio Luxembourg with disc jockey Ray Orchard, who followed Vincent around and taped more snippets for his Friday-night *Capitol Show*, and a press reception held by EMI at the New Bagatelle Club in Mayfair. As the day wore on, Jack Good became more and more worried. 'Oh dear, this won't do,' he thought. The wild man of rock, the banned orgasmic moaner of 'Woman Love', turned out to be a polite, softly spoken man in a sensible winter jacket. And his years of living with disability had taught him almost to mask his limp. Good realised that he had some image work to do.

He later reflected on the problem, and his inspired solution. 'He was a quiet, thin, wan fellow in a baseball jacket, and he said, "Hello, sir, I am very happy and proud to make your acquaintance." . . . I was deeply disturbed and I wondered what we were going to do. I thought he was going to be a dagger boy, the rock'n'roll screaming end . . . I had to fix him.'

Good noticed the leg iron and the slight hobble. 'I was a Shakespeare fan, so hobbling to me meant Richard III. I even thought of giving him a hunchback! . . . Then I thought, "He can be moody like Hamlet." I once played a murderer, Lightbourne, with gloves on . . . so I added that. I arranged for some steps so he could hobble nicely on TV, but he negotiated them very well and hardly looked as if he was hobbling at all. I had to yell out, "Limp, you bugger, limp!" He didn't mind, he limped.' The leather-clad biker image was perfected by mid-January.

However, Joe Brown may have had a hand in giving Good the idea. 'I wore [black leather] all the time because I had a motorbike. Jack could possibly have got the idea from me. I don't lay claim to it, but I've got a feeling it was . . . As if you needed to make Gene Vincent look more sinister than he was!'

And so, after some jet-lagged sleep, it was on to the Tooting Granada the night after his arrival, as guest star attraction on Marty Wilde's show. Also on the bill were Terry Dene, Vince Eager, Dickie Pride and Johnny Gentle. Vincent's inclusion had guaranteed a full house, noisy in their adulation. After an uncertain start to the evening thanks to a reluctant microphone, Vincent turned in a manic, acrobatic, sweaty and fevered set, proof indeed that with Jerry Lee off the scene, at least for the time being, he was the most dynamic performer in rock'n'roll.

'That was some welcome,' he said in his dressing room after the show. He diplomatically did not refer to the failed microphone, claiming instead that he left the stage briefly after a couple of numbers because 'I just wanted to get off stage for a while, that's all.' Joe Brown remembers his first backstage meeting with Vincent after the Heathrow greeting. 'I backed him at the Granada, Tooting. He was a strange man. The first time I saw him he was drunk in a corner with a gun in his hand.'

The triumphant Tooting date was roundly panned by the *MM*'s waspish Norman Heath. 'Gene Vincent, the lesser Presley from Norfolk, Virginia,' he sneered, 'might just as well have stayed at home, judging by his appearance in "The Marty Wilde Show" . . . Admittedly, he was no worse than most of the home-grown rock products – but he was certainly no better. In fact, all he could boast over our boys was a *genuine* American accent. Marty Wilde clicked, but his talents are worthy of a much more sophisticated type of entertainment. Of the rest . . . only Terry Dene impressed. He, too, can look forward to better things.' Oh no he couldn't.

All Vincent fans will admit that he could have off nights, to say the least, but this surely wasn't one of them, in spite of a halting start. The review is a reminder that in those days even the pop press often perversely seemed to send rock-hating reviewers to gigs. Indeed, the

Melody Maker of the day had a weekly column by Steve Race, whose invariable theme was 'isn't pop music awful?' The rock-haters would prove even more common among local paper journalists assigned to review the joint Vincent-Cochran tour. As for Mr Heath's predictions for Terry Dene – in April, just four months later, he was interviewed under the headline 'When a Rock Star Hits the Skids'.

This followed a messy divorce from fellow singer Edna Savage and a tearful dismissal from army conscription following what appeared to be a nervous breakdown. 'There were parties and late nights; there was booze and flattery,' confessed Dene contritely, neatly summarising the *attractions* of the rock'n'roll lifestyle. He was busy planning a comeback after his extraordinarily brief flirtation with fame but it was not to be. Dene found God and went off to bang a tambourine, although for a while he did revive his rock'n'roll career in the 1980s. Indeed, a fanzine review of a holiday-camp rock'n'roll weekend in 1990 starring Buddy Knox compliments Dene, now playing with his backing band the Rapiers, on a 'brilliant set' that began with an Elvis medley and encored with 'Rip It Up'.

Jack Good, unashamedly using his column in *Disc and Music Echo* to promote Vincent, provided a critical counterweight to the underwhelmed Norman Heath, when reviewing the second house at Tooting. 'He looked scared, and his mouth twitched nervously when he discovered that his mike was not working. He found another that was. There was a slight embarrassed pause, then quite unexpectedly he swung his iron-braced left leg right over the mike, spun round a complete 360 degrees and tore into "Be Bop a Lula". The effect was electrifying. A Jekyll and Hyde story come true. The nervous, silent, bewildered Texan [sic] was suddenly transformed into a crouching wildcat.'

Although Good was carefully using his print outlet to build the image of Vincent already forming in his television-producer's mind, he can be forgiven the clear abuse of Her Majesty's fourth estate. Good was an enthusiast, an evangelist, and a far better writer than the jaded, disapproving, Tin Pan Alley bald-heads and the breathless, junior PR gushers who between them filled most of the pop press. It should be remembered that Vincent only worked for this pop Svengali on a handful of occasions – the impresario to benefit most from the iconic image was tour promoter Larry Parnes, who probably found Vincent's appearance just a little vulgar.

'He spins, throws and catches the mike, and swings his leg over it in a single short burst of movement,' enthused Good. 'Then, like a crouching tiger awaiting its prey, he will be stock still for minutes on end.' Good also rubbishes the dismissive notion that a rockabilly singer like Vincent is merely a 'figment of the electronic imagination', overdependent on echo and other technical trickery. He asserts that Vincent's wonderful voice was all his own, more than a match for dodgy sound systems. Good records that Vincent was allowed just five numbers, far too few for an enraptured and demanding crowd.

Marty Wilde harboured bad memories of the gig. 'Gene and I didn't get off to a good start because I had the misfortune to appear with him on his first British gig. For some stupid reason, Larry Parnes wanted me to top the bill ... that was a crazy thing to do ... [Afterwards] I thought, "I hope that never happens to me again."' He later said on Radio 2: 'He absolutely tore them apart. It was bedlam.'

Of course the gig had already been booked and advertised as *The Marty Wilde Show*, with Vincent as a late added attraction, but the bill-topper was clearly and humbly aware of the foolhardiness of trying to top Vincent on his eagerly awaited British debut, and recalls that it took him about five minutes to get into his stride and win over the audience.

David Lands, now a writer on *Jazz Journal*, was in the crowd that night. 'I'd been delighted to see Gene Vincent's name plastered diagonally across the poster – I wasn't that keen on UK rock'n'roll. He came on in the second half and my abiding memory of his appearance was his baggy black trousers. It was quite a shock to see an American rocker wearing what I now understand to be peg-legged slacks, because all of *our* rockers, the teddy boys, were still in drainpipes. The moment he came on stage there was an uproar. I thought Gene looked very unsure of himself, but as he worked his way through songs that were familiar to the fans he began to relax.

'Then he sang "W-e-e-ll ..." and it all came together. Nothing more could be heard from him. The cheers and screams drowned everything and when he swung his leg over the microphone the rest of the performers might as well have gone home. I left the show feeling shattered. I'd seen my first rock'n'roll hero and although at times he looked fragile and uncertain he rocked like no one else I'd ever seen.'

Fortunately for Vincent, the *MM* was kinder to the new single 'Wild Cat' than it had been about his Tooting gig. It was 'a mid-tempo rocker ... put across with Gene's customary dedicated fervour. A natural for the jukebox trade.' Buoyed up by his personal appearances the record reached No. 21 in January, faded and then made a reappearance at No. 39 in March.

On the day after the Tooting show Vincent began rehearsals in London for his *Boy Meets Girls* appearances, which lasted three days.

This confirms that Good was meticulous about mounting the best possible show. On 10 December Vincent travelled to Manchester to the ABC Studios in Didsbury to continue rehearsals, and on the following day the final run-through was held. Then, on 12 December, came the first appearance.

In the Boxing Day edition of *MM*, coinciding with his third *Boy Meets Girls* appearance, Vincent revealed that he had decided to stay in the UK until October. 'I have found that there is tremendous scope in Britain for concert work and TV,' he enthused. There was a reason for this. Larry Parnes had now signed him to a 30-week deal, and the legendary tour began to take shape. The plan was for five weeks in Variety (accorded the dignity of a capital 'V' in those days), a tour of one-night stands 'with a beat package' and a summer season at either Blackpool or Great Yarmouth. 'Gene will give the kids stacks of entertainment,' promised Parnes. 'As Marty Wilde's appearances will be limited next year I needed someone really big to head my beat shows. And for my money there is no one better than Vincent.' In fact, when the tour took to the road it was clear that the distinction between 'Variety' and one-nighters had been eliminated – there were cast changes, but no jugglers or comics, just vocalists and musicians, and rock'n'roll far outweighed more conventional balladeering.

Wilde explained the reason for his unavailability. 'I was going into the West End musical *Bye Bye Birdie* and as I had no work for the Wildcats, Larry Parnes suggested that Eddie Cochran used my band . . . they were delighted. Cochran was Big Jim Sullivan's idol and it showed in his playing – just listen to "Trambone" by the Krew-Kats [a Top 50 instrumental hit in 1961, with Sullivan on guitar].'

And so when he negotiated Wilde's big West End break – as with Tommy Steele, an essential stepping stone in the career-insurance transition from pop star to 'all-round entertainer' – the idea of augmenting the show with Cochran as well as Vincent was already taking shape, consciously or not.

On his three *Boy Meets Girls* appearances Vincent was backed by Joe Brown and the Firing Squad, each time singing 'Be Bop a Lula' and 'Summertime' but also performing 'Baby Blue', 'Frankie and Johnnie', 'Bluejean Bop', 'Say Mama', 'Five Days, Five Days', 'I Got a Baby', 'Rocky Road Blues', 'Right Here on Earth' and 'Wild Cat'. 'I was very impressed with the British group I have backing me on the shows,' he said. 'What a bunch of musicians they are. That Joe Brown is a fabulous guitarist . . . Anything you put before them they'll play, and play well.' Vincent taped his second and third slots, and after a jam session with Cliff

Richard and the Shadows he left for France, where he appeared at the Olympia in Paris, and thence to Frankfurt for a tour of American army bases in Germany.

By this time a young Liverpudlian called Hal Carter was on Parnes's payroll. 'I started as a band boy. I'd go out on tour with the boys, put their gear on stage, run errands for them, get their fish and chips, cigarettes, whatever. I had done Larry a favour, which led to him offering me a job. Marty Wilde needed to get into this theatre in Liverpool but there were screaming fans everywhere. I got Marty in OK, and Larry remembered that.

'Then he called me in and said he'd had a call from Marty saying he wanted me to travel with him as his roadie. Larry asked me my proper name and I told him "Hal Carter-Burrows". He said, "I can't be arsed with all that. I'll call you Hal Carter." So he didn't just name his artists, he even named me! He was right – it's easy to remember and so it's helped me in my own business over the years. I used to get sacked three times a week and I used to fight with him but I learned it all from him.

'Originally Larry had booked Gene Vincent from [agent] Norm Riley to do a tour of the UK,' explains Carter. 'And then he got cold feet a bit and began to worry that Gene wouldn't be enough as a headliner, because we were starting to do mainly weeks, not just one-nighters. He thought that to pull that kind of audience, night after night, with his lads – Dickie [Pride], Billy [Fury], Joe [Brown], people like that – it wouldn't be enough. He talked to Norm, who suggested Eddie Cochran. We knew him from "Twenty Flight Rock". It wasn't actually a hit but it was a very popular record over here. The deal was next to nothing, a few hundred dollars a week.' One report suggests that as his reputation during the tour grew, so did Cochran's wage, to $1,000 a week, and in a newspaper account of his death this was trebled to £1,000.

By this time Parnes had assigned Carter to Billy Fury. 'Basically my job was looking after Bill as his tour manager, although Larry used to use me on different things at times. Then when Norm brought Eddie over he said, "Look, I need somebody to look after the boys." I said, "That's OK, I'm there. I can keep an eye on things." He said he'd pay me twenty pounds a week, which was twice the wages I was getting for Bill . . . It was actually a reasonable wage for 1959. But being American everything was bigger and bolder.'

Parnes was the leading – originally the only – UK rock promoter of the day, a dark-suited operator, discreetly homosexual, who assembled his stable of handsome male stars, with varying vocal ability but uniform good looks. His first big break came when his business partner John

Kennedy wandered into the unofficial cathedral of skiffle, the Two I's coffee bar in Soho's Old Compton Street, and heard an ex-merchant seaman named Tommy Hicks performing. Kennedy and Parnes signed Hicks, renamed him Steele, and launched him as the UK's first home-grown rock'n'roll star.

Steele had played in a skiffle trio with Lionel Bart, soon to be one of the country's most celebrated writers of musicals, and Mike Pratt, who later turned to acting. Together they wrote Steele's first hit, 'Rock with the Caveman', on which a band of session men and disgruntled jazzers attempted to create a reasonable facsimile of rock'n'roll.

'Larry Parnes was a very shrewd cookie,' recalls Hal Carter, 'but he could be a bit naïve on some things. He was a hard taskmaster. He was homosexual but he didn't behave in a gay manner – just like Brian Epstein. You wouldn't know if you didn't know. Larry never ever swore. A sharp dresser, a lot of class. He was very careful with his money, but even though he paid me very little I owe him a great debt. First of all he brought me into the business, offered me a job. He made mistakes like everybody else, but of course at the time no one in this country knew how to promote rock'n'roll. Everything he did he invented. The rock'n'roll business was totally different from the established show business. There was nothing in his background to prepare him – he was a Jewish schmutter merchant. His family had shops on Oxford Street.

'Something excited him about the music, and when John Kennedy found Tommy Steele he brought him to Larry and they became co-managers. John was the PR guy, brilliant, and that's how Larry got involved. I don't know exactly why Kennedy came to Larry, except that he was just around. He was on the fringe of the business anyway, like he was very friendly with Johnnie Ray. He was just there, and it must have made sense to Kennedy to get him involved.'

By the time of Vincent's arrival Parnes had numerous artists on his books. Some were genuinely talented – Billy Fury, who legend has it auditioned for Parnes in Marty Wilde's dressing room in his native Birkenhead and was added to the bill that night, was the UK's most convincing rocker, while Duffy Power matured as a fine blues harmonica player, Georgie Fame is still a star draw and Wilde himself had a long string of hits, and is pulling the crowds today. Vince Eager, Johnny Gentle and Dickie Pride were also on the roster along with Nelson Keene and Johnny Goode.

'It was a very communistic set-up,' says Carter. 'He paid them a wage, and the successful ones subsidised the ones who hadn't made it yet. He kept them on salaries, yes, but don't forget that he looked after everything else. As far as Bill Fury was concerned, his clothes, flat, car, petrol – all that was taken care of. So the twenty pounds a week salary was on top of that, just pocket money. The second year it was forty pounds, and so on. They weren't overpaid, sure, but they *were* looked after.'

Peter Sellers satirised the phenomenon on his album *Songs for Swinging Sellers* when he played Major Ralph Ralph, an ex-military man who brought a touch of parade-ground discipline to the world of rock'n'roll. 'Borrow my fountain pen and ink in where the flesh shows,' he commanded one of his charges, who had been forced to cut holes in his skin-tight jeans because 'my knees were turning green'.

Parnes was more mother hen than commanding officer. He knew that what his shows needed was a red-blooded shot of the original American article, but he had a problem. They were all happily working in the world's biggest record-buying market, out on the road making as much money as they could while their moment lasted. Britain was a distant backwater to them. But Vincent's fortunes were on the wane at home, in the face of the wave of tamer, more manufactured stars like Frankie Avalon and Fabian, and Cochran was his friend as well as sharing an agent in Norm Riley. Parnes also expressed hopes of bringing in another Riley client, Canadian rockabilly Ronnie Hawkins, who had enjoyed two hits in 1959 with 'Forty Days' – a remake of Chuck Berry's 'Thirty Days' – and 'Mary Lou'. No one else seemed very interested except for the tamer performer Jerry Keller ('Here Comes Summer'), who had visited the UK in 1959, but Vincent was surely ideal – eager for the work, and still a dynamic and charismatic performer, even if the fashion at home had moved on.

So the connection between Vincent, Cochran and Hawkins was Riley, a fast-talking businessman in cowboy boots, who had also just signed Bobby Rydell. Once the joint tour was underway in February, he spoke to David Warren of *Disc*, and defined his recipe for success. 'Eighty per cent of our customers are girls, age range twelve to sixteen. That's partly why you don't get many girl rockers – then again, boys don't go for the girls in the same way. Connie Francis began in rock but she soon went over to ballads.

'Gimmicks? With Eddie Cochran it was the way he moves his shoulders and legs. Gene Vincent – well, he's artistic. His gimmick's contortion – you know, the way he bends over the mike and then springs up again.' Riley was clearly impressed with Jack Good's celebrated fashioning of Vincent's new image because he added: 'And, of course, the black leather gloves, black pants and black jacket.'

Vincent returned from Germany and the first element of his extended stay was a twelve-night tour of Granada cinemas commencing on 6 January at Maidstone, followed by Harrow, Dartford, Rugby, Walthamstow, Kingston, Aylesbury, Bedford, Kettering, Grantham, Mansfield and Slough. The support bill was announced as being Wee Willie Harris, Al Saxon, Lance Fortune, Keith Kelly and the Bachelors, with organist Cherry Wainer replacing Saxon in Slough. Don Arden was compere and Vincent's backing band was the Rockets.

Adrian Owlett, later to be Vincent's friend and confidant in the UK, was then a fifteen-year-old at boarding school. 'A friend called through the common-room window, "Gene is coming to Kingston,"' he recalls. 'I went to the show with Ric Sanders, who later played violin in Fairport Convention. During the show, waiting for Gene, the atmosphere built up. There was a quite extraordinary tension in the air.

'At that time nobody could hope to follow Gene – not even Eddie Cochran. We'd never seen anything like it. Once you'd seen him you were wrung out, and anything else would have been an anticlimax. After his show, after the encores, the National Anthem, the house lights coming on, people just sat there unable to move, thinking about what they'd just seen.'

On Boxing Day Cochran had made an appearance on the UK music radar, when it was announced that he had been booked for *Boy Meets Girls* on 16 and 23 January. 'He looks a very good thing for the show,' said Jack Good. 'Eddie has a pretty "tough" voice which should contrast very well with Marty Wilde's.'

Cochran's most recent hit, his third in the UK, had been 'Somethin' Else', consolidating his reputation. Reviewer Don Nicholl had greeted it in *Disc* enthusiastically. 'You want noise? Eddie Cochran has plenty of it . . . as if he was driving a pile home with a steam hammer . . . the instrumental backing is just about as unsophisticated as you can get, with drums splitting their skins. But it will have the jukes rocking.' It had only a three-week run in the chart, however, peaking at No. 22.

But while the record was in favour, Cochran had a ghosted column published in the 16 October edition of *NME*. In it he said that he was lulled to sleep as a baby by 'Hot Pretzels' and 'Beer Barrel Polka' on the family phonograph. He claimed that he was born in Oklahoma City and *moved* to Albert Lea, where he developed his love for hunting, shooting and fishing. In fact, he moved *from* Albert Lea to the big city and back again. His love of hunting landed him in bed for a long time when his brother, struggling with a temperamental gun, shot him in the leg. Cochran persisted with the lie about his place of birth – 'just a guitar picker from Oklahoma City' – presumably because it seemed to have a little more glamour than a small town few had heard of.

On moving to California – 'and as I did not know anyone, I turned to my guitar for companionship' – he soon met schoolmate Connie 'Guybo' Smith, and recalls that their first paid engagement was playing for 'town hall employees' in the South Gate Auditorium. 'My fondest wish is to go to Britain,' Cochran reveals through his *NME* midwife. 'I planned a holiday last summer, but I was too busy. I'll make it yet – and then I'll meet some of those kind people who have written me the best letters I've ever had.'

On the same page is an announcement for the *NME* Annual Poll-Winners' Concert on 21 February 1960, which was to prove a highlight of the tour. The bill was John Barry, Shirley Bassey, Alma Cogan (later to be replaced by Adam Faith), Russ Conway, the Dallas Boys, Lonnie Donegan, Craig Douglas, Billy Fury, Ted Heath, the Mudlarks, Pete Murray, Anthony Newley, Cliff Richard, Frankie Vaughan, Bert Weedon and Marty Wilde – 'Plus! Ronnie Aldrich and the Squadronaires'.

Just a week after the Cochran announcement came the bombshell news that, in its wisdom, 'ABC-TV is dropping its top teen-beat show *Boy Meets Girls* next month. The company is to put on a "family type" show instead.' The announcement was then softened by the assertion that the show would definitely be brought back in April, after a run of *The Ernest Maxim Show*, but amid rumours of falling viewing figures the writing for British rock'n'roll television seemed already on the wall. 'This is the first I've heard,' commented Good. 'I am very upset.'

Good surely had his tongue in his cheek when he responded, in a *New Musical Express* interview, to 'public criticism of singer Billy Fury's erotic gyrations' on the show. When working on television's first show to feature rock musicians, *6.5 Special*, which began in 1957, Good's ambitions to create a real rock'n'roll show had been thwarted by BBC mandarins in favour of a wholesome youth-club atmosphere. As a reaction to these restrictions, he deliberately made *Boy Meets Girls* as raunchy as he could get away with. Fury's crotch was often closer to the camera than his face, for example.

'I fully agree that anything suggestive should be avoided,' he said, po-faced. 'Though, of course, these things are partially in the minds of individual viewers. Frankly, there are one or two things that Billy Fury does that I would rather he didn't. I have, in fact, suggested so to Billy who does tend to get carried away by his performance.' And so it was the shy, nervous Fury who was apparently responsible for embarrassing that shrinking violet, Jack Good.

On 1 January *NME* confirmed the next stage in shaping the tour: 'An exciting teaming of two of America's leading young rock stars has been achieved – with the arrival in Britain next week of Eddie Cochran, who is scheduled to remain here for ten weeks.' Further details of the 'beat-flavoured package show' were given two weeks later, with Sally Kelly and the Viscounts booked for Glasgow, Billy Fury and Joe Brown for the remainder of the tour, and Vince Eager for the one-night stands. Eager, thanks to his popularity on *6.5 Special* and another TV music show, *Drumbeat*, was given third billing, the only name apart from Vincent and Cochran to appear on the posters, though he never had a hit record. Originally Cochran had hoped to bring over his band the Kelly Four, and they were expecting to travel up until the last moment. They were thwarted by the Musicians' Union ruling at the time on exchange visits – British musicians must be offered similar work in America to allow Americans here. Nothing could be arranged in time.

Fury later confirmed that Cochran, not Vincent, turned him on to cannabis resin as well as the more familiar grass. Many years later, when he owned a farm in Wales and was far happier spending his time bird-watching than performing, Fury also became a distiller of moonshine liquor. 'I remember one night I fell into the gutter after drinking it,' says Adrian Owlett. 'Then Billy fell on top of me. He was singing "Be Bop a Lula" at the time!'

Decca chose 'Hallelujah, I Love Her So' as the single to greet Cochran's arrival on 10 January, at which point Vincent had reached Walthamstow on his Granada tour. On the following day Cochran gave a press conference at the record company's head office. There's a famous photograph of Cochran on this occasion, holding a telephone to his ear and a finger to his lips. He is allegedly calling for quiet at the conference while he talks to his parents back home, although it would seem that the photographer is the one making the noise since Eddie gazes, heavy-lidded and handsome, straight into the lens rather than at the distant press pack.

Carter recalls an incident at the Decca reception. 'There used to be an agent, God rest his soul, Hymie Zahl. He ran the office that Norm Riley dealt with in this country, at Piccadilly Circus [Foster's Agency]. Hymie was famously gay, an outrageous queen. He worked with Larry quite a lot. Decca threw this party for Eddie – he was on the same label as Bill. So they did this to welcome Eddie to the country, and invited a few of the other stars, Bill included. Hymie was at the party. First of all in walked Bill. Hymie used to wear glasses that were literally like the bottoms of bottles. He could hardly see at all. He walked over to Bill and said, "Hello, Eddie, so good to meet you," and so on. And he was shaking hands with Bill, who looked at him as if to say, "What the hell's wrong with you?" Because he knew perfectly well who Hymie was. But Bill was very shy indeed, so he didn't say anything to correct Hymie. He was just embarrassed. And then when Ed arrived it was, "Billy, how are you?" He was cuddling Eddie, who must have been wondering what he'd let himself in for.'

Larry Parnes had hurriedly announced his plans for the tour co-headlined by Vincent and Cochran. The distinction made at the time between Variety dates and one-night stands made for a confusing press release: the former were to be at Moss Empire theatres beginning in Glasgow on 1 February, but the joint tour actually began on 24 January at the Ipswich Granada. For the record, a full list of the dates is as follows:

24 January, Ipswich Granada
28 January, Coventry Gaumont
29 January, Worcester Gaumont
30 January, Bradford Gaumont
31 January, Southampton Guildhall
1–6 February, Glasgow Empire
7–12 February, Sheffield Gaumont
13 February, Woolwich Granada
14 February, Taunton Gaumont
18 February, Leicester De Montfort Hall
20 February, Dundee Caird Hall
21 February, *New Musical Express* Poll Winners' Concert, Wembley Arena
24 February, Stockton-on-Tees Globe
26 February, Cardiff Gaumont
29 February–5 March, Leeds Empire
7–12 March, Birmingham Hippodrome
14–19 March, Liverpool Empire
21–26 March, Newcastle Empire
28 March–2 April, Manchester Hippodrome
4–9 March, Finsbury Park Empire
11–14 and 16 March, Bristol Hippodrome

From Leeds onwards, these dates were added to the original schedule as the success of the tour became apparent, and Foster's Agency had to apply for an extension to the Americans' work permits. Meanwhile, on

12 January Cochran began rehearsals for *Boy Meets Girls* and went to Manchester two days later. His first appearance was on 16 January, when he sang 'Hallelujah, I Love Her So', 'C'mon Everybody', 'Somethin' Else' and 'Twenty Flight Rock', and he taped his further contribution to be shown a week later. For this show, as well as the current single 'Hallelujah', he performed 'Money Honey' and 'Have I Told You Lately That I Love You'. The first and last of these had string arrangements dubbed on by the Manchester-based Hallé Orchestra prior to transmission.

For his *Boy Meets Girls* appearances, Cochran was backed variously by guitarists Joe Brown, Eric Ford and Brian Daley, saxophonist Red Price, Alan Weighall on electric bass and Bill Stark on upright, Andy White and Don Storer on drums, plus the Vernons Girls.

Years later Georgie Fame recalled the moment he was recruited for the tour. 'There was a pool of . . . I suppose about fifteen, two or three bands it turned out to be . . . One was Marty Wilde's band . . . which was Brian Bennett, Jimmy Sullivan . . . The other group was the Beat Boys . . . and Billy Fury's the Blue Flames. We were all told to report to this club in Soho . . . and so we were all sitting there, anticipating the great arrival, and sure enough Gene Vincent and Eddie Cochran walked in, and Eddie sat down and played guitar and everybody was astounded . . . it was amazing . . . apart from all his own stuff that he did, he was fantastic playing all that Chet Atkins stuff and the finger-style and the country stuff. He was brilliant at it.' The Blue Flames referred to by Fame were the semiprofessional skiffle group that Brown played in, Clay Nicholls and the Blue Flames.

Talking of Vincent, Fame recalled: 'He used to start off on his knees, the pink spot picking up his face and he'd say, "We-e-e-ll" and the whole place would erupt. He relied on the band a lot because he was not really a musician, but he got 100% because they idolised him.' Parnes initially christened Fame as Lance Fortune, before he became Fame for this tour. A new Parnes vocalist, Chris Morris, took on the Fortune mantle and immediately made the Top Ten with 'Be Mine'.

The line-up for the tour was becoming clearer. The Wildcats were Big Jim Sullivan on lead guitar, Brian Locking on bass, drummer Brian Bennett and rhythm guitarist Tony Belcher. The Beat Boys featured Colin Green on lead (also a member of Vince Eager's band the Quiet Three), Fortune/Fame on piano, drummer Red Reece, bass player Vince Cooze and saxophonist Billy McVay, who later became bandleader Ray McVay.

The one-nighters featured Vince Eager, and his Quiet Three were completed by bassist Tex Makins and drummer Jimmy Nichols. Also on all the one-nighters were compere Billy Raymond, the Tony Sheridan

Trio and vocal threesome the Viscounts – Don Paul, Gordon Mills and Ronnie Wells.

Sheridan was a singer-guitarist, an eccentric performer who had previously played with Marty Wilde and Vince Taylor before forming his first trio with Brian Bennett and Brian Locking. He had appeared with some success on Jack Good's *Oh Boy!* but was sacked from *Boy Meets Girls* because, in the words of a Polydor press release, he 'went haywire (failing to be on time, arriving without his guitar, etc.)'. In the view of musician and author Alan Clayson he had 'a wanton dedication to pleasing himself rather than the customers'. After the tour he, like so many others, moved to Hamburg to work and there he became one of the leading British musicians, coming to be known as 'The Teacher'.

On most of the 'variety' weeks Raymond, Sheridan and the Viscounts were joined by Billy Fury and Joe Brown. On the Glasgow Empire bill, however, they were replaced by Sally Kelly and the 'new' Lance Fortune, and at Finsbury Park by Peter Wynne and Dean Webb. At Bristol Johnny Gentle came in for Dean Webb and the Wildcats missed the last show of all, rehearsing with Marty Wilde for the TV variety show *Sunday Night at the London Palladium*.

'The week-long dates paid for themselves at the weekends, really,' says Hal Carter. 'Sometimes the house would be almost empty early in the week, but everyone was on a weekly wage so the show went on.'

With the tour under way its run was doubled, first to Leeds and beyond, then past the Easter break, having 'opened so favourably', according to *NME*. This explains that fatal break in April – Cochran already had two American television commitments lined up, booked to follow on from the original ten-week schedule. Vincent, meanwhile, was to play the Alhambra in Paris to fill the gap while Cochran was away.

IPSWICH

Cochran won over his first UK audience by saying, 'It's great to be here in Hip-Switch,' provocatively wiggling his hips from side to side. In 1998 Vince Eager, who had been on Vincent's first tour and closed the first half, looked back on the new tour. 'When Eddie came over I asked Larry if I could still close the first half of the show. "No problem." . . . As [Eddie's] act went on I thought, "Oh, God, I've got to follow this." He was just phenomenal.' Eager's show stopper, backed by his band the Quiet Three, was his version of Conway Twitty's 'It's Only Make Believe'. He put everything into it that night and acquitted himself well.

'At the interval I was in my dressing room when there was a knock on the door and it was Eddie . . . He said, "I've got to tell you that was the best version of 'It's Only Make Believe' that I have ever heard." . . . So we struck up a friendship there and then.'

Sixteen-year-old Marge Miller reckoned that Cochran was the star of the Ipswich show. 'When he finished his act we all stood up and shouted, "We want Eddie", and he came back and did another song. When he went off again we shouted. Three times this went on. Then poor old Gene Vincent came on. Although he was top of the bill he was no match for Eddie Cochran.'

After the show that night Cochran granted a very stilted interview to an unidentified local journalist. 'We saw you on the TV last night, didn't we?' quizzed the interviewer, who clearly had not, and when he further asked, 'How long a spot did you have?' Cochran audibly began to prickle. 'How long a spot on the show? I did, I don't know, must have been about twelve minutes or so. Four numbers, I guess it was.'

He was asked what his plans were for when he left the theatre, and presumably did not want the interviewer's company because he seemed to misunderstand the question deliberately, talking about looking forward to a rest and then rehearsing, rather than naming the bar or restaurant.

'What's it like working in front of the Ipswich audiences?' is one of the great questions ever posed to a rock'n'roll star who has just arrived in the country and is bending over backwards to be polite. 'Oh, they're fine. Very appreciative audiences. Good applause, real fine.' He then referred to the age mix in the theatre.

'They're not all squares, the older ones,' suggested the interviewer, sagely. 'No, not all square!' One can sense the warring emotions of politeness, desperation and boredom in Cochran's voice. All he wanted was a drink and a party. He was asked if rock was on its way out, to be replaced by ballads, and he floundered to respond to such a daft generalisation.

'Well, there's always . . . I don't think there are any more ballads now than there ever were, in the charts . . . Rock'n'roll really got a good start about five years ago, and ever since it started they said, "Well, it's gotta be going out in another year." . . . I don't know if it'll do it on the sixth, or not.'

In giving a brief rundown of his film career Cochran arrived at his third outing, *Go, Johnny, Go.* He said that it 'should be here any time now. It was just released over in the States.' 'We'll have to look out for that one, Eddie.' 'Yeh, it'll be coming here pretty soon, I'm sure.' 'Good. It might even play this theatre.' 'I hope so.' 'Thank you very much indeed.' 'Thank you.' A grateful Cochran then joined his fellow musicians.

His genius was soon apparent to all, drummer Brian Bennett for one. 'He taught me a lot about playing rock'n'roll,' he recalled. 'A lot of rock'n'roll rhythm was very simple and he was interested in changing bass drum patterns ... he used to give me very precise instructions about the drum fills he wanted ... Eddie taught me to develop independence between my feet and hands and I'm still grateful to him for that.'

After the Ipswich gig there were three days of rehearsals before the second date, in Coventry, which were held at Max Rivers' club in Gerrard Street, London. Then the tour resumed.

There was little glamour in travel back then, as Carter recalls. 'The train journeys were horrendous. We went most places by train, although we might use a coach for some of the one-nighters. But my work wasn't all that difficult, I suppose. Although I was now meant to be in charge of four guys – Gene, Eddie, Joe and Billy – Joe was a real independent spirit. Everywhere we went he had friends, and he'd go off to see them. It always seemed to be farmers he knew, because he loved shooting – he kept shotguns in the boot of his car. So he'd often go off shooting with his friends. Everyone seems to think he's a cockney but he's not. He was actually born in Lincoln. He came to live in London later on. But when Parnesey started to promote him it was as the cockney kid, and that always stuck with him.

'So Joe would go missing and I just had to look after Ed, Gene and Bill. Other than problems with women and drinking they were usually fine. But I must say that I wasn't a great fan of Gene. I just couldn't get on with him, and he was such a moral coward. Ed was drinking heavily because he was homesick, unhappy. He must have spent a fortune on the phone speaking to the Shrimp, his mum, because all the time, as soon as it got to six or seven o'clock before the show, he'd be on the phone talking to her. He was drinking Jack Daniels like it was going out of fashion.'

A most telling description of the contrast in character between Cochran and Vincent on this tour came from the support act for the final show, Johnny Gentle, now best remembered for his backing group on a subsequent Scottish tour – the nascent Beatles. 'Eddie was a genuine guy – you could feel the warmth from him. He had an interest in the people around him ... Gene didn't do anything like that, he was wrapped inside himself ... he was past his prime and on the slope to oblivion.'

Whereas Jack Good had created a new image for Vincent he immediately realised that such treatment was unnecessary for Cochran, who was already the complete article. It was simply a question of choosing camera angles to present him at his best, judiciously adding a few inches to his modest height by shooting him from below. 'He was not demonstrative,' remembers Adrian Owlett. 'The music clearly mattered more than the stagecraft, in contrast to Vincent who was not a musician as such – although of course he *could* play guitar – but he was a totally theatrical act.'

Good later said of Cochran: 'He had a very strong visual sense of how to present himself. He was in control. He always knew how he should look to make an impact, and he would have made a wonderful actor. He was not your archetypal rock'n'roller, unlike Gene who just did things naturally.'

As Good himself has lamented, it is a tragedy that tapes of *Boy Meets Girls* were reused or destroyed, an all-too-familiar act of cultural vandalism carried out in the interests of economy or space saving. The key was performing the songs live – shows like Dick Clark's *American Bandstand*, which *have* survived, simply presented a succession of current teen stars lip-synching to their latest record. To Good, Vincent and Cochran, the essence of rock'n'roll was in the moment, destroyed by miming and brought back to life by the improvisational tension of live performance. 'Gene and Eddie were delighted to be let loose, as they both hated miming,' Good confirms.

Good has also noted that whereas Vincent was a natural performer, incapable intellectually of conscious work on his act, Cochran was in complete control in the sense that an actor controls his performance to convey the desired effect. This did not make Cochran stylised or forced on stage – he was as charismatic an artist in his own way as was Vincent. But Cochran always had a knowing approach to his stagecraft, whereas Vincent's remained instinctive.

COVENTRY

After the second gig the Coventry press tried hard to sneer. 'There were no frantic scenes when the latest ration of rock'n'roll reached Coventry last night. The two Americans and several British performers who made two appearances at the Gaumont on the same day drew shrieks inside the theatre, but seemed in little danger of losing their shirts outside.' And your point is, exactly?

A member of the paying audience, Alan Sinnett, was more appreciative, and managed to get backstage. 'The lasting memory for me was how genuinely nice Eddie was. I didn't expect Eddie to be interested in us, but he asked questions of us as well as the other way round.'

WORCESTER

Vincent and Cochran were booked into the main hotel in the centre of Worcester, the Star in Foregate Street, handy for the nearby Gaumont. The reporter for the *Worcester Evening News and Times* enjoyed the show, noting that Cochran 'drove the cats wild' and that Vincent said he was going to sing 'Over the Rainbow' 'to prove that a rock'n'roller can really sing properly if he wants to'.

Marilyn Guyatt was at the Worcester show. 'When Eddie first came on the stage the audience was very quiet as we never knew what to expect, but when he started playing everyone got excited. We were just gobsmacked – we could not believe how good he was. His guitar playing was out of this world.'

The *NME*'s Derek Johnson conducted a 'question time' with Vincent early in the tour. Comparing pop television at home and in the UK, Vincent noted: 'The main difference is that the British try to achieve perfection. In the States, they just put you in front of a camera, and tell you to sing.' He identified Jack Good as the key to this contrast, and complimented Joe Brown's guitar playing, even suggesting that a British package tour would be well received in America. After Cochran's death, his girlfriend Sharon Sheeley confirmed that 'Eddie thought Jack was a genius, and credited him with the vastly improved stage act he had acquired while over here.'

As for rock'n'roll's associations with hooliganism and delinquency, Vincent was finger-wagging in his admonishment. 'I think it's a very unfair criticism, and it comes mostly from the older folks. And I would suggest that they cast their minds back a few years to the days when they were doing the "Black Bottom", the "Big Apple" and the Charleston. Let them remember that they were the hooligans and the delinquents of their day!'

BRADFORD

On to Bradford for the fourth date, and the first controversy. Under the headline 'A Badgered "Rock" Star Quits the Stage' the *Yorkshire Post* reported: 'More than 2,000 teenagers at a rock'n'roll concert at the Gaumont, Bradford on Saturday night were astonished when the American star of the show, Gene Vincent, stopped in the middle of a song and walked off stage. His accompanying group faltered to a ragged halt, and harassed compere Billy Raymond hurried from the wings to the microphone to lead a finale in which all members of the company, including a solemn-faced Vincent, took part.

'In his dressing room later, the 25-year-old singer from Norfolk, Virginia, explained his startling exit. "Four guys at the back had been heckling throughout the act," he said. "I didn't particularly mind during my fast numbers, but when they tried to ruin 'Over the Rainbow' I just could not take it any more. It is one of the best things I do and it has been going down very well all over the country. I will never play at this place again." '

From the audience, Terry McGill explains what happened. 'Gene was going down a bomb until at the end of his act. He told the audience that "I'm going to show you that rock'n'rollers can sing, because the critics say we can't." Then he started singing "Over the Rainbow". Quite a few people were upset and started shouting at him to play rock'n'roll. Then they started to shout for Eddie Cochran to come back and then Gene just walked off in disgust.'

Mike Priestley, then sixteen and now a writer on Bradford's *Telegraph and Argus*, recalls: 'Gene was good, a mean, leather-clad rock'n'roller. But he was too old for sixteen-year-olds to identify with as a contemporary. Eddie, though, was one of us. He sang about things we could relate to . . . He was so cool on that cold Bradford day.'

SOUTHAMPTON

By the time of the next date, at Southampton Guildhall, Cochran was suffering from the effects of the British winter. The *Southern Evening Echo* shouted: 'Police Haul Girls From Stage at Soton Session of US "Rock".' It continued: 'Black leather tights [really?], silver waistcoat and laryngitis – that was twenty-year-old Oklahoman Eddie Cochran. Midway through his hoarse croaking into the microphone, he apologised for his affliction. Co-star Gene Vincent appeared in equally dashing attire – black leather jacket, black leather trousers and black leather gloves, as though equipped for a deep-sea dive or a round inspection of the corporation dump.' No, I don't understand it either.

'Best voice of the night?' asked the *Echo*. 'That of Scottish compere Billy Raymond. A pity that he sang only a couple of numbers . . . Show verdict? It became progressively monotonous as it went on – song after song being shaped in the same old tiresome mould.' That's rock'n'roll for you. To steal a line from the musical *Race with the Devil*, it makes you yearn for songs that mean something, like 'Yes, We Have No Bananas'.

GLASGOW

When the package reached Glasgow for the first of its 'variety' weeks, Cochran blundered by referring to being in England, and was brusquely corrected by the crowd. Carter recalls an incident during the week, by which time he was getting a little fed up with Vincent. 'We did sometimes have a bit of fun with him, because he really was a misery, moaning all the time. We arrived at the hotel and checked in. Ed decided he was going to go shopping. Buy some tam'o'shanters and things to take home. Souvenirs of Scotland. Gene wanted to have a bath. He took his leg iron off, stripped and went into the bathroom. Just before he went out Ed took Gene's leg iron and put it on the top of the wardrobe. It was one of those old-fashioned ones which had a carved wooden rim around the top and so you couldn't see what was up there. Off we went, laughing. He was a real practical joker, up to all sorts of tricks.

'We were gone about two-and-a-half hours. We got back and Gene was screaming and throwing tantrums. The manager was scared to death. Gene was telling him he was going to sue for a million dollars – the threat was always a million dollars in those days – because one of the staff had stolen his leg iron. So Eddie got it from the top of the wardrobe, told him to calm down, said it was just a joke. The manager was furious with *him* then. He'd been through all this for nothing. But that was Gene for you. He wouldn't see the joke, he'd just scream blue murder.'

Carter remembers another example of Cochran's humour. 'Eddie Cochran was an absolute darling. A really lovely guy. He was a practical joker but he wouldn't like to hurt anybody. One night Bill was waiting to go on, to open the second half, I think. Ed noticed him looking a bit strange and asked him what was wrong. Bill said, "Oh, just a bit nervous, you know." Ed said, "Nervous? Why nervous? What you've got to do is stand on the stage, plant your legs slightly apart, hands down by your side, look straight out at the audience and say, 'I'm Billy Fury and I'm the guv'nor. The greatest thing to ever appear on this stage.' Be positive. Right, repeat what I've just told you."

'Bill was very reluctant, but he went along with it. He said, "My name's Billy Fury and I'm the greatest thing to ever appear on this stage." And Ed said, "How can you be, Bill – *I* am!" But he apologised straight away when he saw Bill's face. There's nothing nasty you could say about Ed. If he accidentally upset anyone he would always apologise.

'Another time Big Jim Sullivan and Ed were sitting in the dressing room, just chilling out, and Jim said, "Show us a few of your licks on the guitar." Ed said, "No, I can't be bothered. I don't want to play the guitar." And Jim said, "Come on. You've got to be the best guitarist in the world." So Ed said, "Yeh, I suppose you're right." So he played something, lead and rhythm at the same time, and bending the second string, making this incredible noise. Because he didn't use a second string, you see, it was a first. But it wasn't conceited, this "I suppose you're right". There was no way he was bigheaded. It was just a joke.'

The *NME* sent writer Gordon Irving to cover the Glasgow Empire performance, which he watched with mixed feelings. 'Larry Parnes's "Beat Show" . . . descended on Glasgow Empire on Monday with a frenzied swoop, evoking screams galore from the devoted fans.' Irving referred to Cochran's 'forceful singing act' and Vincent's 'leather-clad contortions-cum-singing'. Vincent was 'a more flamboyant showman, almost cuddling his microphone, kneeling and crawling on the stage, and generally leaping about like some leather-clad spaceman from another planet.' However, to Irving 'probably the best act on the bill' were the Viscounts!

Tour compere Billy Raymond, briefly back north of the border for the Glasgow week, had studied music and drama in Scotland. He came down to London at the age of nineteen and landed a job in a strip club, which led to television work as a vocalist on the show *You and the Night and the Music* and an EMI contract as a ballad singer. No BBC or EMI executive ever admitted attending the strip club, but the manager of the club did have some useful contacts.

Raymond appeared on *6.5 Special* and Kent Walton's show *Cool for Cats*, and although his flat-mate Craig Douglas went on to have hits – eleven chart entries, in fact, beginning in 1959 with his cover of Dion's 'A Teenager in Love' – Raymond's success as a singer was more modest. After a falling-out with his manager he was taken on by Larry Parnes as the compere for his package tours.

'I will not make any comments on Gene Vincent apart from that I told Larry Parnes that I'd never work with Gene again,' says Raymond, somewhat primly. Bill Beard of *The Eddie Cochran Connection* reveals that Raymond *did* make some comments to him, but alas his discretion is unbreakable. 'On the other hand,' says Raymond, 'Eddie was an absolute delight – kind, gentle and a gentleman who was so easy to work with and was a lot of laughs. Although he would never say it, I don't think he liked Vincent very much either, but I could be wrong. If he *did* like Gene he was on his own.'

This does tally to a degree with Hal Carter's feeling, quoted later, that the main bond between them was simply that they were Americans in a foreign land, and it is clear that they did not spend much time together when they were off the road – when Sharon Sheeley arrived on her twentieth birthday, for example, Vincent was not at the celebratory party.

Raymond had his own brief spot on the show, impersonating singers like Johnnie Ray and Frankie Laine, and can still remember Cochran's good-natured disposition. 'On many occasions Eddie would watch me from the side of the stage and I'd come off and he's give me a hug and say, "Bill, how do you cope so well with that noisy crowd?" I used to say, "Ed, you think they're noisy for me – wait until you go on." '

SHEFFIELD

Local newspaper journalists by and large remained resistant to the thrilling power of rock'n'roll. Said the *Sheffield Star*: 'If hip-swinging acrobatics around a microphone is the hallmark of a beat singer, then 25-year-old Gene Vincent would take a lot of beating, for Gene did every sort of microphone gymnastics imaginable. Personally I was not impressed . . . Eddie Cochran's harsh singing and jogging movements were a little wearing to both the ear and the eye. Vince Eager gave a first-class performance.'

One honourable exception was eighteen-year-old cub reporter Carole Commander, who was invited to meet the artists before their first Sheffield performance at a buffet party, in the Green Room Restaurant above the theatre. She was hugely struck by Cochran in particular. 'I shall always remember meeting this good-looking, blond-haired, blue-eyed guy. He looked fantastic dressed in brown leather jeans with matching flying jacket and an orange open-necked shirt . . . There was something about him that was sincere and friendly – the boy-next-door type. We spoke as though we had known each other for years . . .'

According to Sheffield fan Mick Jackson, Cochran opted for 'Some-thin' Else' as his opening number and was dressed in fawn leather waistcoat and trousers. 'His guitar playing was superb throughout his entire act and sounded much better than on a lot of his records, because it was really loud and blasted out of the amps . . . Vincent was also great, but I preferred him with the Blue Caps.'

WOOLWICH

John Green met both his heroes backstage at the Woolwich Granada, noting – as did so many others – how short Cochran was, before settling down for the second house. 'The show was the best I've ever seen. Eddie started his part with the theatre lights turned down low, and the curtains closed. Then the opening riff to "What'd I Say" began. Slowly the curtains began to open. A spotlight came on to show Eddie with his back to the audience, still playing the riff. Suddenly, as the house lights came on, he spun round to face the audience, and belted into the song proper. What a great effect. The fans went nuts!

'Eddie looked and sounded great. Moving his guitar and his shoulders in a circular motion, like a train chugging along . . . Eddie didn't move around too much on stage. He didn't have to. And, dare I say it, Gene Vincent was even better. He was a maniac on stage. Crouching, throwing his leg over the mike stand, banging it on the stage, falling on to his knees and urging the band along, he was *the* rock'n'roll hero.'

With Jerry Lee Lewis just beginning to rebuild his career and Little Richard bashing a Bible, and in spite of the refreshingly conflicting opinions expressed here, surely Vincent was the only artist in early 1960 who could possibly hope to follow Cochran.

Charlie Wills was also at the Woolwich gig. He was serving in the army at the time and, come the day, he did not have a pass allowing him to leave the camp. He was caught going over the wall by the orderly sergeant – 'probably the only NCO in the regiment who was decent enough to let me go when I explained where I was going – my eternal gratitude is due to Sergeant Dennis Plaisted.'

Wills recalls that the show was opened by Tony Sheridan and his group, followed by the Viscounts, after which the Wildcats went into their introductory riff with Cochran. 'As he spun round to face us the full set of spots were switched on, reflecting in many rays from the magnificent Gretsch guitar he held high across his chest.' Cochran told the audience that he had laryngitis and eyestrain, but 'his problems certainly didn't affect his act, which was superb.'

Surprisingly, Vince Eager was still closing the first half, as if he hadn't learned his lesson by now. Billy Raymond opened the second half, and then 'one of the truly outstanding moments of my life . . . the greatest singer the whole world has ever known.'

The Wildcats were back on duty, leading Vincent into a slow version of 'Be Bop a Lula'. 'His left leg stretched out behind him while he sang, his face turned upwards to one side, his huge eyes staring towards the ceiling, then a sudden swing of that leg, in spite of its iron brace, over the top of the mike . . . As a complete contrast, near the end of his act he sat quietly down on the edge of the stage and sang "Over the Rainbow" . . . if there's a more beautiful sound on this earth I've never heard it.' Wills recalls that the ensemble encore that night was 'What'd I Say', and thanks to the fact that it was now dark he climbed back into barracks undetected.

TAUNTON

And so the caravan moved on to my home town, Taunton, where the band stayed at the poshest place in town, the Castle Hotel, a stone's throw from the theatre. I remember just a few snapshots in motion – the riff to 'What'd I Say', the impact of Cochran as the very image of rock'n'roll, the wildness of Vincent as he hammered the microphone stand into the stage.

Fortunately Barry Holley has a more efficient memory. 'Taunton in February 1960 on a Sunday had less life than an undertaker's back parlour on a mortician's day off . . . Killing time around the market square it never occurred to us that these American stars might be hanging [round] the streets in a vain effort to find an open pub . . . The stage was not very deep and we were just a couple of rows from the front of the stalls. The musicians seemed to be on top of us . . . People have said that Eddie started his act with his back to the audience. At Taunton I don't think they even used the curtains. A voice announced him and he just burst on to the stage . . . playing that familiar "What'd I Say" riff on his big guitar, and singing in that raw, rough style.

'Those first few moments of a high-voltage and magnificent stage presence was like some religious revelation . . . in that basic cinema we were face to face with a fantasy that had turned into a brilliant reality. We sat there entranced and overwhelmed, immersed in a tidal wave of glorious sound.'

The *Somerset County Gazette* maintained the churlish attitude of so many local papers. 'Gene Vincent and Eddie Cochran, the two American stars of the rock show, proved to be little above the average standard of home-grown products . . . Vincent tried to overcome the handicap of having to leave his echo chamber behind by an attempt to create an air of brooding mystery about himself. Dressed as though he had arrived at the theatre by motor cycle and had paused only to remove crash helmet and goggles before going on stage, he adopted a semi-crouching position, went through the usual motions of making love to the microphone, and disdained even to say the customary few words of greeting or farewell to the audience. However, he did succeed in creating a mystery – what were the words of his songs?

'In fairness to Eddie Cochran, who was also disappointing, it must be recorded that he had been suffering from laryngitis ever since his arrival in England. But despite this he was more comprehensible than Vincent was, and he was also versatile.' The *Gazette* felt more comfortable with the safer appeal of Vince Eager and Billy Raymond.

After the Taunton date there was a further break in the tour for broadcasting commitments. On 15 February Vincent appeared on the

BBC radio show *Parade of the Pops* and on the following day he and Cochran were at the BBC's studio in the Haymarket to record segments for *Saturday Club* at the BBC's studios near Piccadilly Circus. They then travelled to Manchester for further *Boy Meets Girls* rehearsals before moving on to Leicester.

They did a further *Saturday Club* recording a week later, after the *NME* Poll Winners' Concert, and the sessions were broadcast on 5 and 12 March. The first segment started with Vincent launching into 'Say Mama', before the stilted interview described below. Vincent then sang 'Summertime'. After Cochran was introduced he sang 'Somethin' Else' and 'Hallelujah, I Love Her So'. The rest of the first recording consisted of 'Be Bop a Lula', 'Twenty Flight Rock', 'Rocky Road Blues' and 'C'mon Everybody'. On the second show Vincent sang 'Wild Cat' and 'My Heart' (with Cochran on guitar) and Cochran performed 'What'd I Say' and 'Milk Cow Blues', interspersed with the interview below. These perform-ances, plus their *Boy Meets Girls* contributions, are available on the Rockstar CD *Rock'n'roll Memories*.

Brian Mathew, host of *Saturday Club*, recalls: 'We did a session at which they both appeared and we recorded Gene Vincent first. As he was leaving the studio Eddie Cochran got on the tiny stage. He shouted . . . "Hey, Vincent, you ain't going nowhere. I got your crutches. You're going to jam with me." Gene went back and jammed with him for ten or fifteen minutes.' Unfortunately, the studio engineer did not think to switch the tape machine on.

By the time Mathew had struggled with the uncommunicative Vincent and a tongue-tied fan it must have been a relief to talk to the more forthcoming Cochran. He began: 'Well, Gene, we're very pleased to have you back on *Saturday Club*. Last time we met you'd only just arrived in the country. Since then you've been travelling around quite a bit, haven't you?' Vincent replied simply, 'Yes, sir.' 'Well, how are you finding the audiences,' prompted Mathew. 'Are they liking what you've been giving them?' 'Very much, sir. They've been very nice to me.'

'Now, what about an accompanying group? You're using the one we have here – Marty Wilde's Wildcats?' 'Yes, sir. Uh, huh.' By this time the ultra-professional Mathew was almost audibly sweating. 'And how do they suit you?' 'Oh, just fine.' 'Well . . . that's nice to know.'

Mathew announced that Eddie Cochran was also on the show, and moved on to a group of young fans from the Star Teenage Club in Sheffield, asking one, 'Is there any particular number you'd like to hear, Cynthia?' Silence, followed by an awestruck croak. 'Well, there must be one. One of his better-known ones.' He turned to the more forthcoming

Glenda, who requested 'Twenty Flight Rock' right on cue. But then Mathew returned to Cynthia. 'Do you want to send a dedication with this one, Cynthia?' More dead air. 'I know you didn't know you were going on air . . . For your friends in Sheffield, maybe?'

'Er . . . well, there's Hazel.' 'Yeah?' 'And . . . er . . .' 'She's in Sheffield? Well, fine. That'll do,' says Mathew, moving hurriedly on to Cochran, although his interview was held over until the second show. 'We've already heard how you play a lot of other instruments, is that so?' 'Well, hold on,' Cochran replied. 'I play bass and drums, and piano, and guitar a little bit . . .' He then said that he only played anything other than guitar in his nightclub act. This would seem to be one of the early hints that the dangers of constant touring were getting to him, and that he was planning to play more intimate shows closer to home.

He then gave a sad forecast of his immediate itinerary. 'I'll be here until April seventeenth, then I go home for ten days. Then I'm back near the end of April and I stay here for ten more weeks,' said Cochran. 'What do you have in mind for your career when you get back home? Is there anything in particular you want to do?' 'Yeah, I'd like to be successful . . .'

Billy Fury was also booked to appear with them on *Boy Meets Girls*, and Carter accompanied the three from London by train. 'We were on the train, me, Bill, Gene, Eddie, and we were sitting in First Class, drinking. Bill wasn't a great drinker. In those days scotch and Coke was the 'in' drink. But Gene and Eddie were drinking Jack Daniels with Coke chasers. They didn't mix them. Bill was just on Coke. What they'd do, they'd shout, "What's that?" and point out of the window. Bill would look and they'd chuck scotch or JD into his glass. I don't know how many times they did this but Bill was stoned out of his brain. Gone.

'We were going through a station and they were doing something to the track. They were putting new stones down, all white, brand new. Ed looked out the window and said, "Jesus, it's snowing." Bill said, "No it's not." "I'm telling you it was snowing back there." Then we pulled into Manchester and I heard Bill shouting, "There's no snow." He was down between the carriages, kneeling on the track. That's how drunk he was.

'We got a cab and they were staying at one of the big hotels. We checked in and Bill and I were staying in a boarding house. Just outside the city. Ed said to me, "Can you get me some comics?" Not papers, comics. I said, "Ed, it's midnight. You won't get comics at this time of night." So he told me to go and check. I told Bill to come with me but Ed said, "No, he stays here." He knew what I was going to do — make a run for it. So Bill was a hostage!

'I found some comics somehow. Maybe it was just a pile of magazines, I can't really remember. But in the meantime they'd left their room. And in that hotel around every door was a big leather screen, to stop the draught or whatever. And the fire extinguishers were in glass cases on the wall. This was a posh hotel, so the guests had put their shoes out for cleaning. The three of them had taken all the shoes and filled the glass fire compartments, so all you could see was shoes, and then put others as if they were walking around the top of these draught excluders. Of course there was murder the next day. You can imagine. Half of the guests had brogues, very similar to each other, and they'd be walking around with a size seven and a size eight or whatever. Of course I had all the headache of sorting it out.'

Why, in Carter's view, did this strange friendship between two such different people develop? 'It was indeed a strange friendship, but I think they both liked having another American for company, someone from the same part of the world, both in Australia and the UK. They used to fight, though. One time Gene gave Eddie a black eye. It was supposed to be a fun fight but he got carried away. Ended up smacking him one. I feel that Gene abused the friendship in many instances, but they did stay together. There was an instance where they wanted to change the running order, to have Gene close the first half and Ed close the show, but Ed wouldn't have it. No, he said, Gene closes the show. He knew Gene would have been upset. That's the kind of guy Ed was.' Well, later in the tour Cochran was indeed occasionally persuaded to close the second half, but he clearly was not happy about it, because it did not become the norm.

LEICESTER

About the show at the De Montfort Hall, the *Leicester Mercury* was even more dismissive than the *Somerset County Gazette* had been. 'What a Show to Go Frantic About' tut-tutted the headline. 'Now I am no square,' began the reviewer, evoking the same expectation as when some public-bar buffoon says, 'Don't get me wrong – I'm not a racist, but . . .' 'I can appreciate a tune with a foot-tapping beat as much as anyone,' continued the hep-cat critic, 'but last night's exhibition of "talent" sickened me. It was not so much the singing, because there was so much yelling going on I could hardly hear it, but the fact that these "singers" seemed to get such enjoyment out of leg-kicking, face-pulling and making the youngsters scream. I cannot believe this is true entertainment . . . I can only hope that last night's audience were not typical of Leicester's young people.'

One of those young people, John Williams, recalls that 'Eddie Cochran brought the house down', but that Vincent 'struggled unsuccessfully to create the magic Eddie brought to the first half'.

After playing Leicester they returned to Manchester to tape their contributions to the *Boy Meets Girls* transmitted on 20 and 27 February, staying at the El Morocco Hotel in Didsbury. For the first show Cochran performed 'Hallelujah', 'Twenty Flight Rock', 'Summertime Blues' and 'Milk Cow Blues' while Vincent did 'My Heart' and 'Dance in the Street'. For the finale to the show they were joined by host Marty Wilde, Billy Fury and Joe Brown for Willie Dixon's 'My Babe', which they occasionally used as the closing ensemble number on stage.

For the second house the most notable contributions were a rare duet, on the Big Bopper's 'White Lightnin'', and the fact that Cochran performed Terry Randazzo's 'I Don't Like You No More'. This is a smooth, big-band cabaret number, closest in character among Cochran's familiar repertoire to 'Hallelujah, I Love Her So', and hints at one direction he may have been intending to broaden out towards from his rock'n'roll base.

Cochran appeared on *Parade of the Pops* on 22 February, backed by Bob Miller and the Millermen from the Light Programme's Sunday-morning pop show *Easy Beat*, and on the following day both artists recorded two further *Saturday Club* performances. It was a grinding schedule, squeezing as much value out of Vincent and Cochran as possible. In between these commitments they had to travel as far as Dundee and then straight back to London for the Poll-Winners event!

DUNDEE

Dundee's Caird Hall was the scene of a serious riot, seemingly a Dundee speciality – two years earlier Tommy Steele had been injured when a hysterical crowd invaded the stage. This time, the trouble was brewing for most of the evening. Three people fainted during Cochran's act (two of them men!), and during the second half six more were ejected from the hall. Then a girl jumped on to the stage towards the end of Vincent's spot and threw her arms around him. This prompted dozens more to leap on to the stage, and theatre attendants and backstage staff grappled with them. Cochran and Vince Eager joined Vincent on stage and launched into the final number in an attempt to restore calm. It had the opposite effect, however, and the stage was overrun.

The police arrived to escort the performers to their dressing rooms, followed by fans, who hammered at the locked door separating the stage area from the safety of the dressing rooms. Fighting broke out and girls fainted in the crush. Meanwhile, back in the auditorium, teenagers on the stage began body-surfing, hurling themselves into the milling crowd below.

A large bust of the hall's benefactor, Sir James Caird, was uprooted from its niche and damaged, as were fittings in the lavatories. It took half an hour for the police to restore some sort of order. Hundreds waited in the square outside for Vincent, Cochran and Eager to emerge, but they slipped out of a back door into an adjacent garage and a waiting taxi. When the taxi emerged into the street, however, the fans spotted them, banging on the doors in an unsuccessful attempt to open them.

A spokesman for the city council said that this was 'the last straw' as far as rock'n'roll in Dundee was concerned. A member of the audience, James Clark, recalls: 'We were dancing in the aisles, stuff like that. When Gene Vincent came on we all climbed on the stage, and Eddie just happened to be standing in the wings next to me, so I said to him, "How's it going, Eddie?" He said, "Crazy, man, but I don't like this fighting." I said, "It's not fighting, just pushing and shoving." . . . It was brilliant.'

WEMBLEY

Vincent and Cochran travelled down to London overnight for the *NME* Poll-Winners' Concert at the Empire Pool, Wembley the following afternoon. Not surprisingly, the *NME* itself was rather more appreciative of their efforts than most of the local press had been. 'Eddie Cochran . . . proved to be one of the most animated performers America has sent us for a long time. Wearing black leather trousers, tartan shirt and silver waistcoat, he swung his guitar in a circular fashion across his body and pranced across the stage . . . Gene Vincent looked like he'd just parked his motorcycle! His vigorous act had all the pace and drive one associates with that vehicle . . . Gene's presentation is unusual, to say the least. He's bent double over the mike a lot of the time, and at one point ended up lying on his back with the microphone held above him!'

STOCKTON-ON-TEES

Three evenings later the tour resumed at the Globe in Stockton-on-Tees. Among the crowd was trainee police officer Charlie Robbins. 'Gene Vincent, who was then a well-established performer, was my main incentive to attend, but I was very pleased with Eddie Cochran, who sang equally well and appeared to be a better instrumentalist. This was the first time I had encountered screaming girls in the audience . . .'

CARDIFF

The caravan reached Cardiff two nights later, and the local press was in its usual censorious mood. 'Teenagers – Your Theatre Manners Are Shocking,' shouted the *Cardiff and Suburban News*. In this case it was indeed the behaviour of the fans rather than the performers that the reviewer objected to, citing the hurling of lit cigarettes on to the stage during Tony Sheridan's act by youths impatient for Gene Vincent. 'The beat show descended on Cardiff with a frenzied swoop, evoking screams galore from the majority of the 2,000-strong audience. Vocals could not be heard against the instrumental backing and shouts . . . Eddie soon had the customers in the beat mood. Vincent is a more flamboyant showman, almost cuddling his microphone, kneeling and crawling on the stage . . .'

Paul Barrett, later to become a notable rock'n'roll manager and promoter in Wales, launching, for example, the career of Shakin' Stevens, confirms that this was one of Vincent's better nights. 'I cannot recall the support acts at all. They were blown from my memory by the performances of Eddie and Gene. Gene was wonderful, so good it makes his decline even harder to bear . . . [forty years later] I have seen nothing better.'

Later, Vincent and Cochran gave interviews to local hospital radio presenter Vic Dawe. 'Give me stage shows every time,' said Cochran. 'When an audience is enthusiastic I get something from them and in return give a better performance.'

LEEDS

By the time the package reached Leeds for its week-long run at the Empire, Cochran's homesickness had got the better of him. He had already been away from home longer than he expected when he arrived. He and Vincent were staying at the Queen's Hotel in City Square. 'The only time Eddie was incapable of performing through drink was one night in Leeds,' says Hal Carter. 'I'd gone over to the hotel to pick them up and get a cab to bring them to the theatre. When I got there he was out of it, blotto. I said to Gene, "You should have stopped him, taken the bottle off him or something." It was one of Eddie's bad days, when he really was depressed. But Gene had just let him drink. So I was pouring black coffee down him and we got him over to the theatre. We laid him down on the floor of the dressing room. We didn't have a couch or a put-you-up in those days, just a couple of chairs. Laid him on the floor. He always had one of these washing bags with him, a leather one. I'd never seen one before, this black bag with all his washing stuff in.

'You know in the westerns when they caught a villain they'd lay him out on a board so that he looked alive, eyes open, but he was actually dead. Well, Eddie was on the floor with his leather bag under his head looking like that, as if he was laid out ready to go to the morgue. And then we dressed him and lifted him up, put his guitar around his neck, took him down behind the curtains, plugged his guitar in. The band struck up and he just went into performance mode. His eyes were black through not sleeping so he had the sunglasses on, and he did his whole show, and then at the end he used to go down on his knees to finish off. This time there was no way he was going to get up. He'd gone down on his knees, we pulled the tabs across and lifted him up, ran off and opened the tabs again and he did his encore bit. Down on his knees again, close the tabs, run on, stand him up – we did this twice or three times.

'God bless him, from that day to the day he died he swore he didn't remember anything about doing the show. In fact he swore that he didn't do the gig at all, that we were winding him up. But he did. God knows what he'd been drinking because he could polish off a bottle of Jack Daniels and it would seem to have very little effect.'

Big Jim Sullivan confirms that both stars had a huge thirst. 'Eddie and Gene used to drink a bottle of bourbon before they went on stage. They were the first men I'd ever seen who really drank.' In Sullivan's recollection Cochran's drunken episode occurred at the Liverpool Empire, and he seemed to sober up after a couple of numbers. Of course, they could well be separate incidents. 'I don't think that Eddie wanted to be over here for one minute,' says Sullivan. 'And I don't think Gene gave a shit.' Sharon Sheeley confirms that Cochran got more and more homesick. 'When he first got there he loved it . . . but after months of the cold and the hard tour . . . he was burned out. He just wanted to get home.'

The *Yorkshire Evening Post*, presumably on a different night to the drunken one, complimented Cochran on his 'vigorous, open-air approach', but noted that 'Mr Vincent looks frankly macabre in a suit of black leather and gloves to match. Legs spreadeagled, he sings from a crouching position, rarely facing the audience and occasionally shaking his head from side to side in a rhythmic frenzy.'

Cochran was so good on the night that fan Billy Walker attended that he obliterated memories of all the other acts, Vincent included. 'He moved around the stage with ease, gliding slowly across, playing and rolling the guitar around his hips . . . At one part in the show a girl threw Eddie a bunch of roses. He picked them up and said, "Thank you very much." ' One notable feature of the residency at the Leeds Empire is that, for the first time, Cochran closed the show.

Cochran's professionalism during this tour is remarkable. He was plagued by laryngitis, very homesick, often drunk, and obsessed by thoughts of Buddy Holly's death. And yet – those anti-rock reviewers apart – no one ever accused him of putting on a lacklustre show. As soon as he strapped on his guitar and hit the lights he was transformed.

Joe Brown recalls that escaping from the theatre into a waiting car was sometimes a problem, and that after one of the Leeds shows the fans caught up with them. 'We stopped at the traffic lights. Gene . . . was in the front passenger seat, Eddie and I were in the back . . . Eventually [the door] flew open and there's a lot of people all jumping around, reaching in the car. Lights change, driver puts his foot down and shoots off . . . Everything was quiet and all of a sudden Gene said, "Eddie. Eddie . . . they got my pants!" They'd reached in and grabbed his leather trousers and whipped them off.

'He was sitting in the front of the car with his grubby Y-fronts on and his leg iron on our way to this posh hotel in Leeds . . . I have this picture of him going up the stairs to his room with no trousers on and his leg iron going clonk, clonk.'

BIRMINGHAM

And then it was on to Birmingham. 'Gene was always moaning about something or other,' says Hal Carter. 'Now Ed was so good-looking, I always felt that Gene didn't like the attention he was getting. We'd finished Leeds and we were going to Birmingham for the next week. We'd all gone to the station to get the train, and when we got there there's this bird with us. Gene was going for her. I said, "Gene, leave it out, forget it. We're going to a new town. You know what it's like in the States, taking a girl across the state line." I was trying to frighten him. I just didn't want the hassle. He was complaining, "Oh, c'mon, man." I said, "No, off you go."

'There were fans there and they were signing and I hovered about just keeping an eye on things. The stationmaster told us to get on board and I put them in one compartment and then Bill and I went into the next one to get a bit of peace. Next thing I heard this noise of giggling and laughing. I went in and there was this bird. I said, "Oh, shit, Gene, what have you done?" He said, "No, no, man, it wasn't me." I went back into the other compartment. I thought we'd just have to get rid of her when we got to Birmingham. I found out while I was still on the train that Gene had given her the money to buy a ticket. So I was not best pleased.

'Anyway, we got to Birmingham and I hustled them into a cab for the hotel. Just round the corner. Whipped them inside the hotel. We checked in and we were just sitting there with some sandwiches and coffee. They were lying on the beds and the phone went. I picked it up and it was this chick. "I need to speak to Eddie." "You can't. He's not here. You've got to go. Go back to Leeds. And if you don't, I'll call the police." She said, "Please yourself. But when they find out I'm only fourteen you'll all be in trouble." I dropped the phone. What to do? I shouted at Gene, "She's fourteen. Now do you understand why I told you to leave her?" I'm trying to think on my feet. And Vincent said, "Goddam it, Eddie, I told you not to bring that motherfucker with us." He started having a go at Ed. I couldn't believe what I was hearing. But he was shitting himself.

'Ed took the phone and said, "Look, I'm sorry, honey, but we've got to rehearse and then we've got a show to do, you know? You write to me and I promise that I'll write back, OK?" He did this whole spiel beautifully, and got rid of her. But Vincent, as soon as there was a problem, he said it was Eddie's fault. But it wasn't. He was the one who gave her the money. He coaxed her to travel with them. That's why I called him a coward. He'd try and wriggle out of anything.

'I think he had a mental problem. Not mad, but disturbed. Problems with his life. He was always a victim of something – people ripping him off, whatever. That's the vibe he gave off, "I'm a victim." Using the leg to get attention. I could never warm to him. And Sharon didn't like him. He didn't like her, either, because she was taking Ed away from him. No homosexuality, I don't mean that, but just that he relied on Ed totally during that tour. Someone to stand up for him.'

It seems that this close call with the underage girl, with its Chuck Berry overtones, did nothing to reduce Vincent and Cochran's libido, creating more headaches for Carter. 'First night in that hotel. We got there on the Sunday and I left them there because I wasn't staying with them. Bill and I always stayed in Mrs Green's boarding house. She was great. So I booked them in, took them to their rooms, made sure they had room service, all set. Eddie got rid of the girl. I said I'd be back the following lunchtime to go to the theatre for a run-through. I left them to it and came back on the Monday afternoon.

'The manager had steam coming out of his ears. "Get them out of here. Out! I'm not having this, interfering with my staff." I thought, "Oh, shit, what the fuck's going on now?" I went flying up the stairs. It turned out that all the chambermaids and the waitresses had converged on their room, this big double-room suite, and they'd been partying. Like a

Roman orgy. Then the housekeeper – they're all the same, 55-year-old virgins, don't want to know about this disgusting sort of thing – she'd gone in and thought she's cleared the place but she hadn't. She couldn't believe there could be any more in there but there was one in the wardrobe, two under the bed, one in the shower with the curtain across. When she came in she only saw the ones who were visible, and sent them packing. But as soon as she left Gene and Ed were at it again, partying with the ones who were left. She came back and went through the place with a fine-tooth comb, finally got them all out.

'So then I had to find them another place. I spent all afternoon trying to get another hotel, but it was convention time. Everything was full, best hotels, cheap hotels, it didn't matter. Mrs Green's was full as well, because that time Joe stayed with us, Dickie, I think Georgie Fame. I eventually found another boarding house, a twin room. I had a look at it and I couldn't believe it. You had to close the door to get into bed. You had to climb over the beds to get to the sink unit. The bathroom was along the hall.

'But I was desperate, so I said I'd take it. I took them over there in a cab and said I had to get straight back to the theatre. I ducked out. I didn't want to be there when they saw the room. The whole Monday night show, believe me, I was invisible. Especially from Gene, I expected he'd have a right go at me. But apparently the landlady had made a real fuss of them, was really chatty, having a couple of stars in her boarding house. It had become a home from home within two days!'

The digs were in Sparkhill and the landlady was Mrs Lovesey. It was here that the daughter of one of Mrs Lovesey's friends, Rita, came to meet her heroes. She and her husband-to-be Phil Peachey were walking past the house and recognised Joe Brown in the garden. He invited them to return after the show that night for some supper. 'We went into the front room,' recalls Rita, 'and all I could see was this chap lounging back in a big armchair. I thought to myself, "My God, that's Gene Vincent!" . . . Eddie and Gene both got up and shook our hands . . . We had quite a long chat with them both, more so with Eddie as Gene looked as if he was ready to flake out at any time.'

Cochran talked about his future recording plans, and seemed genuinely delighted to meet a couple of fans so informally. Phil became friendly with Joe Brown after that day, and through him the couple met many more of Mrs Lovesey's guests including Dion, Del Shannon and Buzz Clifford.

Another fan, Keith Powell, remembers that although Vincent topped the bill on the first night at Birmingham, they swapped places once more from the second night on. Although the show programme still announced the original running order, it is clear that by this point on the tour Cochran's star was in the ascendant. Powell later formed a band, the Valets, who backed Vincent towards the end of his life. 'The crash had taken quite a toll of him physically and mentally. He was a strange man, but still a great artist.'

LIVERPOOL

In Liverpool Vincent and Cochran were billeted at the Adelphi Hotel. Jim Newcombe was at the Empire show on 15 March. 'The curtains opened on a darkened stage. Three guitarists stood bending over at the waist, facing away from the audience. The now familiar intro of "What'd I Say" began to pound across the footlights. As the tempo increased, the three whirled round as one and we got our first glimpse of Eddie. He was the middleman . . . Eddie didn't move very much but stood there, legs braced, as wave upon wave of sound swept over him . . . He had a peculiar way of shrugging his shoulders to accentuate his songs . . .

'Eddie asked if there were any sixteen-year-olds in the theatre and a forest of waving hands greeted his dedication of Chuck's "Sweet Little Sixteen". He played his guitar with a circular motion . . . During the guitar breaks Eddie would step away from the mike to stand near Big Jim [Sullivan] while they watched each other's hands for the chord changes . . . All too soon his spot was over. We needed the interval to cool down. Thirty-five days later Eddie was dead.'

Newcombe was remembering the performance eleven years later, a decade that had seen everything from Merseybeat to posturing stadium rock, but his recall was clear and fascinating. Cochran, the reluctant showman, was nonetheless a master of simple stagecraft. The musicians respected and bounced off each other, encouraged by the star, but the star behaved as an equal. And then there was that beautiful *noise*. Buddy Holly had introduced us to it in 1958, and Cochran was now confirming the unparalleled excitement of rock'n'roll music.

Not that the correspondent of the *Liverpool Daily Post* got caught up in it. 'Larry Parnes, whose claim to fame is that he has discovered more teenage pop singers than anyone else, has conceived of the idea of putting a whole flock of them into one show. Mr Parnes's claim is dubious because on the evidence of last night's effort any untalented kid who can clutch a microphone or guitar is a potential starlet . . . There is bubbling youth, a riot of noise and an almost complete absence of talent . . . I did at one point, while one of the Americans, oddly attired in a black leather suit, was crawling about the stage clutching a microphone, catch a few phrases of a fearfully maltreated version of "Over the Rainbow". Apart from that I have no idea what anyone was singing about . . . In all charity, this is not entertainment. It was enough to torture the spirits of any of the great stars of the past who may still hover about this theatre . . .' Disc jockey and fan John Peel disagrees: 'Eddie was great, Gene Vincent even better . . .'

NEWCASTLE

A day's travel north brought the company to Newcastle, where the two stars were put up at the Turk's Head Hotel in Grey Street. Ann Matthews was at the Saturday show. 'Joe Brown was near the beginning, full of bounce and good fun and he seemed to enjoy himself as much as we did. When Eddie Cochran came on dressed in silver lamé trousers and waistcoat and black shirt and dark glasses the girls went wild . . . he was very sexy. Billy Fury was also on the bill. He was dressed in a gold lamé suit . . . what he did with those hips while singing was nobody's business! But finally we had Gene Vincent. Our favourite – I've always had this thing about black leather since that night. He was stupendous. His left leg was in plaster, but it didn't hinder him at all . . . The show ended with everyone on stage for the finale, which was "Shake, Rattle and Roll". You didn't know who to look at! What a show . . .'

Steve Aynsley, who has worked on such fanzines as *Git It!* as well as being a fan-club organiser and performer, recalls that the Newcastle running order was Billy Raymond, Tony Sheridan, Joe Brown and then Eddie Cochran – in other words the old order had been restored – before a second half of Georgie Fame, Billy Fury and Gene Vincent. It may be that the theatre manager was unwilling to disturb the bill as printed in the programmes, but there is also Hal Carter's suggestion that Cochran was unwilling to upset Vincent by upstaging him to take into account.

MANCHESTER

Jack Good caught up with the package in Manchester, by which time the two stars were worn out by the rigours of life on the road. 'I have never known such a loyalty to the maxim that "the show must go on",' he reported. When Good arrived at their hotel, 'I found them both in bed. Gene had not recovered from an attack of pneumonia followed by pleurisy. Eddie was suffering from insomnia, and terribly strained eyes.'

Any wife will attest to the fact that, to men, a cold is flu, and so maybe flu becomes pneumonia. But there is no doubt that Vincent was a sick man by this stage of the tour. Not far behind him in the drunken, bug-ridden stakes was Cochran, but Good shrewdly noted insomnia as his main problem. By this time Cochran was becoming consumed by the idea of death on the road, thinking all the time of Buddy and Ritchie Valens, dreaming about crashing. He now had two weeks to live.

The pair were staying at the Milverton Lodge, and after Cochran's death hotel manager Arnold Burlin recalled: 'Cochran was obsessed and in a dreadful state over a strong feeling he had that he was going to die. He told me: "I feel so horrible – there is nothing I can do about it, but I know I'm going to die."

Mr Burlin stated that Cochran got 'het up over his sense of impending doom. He first came to see me on the Thursday morning, and looked pale and drawn. He said he hadn't slept all night – and then blurted out that he was going to die. We couldn't do anything to allay his fears, and he got worse. It was the same on Friday and Saturday, although he managed to get some sleep after we called a doctor, who gave him sedatives. He must have played to fans with that awful fear in his mind. It wasn't as if he was ill – he was perfectly fit . . . He said he had never had such a feeling in his life before. He told me, "You know, I am going to die and I just don't know what to do about it." '

Given that Mr Burlin had the benefit of hindsight and was perhaps tempted to add a gloss to his recollections, and that people do not actually use phrases like 'allay his fears', this evidence does add to the feeling that Cochran was in a fatalistic mood during the last days of his life. Another story has occasionally been aired that he once hammered on a hotel manager's door in the middle of the night, screaming that he was going to die. This would seem to be the 'Chinese whispers' version of Mr Burlin's account – he was undoubtedly severely depressed and brooding, but midnight screaming seems far-fetched. On the other hand, Jack Good once said: 'I never saw Eddie with a sense of doom.'. This does not of course mean that Cochran definitely did *not* have it.

And yet the pair's extraordinary, pill-fuelled energy and sheer trouper spirit – which the dissolute Vincent shared with the ultra-professional but frightened Cochran – saw them through that show. Jack Good was not looking forward to it, having visited them in their sick beds, but he need not have worried.

'They were superb. Eddie Cochran was amazing . . . even more dynamic than I have ever seen . . . And how he used those bloodshot eyes. For the first twelve bars of his act he crouched with his back to the audience, while the Wildcats – greatly improved – whipped up a storm. Then on the first words of "What'd I Say" Eddie swung round . . . and there was a gasp . . . he was wearing dark glasses . . . It looked fabulous and outrageous ... This beat everything for turning a disadvantage into an advantage ...' Good likened Cochran to Rocky Marciano, delivering a knockout blow to the audience.

He then waited impatiently for the star, Vincent. 'Pain-wracked as he was, both from his chest and his leg, for the umpteenth time in plaster through his iron brace breaking, Gene drove himself and his audience unmercifully ... [He] is like a demon possessed by the beat. His face pours with sweat ... contorted to an agonised smile, his huge eyes staring at a vision only he can see. Vincent is the most extraordinary eccentric and terrifying spectacle on the stage today.'

In my view this spectacle reached its peak on this often harrowing, drunken, arduous and ultimately tragic tour. Vincent was at the height of his lunatic power as the most 'possessed' rock performer of all time. The later calculations of 'shock rock' stars, all make-up and special effects – however expertly striking, as in the case of Alice Cooper – and the posturings of screeching stadium stars are just that; calculated postures. On Vincent's 'bad nights' Cochran may well have upstaged him with his wonderful stagecraft and more well-rounded talent, but Vincent's remains one of the few lasting images of rock'n'roll.

Vincent could not have plotted out his effects and moves and characteristic 'gimmicks' however hard he tried. 'When I get to work my moves are spontaneous,' Vincent confirmed in a ghosted column. 'They're not rehearsed or worked out beforehand.' The marvellous Screamin' Jay Hawkins was an actor playing the role of a rock'n'roll madman compared to Vincent, who simply *was* a rock'n'roll madman. Most of his records, most of his post-1960 performances, can only hint at the demon who stalked the Hippodromes and Empires of 1960 Britain.

Great visual art can be born from the cool, precise calculations of Vermeer or Raphael, but also from the passion of Bosch and El Greco. Vincent seemed driven by desperation, descending into hell, clinging by his fingertips to the rim of rock'n'roll heaven. Vermeer would have found him gross, but Bosch would have been in the front row, punching the air, urging him on. No wonder Vincent was always drunk. His whole life was a rehearsal for death, screaming defiance at it while on stage, waiting for it quietly in his private moments, then raging again as the drink took hold, waving a gun or lashing out with a knife. 'Only Eddie and I could take Gene's gun away from him,' says Joe Brown. 'I've been called out of my dressing room a couple of times to get the gun off him. I was daft when I think about it.' He would admonish Vincent: 'You can't keep poking it in people's ears. They don't like it. It frightens them.' Vincent would always claim that he would never hurt anyone. Brown also says: 'Eddie was like a bit of a mother hen with Gene . . . [Gene] drank too much and it was a bit dangerous leaving him on his own . . . We had to look after him a bit, really.'

The *Manchester Evening News* broke ranks with the majority of local papers by complimenting the show. 'Americans Gene Vincent and Eddie Cochran led the assault. Vincent had to combat intense pain from his plaster-encased foot among other things, but this seemed to needle him into a tremendous performance. He started off using the microphone as a crutch and finished using it as a club, hammering the stage in time with his accelerating beat. Cochran was more relaxed, but equally effective . . .'

After the Friday performance in Manchester, Vincent, Cochran, Fury and Brown travelled to Oldham, mingling with the crowds at the Oldham Carnival Ball and signing autographs. This caused so much excitement that a police motorcycle escort was needed to get them safely away.

LONDON

From Manchester the company travelled to London. 'Everybody's been real good to us, and that's how we got on our feet again so quickly,' said Vincent when Keith Goodwin, of the *New Musical Express*, pitched up for the latest medical bulletin from 'the likeable pair' at their London hotel. 'It's been pretty tough these last few weeks,' admitted Cochran. They were both enthusing about Brenda Lee, and her record 'Sweet Nuthin's'. 'Are Gene and Eddie fans of this curly-headed, fifteen-year-old bundle of dynamite?' mused Goodwin. ' "You bet!" ' they chodused.

Both Vincent and Cochran complimented the standard of rock'n'roll singing and instrumental skill in the British outpost of the art, mentioning Joe Brown in particular. Vincent noted that his 'wild rock songs' went down best – the UK was quickly developing a male-rocker culture alongside the familiar swooning girls. This was the main reason why the reputation of Holly, Cochran and Vincent was seen as timeless in Britain, transient at home. Swooners swoon for the latest chart sensation, but rockers recognise and stay faithful to class.

Indeed, Cochran spotted 'the same fans at theatres all over the country', suggesting a depth of support that already transcended that for a current star at the local Odeon. 'They must have travelled miles to see us,' he marvelled. Yes, and in the main by bus and train, because we didn't get a Thunderbird for our eighteenth birthday over here.

Their only reservation about touring the UK was just that – the travel. 'Most of our journeys are by train,' said Vincent. 'I don't like British trains. They're not comfortable.' But as long as Jack Good represented the country, then they were happy. 'He's the greatest guy I ever knew and he produces the best beat show of all. There's nothing to compare with Jack's show in the States,' said Vincent. 'He's a brilliant guy,' agreed Cochran.

Elsewhere Vincent repeated his praise of Good. 'That man has more musical sense in his little finger than I could acquire in a lifetime . . . [He] has given me confidence.' Vincent stressed that he was a shy man – which indeed he was, when sober – and this is more confirmation of Good's skill in exploiting the potential he saw behind the reserved façade.

The teenage fanzine *Valentine*, just three weeks before Cochran's death, cast his horoscope. Libras are 'thoroughly human types', it said, thereby ruling out any possibility of a trace of budgerigar in his genes. But a chilling note is struck in a 'personal message' from Cochran amid all the superstitious tosh, and it was picked up as the title phrase for Julie Mundy and Darrel Higham's 2000 biography. In Cochran's own hand, it reads: 'Best always to the readers of *Valentine*. Don't forget me, Eddie Cochran.' With hindsight, this apparently throwaway scribble is almost unbearably poignant.

Adrian Owlett recalls seeing the show during its run at the Finsbury Park Empire. 'I was with a young teddy boy, Colin King. We spent all day just hanging around. At one point we went for a coffee, to a place under the railway arches. And there was Gene, Eddie and, I think, Big Jim Sullivan. An extraordinary piece of luck. I introduced myself, and I showed them some photographs I'd taken at Gene's Kingston show. Gene introduced us to Eddie, and we had a chat about what they were doing. Eddie stood up at one point, and I remember being shocked at how small he was, maybe five foot six. He had this tiny pipe – I didn't know it at the time, but it would have been a dope pipe. He sat there like a little old man, smoking this little pipe, in full stage make-up. They were doing a run-through that day.

'When we went back to our table, naturally we earwigged their conversation. It was centred on music, about Duane Eddy, Bobby Darin. They were both drinking tea, and Gene told me later he'd never drunk it before coming to England. He was wearing a check bomber jacket and a scarf – there was quite a nip in the air, particularly for an American. Eddie was wearing the flying jacket he wore on *Boy Meets Girls*, and blue jeans.

'We hung around the stage door in the afternoon, and heard Eddie rehearsing. I remember "What'd I Say". There were two shows that day, and we went to both. Eddie changed his shirt from red to black, and also his opening number. For the first show he opened with "Somethin' Else" and for the second with "What'd I Say". He would lead into the songs on guitar and the band picked it up from there. But at that time Gene *always* opened with his slow version of "Rocky Road Blues".

'There were big posters on all the tube platforms advertising the tour, and as you approached the Finsbury Park Empire, right at the top of the building was this V-shaped billboard with the words "Vincent–Cochran".

'The build-up to Cochran, who closed the first half, was more "variety" than rock'n'roll. Not really suitable. But then the curtains were drawn, sudden bright light, and he started playing. Wow! Not as riveting as Gene, not as spectacular an entrance, but the guitar was stunning. And also he could talk to the audience, which Gene couldn't. Though Gene could deal with hecklers. His best line when, say, there was a hold-up for some reason and someone shouted "Get on with it", was to say, "Son, I could make a fool of you but your ma and pa beat me to it."

'Eddie did that train movement with the guitar [mimicking the pistons of a steam engine] but when he did that it was Big Jim Sullivan or Joe Brown actually taking the solo.' Brown confirms this: 'Eddie used to play rhythm on stage and he hardly took any solos.'

'For Gene,' Owlett continues, 'there was a difference in build-up. As it had been at Kingston, there was this tension in the air. A pin spot roved around, picking up nothing in particular, until it hit the drummer, Brian Bennett. And there was Gene, crouching down next to him. As the song started the light just exploded, all over the stage. No, no one could follow him!

'After the show, well, we were fifteen-year-old groupies, if you like. We hung about at the stage door and saw Gene and Eddie leave in a taxi. But we knew that they were staying at the Stratford Court Hotel, just off Oxford Street, so we went there. Two o'clock in the morning – we couldn't get home to Walton-on-Thames anyway. Then a lot of the cast turned up and went upstairs. We could hear a jam session going on in their room. We walked down to Waterloo Station and got the milk train home to end a fantastic day.

'A few days later I heard the midnight news on the wireless, at Easter. There had been a car crash and two American rock'n'rollers had been killed. No names. It could only have been them, of course. To my shame, when it was confirmed that Eddie had died and Gene was alive, I suddenly felt relieved. That Gene hadn't been the one to die.'

The first night at Finsbury Park Empire, 4 April, was Sharon's twentieth birthday, and she had just arrived to join Cochran for the rest of the tour. She, Cochran, Duane Eddy and Eddy's musicians went to the Condor Club in the West End to see Terry Dene performing. 'When we got back from the club,' she later recalled, 'Duane went to bed and Eddie and I sat in the hotel lobby. We ordered and drank three bottles of champagne.'

They stayed up so late that a chambermaid appeared with a vacuum cleaner. 'Eddie had an idea. He talked the maid into lending him her cap and cleaner and up he went to Duane's room. He started to clean up while wearing the maid's cute little cap, saying, "My goodness, Mr Eddy, you're very untidy, aren't you?" '

Keith Woods was at one of the Finsbury Park shows. He had already seen Vincent on *Boy Meets Girls* and 'overnight I changed my hairstyle, my clothes, everything. I came out of my shell overnight. I even walked with a limp to school!'

He recalls that the review in his local paper, the *Tottenham Herald*, opined that balladeer Peter Wynne 'will be a star long after Eddie Cochran and Gene Vincent are forgotten'. Woods notes that Cochran included 'Fever' in his set and 'I remember in particular a really brilliant "Hallelujah, I Love Her So" and a really rocking "C'mon Everybody". Then Cochran went to the left-hand side of the stage and he held his guitar up and danced across the stage on one leg . . .'

Vincent also included an unfamiliar number in his set – Jack Scott's reverberating ballad 'What in the World's Come Over You', which had just entered the UK charts. 'At the end of the show they came on together and they did "What'd I Say" and "Shake, Rattle and Roll". Eddie came on stage from the left wing with Vincent on the right and Vincent was smashing the mike stand on the stage with all his hair flying amok and Cochran danced across towards him with one leg up and they more or less met in the middle of the stage.

'The old Finsbury Park Empire stage was really shaking and because of all the dust coming up from the stage floor they were almost obliterated from view. The audience was going wild . . .'

In an unidentified newspaper cutting reporting the Finsbury Park gigs, the writer says: 'The Empire's programme costs a shilling. Although I must on principle object to this extortion, it is also fair to say that the programme is more interesting than usual and the biographical material no doubt holds a teenage appeal. But I think it is extortion all the same.'

David Lands saw the Vincent–Cochran tour seven times in and around London, as well as the *NME* Poll Winners' Concert, and was at the Finsbury Park Empire. He recalls: 'Vincent took my breath away every time he appeared. By now his act centred around his mesmerising version of "Over the Rainbow". The audience were stunned into silence as his delicate voice filled the theatre. What really captured them was the way Gene gazed up beyond the gods in a trancelike state and kept the rowdy rockers spellbound.

'After two or three shows Cochran had developed his act. I'll never forget the darkened stage, the thumping intro of "Somethin' Else" and the spotlight hitting Eddie's back. His outfit was memorable – one time it was a mauve shirt, a silver waistcoat and leather jeans. After the intro he swung round to deliver the opening line – "Looka here!" To cap it all he wore sunglasses. Some image – we'd never seen anyone wearing them on stage before. He was cool. But despite this, and the fact that Eddie was a marvellous musician, it was Gene who had the magnetism on stage. He was menacing, his act was full of drama, and when he swung that leg over the microphone or stared into the distance we were captivated. I've seen most of the greats over the years but I've never seen anyone surpass the magic that Vincent brought to the stage.'

Joe Brown has a painful reason to remember the leg-swinging gimmick. 'He had a piece where he'd swing his iron leg over my head. He was very accident-prone and he was breaking that leg all of the time. One night it was in plaster up to his thigh. He swung it up in his usual way but he caught me on the side of the head. It knocked me flat and squashed my guitar.'

Among those who visited Cochran and Vincent during their week in London were the Crickets, also on tour at the time. Drummer Jerry Allison recalls: 'We actually saw Eddie three or four days before the accident. We stopped by the hotel – in London, I guess it was. We hung out with him and Gene Vincent for a while. They'd been here about six weeks or something [and] they were real anxious to get home . . .'

BRISTOL

By the time of the scheduled break in the tour after the Bristol dates, both Vincent and Cochran were more than ready for it, exhausted by all the travel by rail and road. In addition, in spite of the presence of Sharon, Cochran was still very homesick indeed, quite capable of spending a thousand dollars on phone calls home in a week, passing the lonely hours talking to his mother, brother Bob and sister Gloria from his room in the Grand Hotel. They did enjoy a day's rest on the Friday, however, because it was Good Friday, when all theatres in those days remained dark.

A member of one of the Bristol audiences, Edward John Penny, vividly evokes Cochran's sense of stagecraft, building up the atmosphere and excitement, making the crowd wait for the cathartic launch into the first verse of 'C'mon Everybody'. The way he started his act here contrasts with the back-to-the-audience pose for 'What'd I Say'.

'The stage was dark, a spotlight picked up the head of a guitar to the right of the stage . . . the beat got louder and Eddie, who was dressed in an orange jacket, black slacks, a dark shirt and his dark shades, moved slowly across the stage rotating his guitar to the beat. He stepped up slowly to the microphone in the middle of the stage – no voice, just the drumming beat of the guitar . . . a strobe of light fell on him, the guitar and the microphone – the rest of the stage was in darkness. The noise of screams and whistles, feet stamping to the beat, it was fantastic.

'The beat stopped; his arms reached out to his sides. Eddie lifted his right arm very slowly as he looked straight ahead. His hand came up to the frame of his shades and very slowly took them off . . . Eddie smiled and looked all around the audience. I think he said something but I couldn't hear for all the noise.

'The music started and he began to play and move to the rhythm. It was absolutely breathtaking. You felt the music deep down inside of you, and you just had to move to it . . . Everybody was moving and dancing to the music. I have never felt that sort of excitement before, to hear one of the greatest rock'n'rollers there ever was . . . watching him move and play the guitar like no other . . .'

The critic of the *Bristol Evening Post* noted sagely that Vincent's bent-double position 'puts the diaphragm at its greatest disadvantage'. Seeing Cochran's dark glasses, the writer wondered whether the audience was being palmed off with 'Mr Terry Dene or that nice Mr Marty Wilde, back from his honeymoon incognito. But it was Eddie all right, apologising for a sore throat . . .'

Early in 1971 Vincent was to reveal some surprising snippets to Terry Clemson, the guitarist who backed him on two tours in the year or so before his death. 'I remember him talking about Eddie Cochran,' recalls Clemson. 'He described themselves as almost like brothers. He claimed that Eddie had no intention of ever marrying Sharon Sheeley. In fact, he said, on that tour often he and Eddie would share a hotel room while Sharon stayed alone.'

Vincent told a similar tale that year to *International Times*. 'She said she was engaged to him, which was the biggest goddamned lie I'd ever heard in my whole life. I never heard such a bunch of shit in my life.'

This reflects Hal Carter's memories of the relationship. 'Sharon was besotted with Eddie, but he was a bit of a playboy. All the girls liked him. She wasn't with him all the time when she was over here. She'd go off sightseeing. And Bill Fury fell in love with her. So he was lapdogging. Ed was a ladies' man, but he did like Sharon very much. More than that, in fact, but the temptation was often too much for him. She knew about it but looked the other way. But it was her he invited to come over because he was homesick and lonely. He wouldn't have asked anyone else to come over. I couldn't see him getting married, though, not for a long time, until he'd got it all out of his system.'

Vincent also confirmed to Clemson the more familiar tale of the communication cord. 'He said that on one of their train journeys they became fascinated by the communication cord, and Eddie kept pulling it to stop the train. When the guard came round to see what the problem was Eddie would just smile and pay the five-pounds penalty. This apparently happened several times on the journey.'

Hal Carter was absent for the Bristol dates, and his place as road manager was taken by Patrick Thompkins. It was he who handed the flight tickets for America to Cochran, who was overjoyed. For the last leg of the tour substitute artist Johnny Gentle arrived by car, and Cochran – who had had enough of coach travel – asked if he could give him, Vincent and Sharon a lift back to London.

Gentle recalls: 'Eddie asked me if I could take him, Sharon and Gene back to London, but I couldn't because I'd got a full car.' The four were Gentle, Peter Wynne and their girlfriends. Another version of the story, however, asserts that a taxi was always the chosen option.

In a chilling addition to the story Gentle says that he was very short of petrol, it was after midnight and the garages were closed. He asked a policeman if he knew of anywhere, and was told that there was a breakdown truck up ahead. The truck driver gave Gentle permission to siphon fuel from the wreck, and he only realised who had been in the car a day later.

Why was Carter not around? 'I finished the Vincent–Cochran tour early, after Manchester, I think,' he says. 'Jack Good had come up with this idea for a new TV show, *Wham!*, and he wanted Bill and Joe to do it. He needed them that week, the week of the Bristol dates – because those dates were arranged after Larry had agreed to let Jack have Bill and Joe. And of course I worked for Parnes first and foremost. So he brought in Johnny Gentle to replace them in Bristol, and I organised Pat [Thompkins] to look after Eddie and Gene for the week.'

With no lift available the next alternative might have been a train, but by the time the show finished the last Easter-service train from Bristol

Temple Meads to Paddington had long gone. Although their flight was not until 1.00 p.m. on the following day, Cochran was anxious to get going, and so Thompkins booked a cab to take them from the Hippodrome in Bristol at 11.00 p.m. on the Saturday.

Billy Raymond recalls the occasion. 'We were all packing up, chatting and laughing, and there was no real hurry due to Eddie and Gene's departure time. I knew that Eddie was going to Heathrow for an early flight in the morning. At the end of the hilarity Eddie and I hugged each other – he was a lovely "huggy" person, but there was nothing sexual about this.

'We talked about us all being together in ten days time for the Moss–Stoll tour and, sadly, the show became *A Tribute to Eddie Cochran*. I was driving my own car home, to the Strand in London. I didn't get there until about five in the morning and crashed into bed, taking the phone off the hook. I put the phone on around three in the afternoon and it rang immediately. It was a friend asking me how the tour was going. He then dropped the bombshell . . . I have to admit that I cried for days.'

Pete Purnell has a poignant memory of the last night. 'After the show was over we were determined to get [Cochran] and Vincent's auto-graphs, so we waited with our car outside the stage door. After some time they came out, but they did not sign anything and hurried into a Mark II Ford Consul taxi that was waiting. Eddie did throw out some publicity photographs. I grabbed two and still have them today. Anyway, because we thought they were probably going to a hotel, we got in our car and followed them at great speed, through the centre of Bristol, on to the Bath road, but we gave up the chase after three miles. It wasn't until the Sunday morning that we heard the news of the car crash . . . it was a show I shall never forget.'

Cochran forgot his leather jeans that night, and even forgot where he had put them – under the mattress back at the Grand Hotel, to press them overnight. He rang the porters' lodge at the hotel and the phone was answered by pageboy Pete Williams. 'He asked me if I would go up to his room and see if I could get his leather jeans . . . I looked everywhere but I couldn't find them. So I phoned the stage door at the Hippodrome . . . they told me they would get Eddie to ring me back. A little while later the phone rang . . . Eddie said, "It's my fault. Look under the mattress, that's where they are." . . . I wrapped the jeans in brown paper and legged it to the Hippodrome . . . I was told I would have to wait as Eddie was on stage. Gene Vincent was sitting on a wicker basket watching Eddie perform, so I sat next to him.' When he came off stage a grateful Cochran gave Williams a generous tip.

'They were meant to go from Bristol straight to the airport,' says Carter. 'They had everything with them. But Ed wanted to go back to the flat in Jermyn Street first. Pat had hired this taxi service to take them backwards and forwards to the theatre, so he asked the driver how much it would cost from Bristol to London. Twenty-five pounds! But the driver, George Martin, instead of going to the firm and telling them he had a night job, went to a mate and borrowed *his* car.' Years later Vincent had slightly different recall. 'I [not Cochran] was supposed to pick up some suits . . . we hired a car, what we thought was a taxi . . .' But the implication that it was not a regular taxi tallies with Carter's account.

It should be said that this version is contradicted by the frequent assertion that there was confetti in the car from a wedding earlier in the day, suggesting that it *was* a taxi, and that one of those making the claim was Sharon Sheeley.

'When he crashed he was going the wrong way,' continues Carter. 'He'd turned back along the A4. The A4 was always chock-a-block, and if you got a lorry there you could be stuck for hours. So what he did, instead of taking the A4 from Bristol, was to use the back road from Bristol to Bath, and the back road from Bath to Chippenham.

'He came down under the viaduct and he saw a sign saying "A4" and he turned right. Instead of going over the bridge and turning left, he was actually heading back towards Bristol. Then he braked too hard when he realised he was going the wrong way. The tyre went and he hit the kerb. They'd just redone the road with new chippings, so he was sliding. It was just a horrible chain of events.' The car hit the kerb on the other side of the road and skidded backwards until it crashed sideways into a concrete lamppost on Rowden Hill.

As the press photograph of the wrecked car makes clear, the impact broke the nearside rear-window arch and smashed the rear door. Although Cochran was sitting in the middle of the back seat, with Sharon the most vulnerable of the three, he instinctively threw himself to his left to protect her. His head hit the roof, probably causing the fatal injuries, and as the car continued to spin and the door gave way he was thrown out on to the road. Sharon had her pelvis broken and Vincent fractured his collarbone as well as aggravating his chronic leg injury. Remarkably, Martin and Patrick Thompkins climbed out of the front seats almost unscarred, physically at least.

Vincent later recalled: 'When the three of us travelled together Sharon always sat in the middle but, because of the crowd of fans, I got in the cab first, then Eddie, then Shari last. With Eddie in the middle, the only way he could have flown out of that door was if he tried to cover Shari. The only way I came out alive was because I had taken a sleeping pill. After the crash I woke up and carried Eddie over to the ambulance even though I had a broken arm. I was in such a state of shock that I thought nothing was wrong with me.'

By 1971 the theory had altered slightly. 'Usually I got in first, then it was Eddie and her. But this one night, I don't know what happened, but she got in first, then Eddie and me. Eddie was killed 'cause he was in the middle. Now there's only one way he could have been killed. That was throwing himself across her body. It's the only way! We've tried to figure it out. Nobody's really told the truth . . .'

During the same interview he described the events immediately following the crash once more. 'Eddie went out the door . . . skidded two hundred and fifty yards on the back of his head. I was thrown on the grass and had my whole left side broken up. I picked Eddie up and carried him. When we got to the hospital I told the doc, "I'll give you a million dollars if you can save his life." He said he was dying . . . I had a doctor flown in by helicopter . . . a brain surgeon. He operated, then Eddie died. Two hundred and seventy-two concussions across the back of his head.'

Vincent had had many years and many repetitions to embroider this tale. More objective accounts of the scene suggest that he was unconscious, and as for flying in a brain surgeon – did he have his name in his address book? – he is quoted below as lying in bed after regaining consciousness thinking that the patient across the aisle was Cochran, not knowing he was dead.

Rob Finnis reported in 1988 that a local couple, Dick and Phyllis Jennings, were driving home and were soon on the scene. Cochran was gurgling, and bleeding from the mouth and ears, Sharon was sobbing his name and Vincent lay silent. The Jenningses made them as comfortable as they could and a woman in a nearby house summoned an ambulance, which arrived promptly from the depot in town to take the injured trio first to a nearby cottage hospital, and hence to St Martin's Hospital in Bath, where a doctor was already waiting to examine them.

The police accident report was filled out in Chippenham by Police Constable R.S. McIntyre.

Fatal Accident at Bath Road, Chippenham at 11.50 p.m., 16 April 1960. At 12 midnight . . . I was called to the scene of the accident . . . I found that a cream-coloured Ford Consul saloon, reg. no.

RBO 869, travelling from Bath along the A4 towards the direction of Chippenham, was the only involved vehicle, and that it had not been moved prior to my arrival.

I took its position, the vehicle being on the driver's nearside facing obliquely towards the crown of the road and in the direction of Chippenham. The rear nearside of the vehicle was tight into the driver's nearside kerb. The rear nearside of the vehicle was extensively damaged – the nearside doors being smashed and the rear window torn out, the rear of the car being completely twisted.

I examined the road and found skid marks commencing on the Bath side of the location and extending for 50 yards, these marks veering over to the driver's offside of the road and then back to the driver's nearside. I found traces of paint on a lamp standard located on the driver's nearside kerb, this paint being cream in colour.

The width of the road was 30 feet, there being a pavement on either side. The location is a gentle rising left-hand bend when travelling towards Chippenham and is well inside the built-up area. The weather was fine and the road dry. The occupants of the car were all taken to the Chippenham Cottage hospital and later transferred to St Martin's Hospital, Bath, where the deceased died during the afternoon of the 17th April 1960. Driver George Martin was uninjured. The other passengers in the car being Sharon Sheeley (aged 20), Gene Vincent Craddock (aged 25), both US citizens under the care of Fosters Agency, and Patrick Thompkins (aged 29), these persons being detained at St Martin's.

The deceased is a US Citizen and was by profession a well known 'rock'n'roll' singer. His personal manager is a Mr Riley of Room 212, Stratford Court Hotel, Mayfair, London. Mr Riley may be called to give evidence of indentification.

Cochran never regained consciousness and the cause of death was given as lacerations to the brain caused by the impact of the crash. He died at 4.10 p.m. on the Sunday. Given the nature of his injuries it had been hoped at one time to move him to Frenchay Hospital in Bristol, which then as now had a reputation for treating neurological injuries. He was considered too weak to move, however. The postmortem two days later, carried out by Dr C.D. Cross, identified further abrasions and bruising, as well as internal haemorrhaging.

Also early on the scene had been a police cadet, David Harman, who retrieved the precious Gretsch guitar, miraculously unharmed. Later, he became singer Dave Dee, who with Dozy, Beaky, Mick and Tich had a string of hits throughout the second half of the 1960s. The guitar remained at the police station for a while before being returned with the rest of Cochran's possessions.

Cochran had suggested that Vince Eager went back with him to America during the break in the tour to do some recording. Eager says that he was at Heathrow when he heard about the crash. At this stage Cochran was still alive. Eager's driver Noel took him to St Martin's Hospital. 'The doctor told me that Gene is not too bad, but Eddie is in a bad way and that he is not expected to survive . . . At about three o'clock I started to leave the hospital . . . Everyone arrived – Larry Parnes, Billy, Norm Riley . . . The press had found out they were there . . . Then Larry took over as he used to like doing. The first thing he said was that Eddie's next record was to be "Three Steps to Heaven" – and that was before Eddie had died! Of course I just flipped . . . I had a big row with Larry on the steps of the hospital and I never worked with him again. I just got into the car and left everybody there.'

When he was talking to Spencer Leigh, however, Eager's chronology was different. He said, 'I was going to the States with him for five weeks,' which could not have been during the ten-day break. Both memories could be accurate, however, if they refer to separate occasions.

On 18 April the *Los Angeles Times* reported: 'His body will be flown home, probably in the care of British singer Vince Eager, who was to have flown to Los Angeles with Cochran.' Eager did consider travelling to the States but changed his mind, concerned that Larry Parnes might make publicity capital out of it.

In Eager's view Cochran looked after Vincent, in contrast to those who felt that they were not as close as is usually assumed. 'Gene would still be alive today if Eddie had lived, because he was like a father to Gene. If he was having a drink and Eddie said no more, Gene wouldn't drink. Of course when Eddie died there was nobody. Gene went to pieces.'

From Buddy Holly to Otis Redding, the *Daily Mirror* of all the British newspapers was the most likely to treat the death of a pop star as a front-page splash, and Cochran was no exception. ' "Rock" Star Dies In Crash' was the headline on Monday 18 April, illustrated by a smiling Cochran, a picture of Sharon Sheeley and the grim wreckage of the car. 'American rock'n'roll singing star Eddie Cochran, 21, died yesterday after a car taking him to London Airport crashed.'

The paper reported that Sheeley was in a 'fair' condition in hospital, and that the news was broken to her mother in Hollywood by the mother of Ritchie Valens. 'Eddie was the first and only boyfriend Sharon ever had,' said Mrs Mary Sheeley. 'They were unofficially engaged.' The time of death was put at four o'clock the previous afternoon. Vincent was quoted as saying: 'I hope to be out in three or four days.'

The front page was completed by a report indicating a disastrous Easter holiday on the roads. 'At least 33 people have been killed and 632 injured on the roads since the Easter Holiday started on Good Friday,' it stated, and it seemed that Cochran was one of twelve who died on the Sunday. Given that traffic density was roughly one-tenth of that today, it was indeed a black weekend. In June, at Bristol Assizes, George Martin was convicted of speeding, fined £50 and banned from driving for fifteen years. He was also threatened with a jail term if he defaulted on the fine. The ban was quashed in 1969.

The *Daily Sketch*, tabloid rival to the *Mirror*, also gave the tragic event due prominence, and reporter Edward Connolly described it in more sensational terms, under the splash headline 'Crash Kills Boy Rock Star': 'Eddie Cochran, the 21-year-old rock'n'roll star, died in hospital yesterday after being hurled from a crashed car. He had terrible head injuries. For hours doctors in St Martin's Hospital, Bath, fought to save his life. But he was too weak to stand an operation.

'In another ward lay Sharon Sheeley. She, too, was seriously hurt in the crash. Her song "Poor Little Fool" put Ricky Nelson in the pop hit parade and she was going to write songs for Eddie. They had been school chums in America. And Eddie's mother said last night they were "more than friends". The £1000-a-week star was on his way to Hollywood for filming after a two-and-a-half month tour of Britain.'

After the loss of his best friend, Vincent evoked the old showbiz cliché 'the show must go on'. 'I shall rejoin the show even if it means that I have to go on stage strapped up,' he promised. But in the meantime he discharged himself from hospital on the Tuesday with the intention of accompanying Cochran's body back to Los Angeles. However, he could not book a suitable flight and the body was not released in time.

Cochran's close friend Johnny Rook got the news from his brother Charles, who had heard it announced on the radio. Rook rang the Cochran home in Buena Park and Red, Cochran's brother-in-law, asked him to fly out there right away. When he entered the house Rook remembered a promise he had made to Cochran, to look after his mother if anything should happen to him as it did to Buddy Holly. Then the phone call came to say that the body was on its way from England.

Cochran's body eventually reached Los Angeles on the following Saturday. Brother Bob went to view it, and came back saying over and over, 'It doesn't look like him.' They decided on a closed-casket funeral, and on Monday 25 April, Cochran was buried in the Forest Lawn Memorial Park in Cypress, not far from the family home. There were about 250 mourners, including Mrs Concepcion Valens, Ritchie's mother, and the short service was conducted by the Rev. C. Sumner Reynolds of Maywood Methodist Church. The grave, some 300 yards to the left of the main gate, is shaded by a huge tree.

On the gravestone is a touching motto: 'If mere words can console us for the loss of our beloved Eddie then our love for him was a false love.' The effect of this cryptic message is somewhat diluted by the poem that fills most of the stone, included here for the sake of completeness.

Heavenly music filled the air
That very tragic day.
Something seemed to be missing tho'
So I heard the Creator say:
'We need a master guitarist and singer
I know of but one alone
His name is Eddie Cochran
I think I'll call him home.
I know the folks on Earth won't mind
For they will understand
That the Lord loves perfection
Now we'll have a perfect band.'
So as we go through life, now we know
That perfection is our goal
And we strive for this
So when we are called
We'll feel free to go.

A year later Vincent was to recall his stay in hospital in touching terms. 'I suppose I was in a daze,' he said, 'but I kept thinking the guy in the bed opposite mine was Eddie. Seeing him there gave me comfort. It wasn't until I asked a visitor one day, "Why don't you go over and see how Eddie's getting on?" that I learned the truth.'

Sheeley said that she knew the worst straight away, however, while still in the ambulance. 'I knew he would die. I can't explain how, but it was a strong instinct I had and when the doctor came into my room a day or so later, he didn't have to break the news to me. I knew.'

Cochran's co-stars paid tribute to him. Marty Wilde said: 'Eddie had a fabulous stage act. He was a raunchy, loose-limbed guy who enjoyed himself. There was nothing pretentious about him. He was an extremely good musician . . . ahead of most people musically, and I don't think he would have stayed with rock'n'roll. You'd have heard a lot more from him in the 1960s.'

'I rate Eddie Cochran very highly as a rock'n'roll guitarist,' said Joe Brown. 'He was great. He could play a good lead guitar but he said to me, "You play lead, I'll play rhythm." ' Brown also confirmed the story about how Cochran strung his guitar unusually. 'He used to put a second string instead of a third string on his guitar so that he had an unwound string and he could bend it and get those bluesy sounds you never heard in England. That was the greatest thing I learned from Eddie and, as a result, I got loads and loads of session work.'

Big Jim Sullivan said: 'He was a guitarist of exceptional talent and originality . . . I don't think that Eddie ever reached the heights that someone of his formidable talent could have achieved . . . At that time I didn't realise how much an effect Eddie was to have on my career . . . I look back at that time and see how the American influence came to England. The British guitar scene progressed because we only listened to the best that the Americans gave us . . . We did it our way with the emergence of the Beatles and many other UK artists. If you ask these musicians who were their influences, I bet they will mention the same names, and among those names would be Gene Vincent and Eddie Cochran. Well, I played guitar for both of them and without doubt they changed my life!'

Vince Eager remembered his friend: 'The thing about Eddie was that he wasn't typical star material . . . he loved going into transport cafés and coffee bars. I never once saw the star-edged prima donna bit that so many others in the business had . . . [and his] guitar playing was truly amazing.'

Georgie Fame added his tribute: 'Eddie was a wonderful guitarist and a terrific performer. He was a really nice guy and more than anyone else he was responsible for introducing Ray Charles's music to the masses of England.'

On his discharge from hospital, his projected Paris dates cancelled, Vincent flew from London to New York, where he was reunited with his partner Darlene and her daughter Debbie. From there they flew to Portland, Oregon, and on to Vancouver for a recuperative holiday. He told local paper the *Columbian* that he was determined to complete the tour 'even if I have to sit down'. Darlene's parents lived in Hazel Dell, Vancouver, and Vincent stayed with them before preparing to return to London.

Vince Taylor, a veteran of Good's forerunner to *Boy Meets Girls*, *Oh Boy!*, was announced as joining the resumed tour, while Jerry Keller was booked as Cochran's replacement. Taylor, who with his band the Playboys had produced one of the meatiest cuts of British rock'n'roll in 1959's 'Brand New Cadillac', later relocated to France where for a while he was second only to Johnny Hallyday in the rock pantheon. The early Playboys included the rhythm section of drummer Brian Bennett and bassist Brian Locking, later of the 1960 Wildcats touring with Vincent and Cochran, and later still of the Shadows.

Meanwhile Joe Brown was sounding off about pop music in the *Melody Maker*. 'To me country & western is the only music. I don't like modern jazz. Shocking waste of good musicianship. Clever and all that – but me, I'd take it to the taxidermist. I'm afraid rock is dying and it's a damned shame.'

Brown was only reluctantly reflecting a feeling abroad in the aftermath of Cochran's death and reflected in the attitude of the television moguls – that rock'n'roll was reaching its sell-by date. Not true, thank God, as the blues revival, Merseybeat, Creedence Clearwater Revival and Canned Heat, among many other examples, would triumphantly spend the remainder of the decade demonstrating. The mistaken idea that rock'n'roll was a fad like the hula hoop, rather than a sturdy plant growing from the bedrock of the blues and hillbilly, was commonly held at the time. Although ABC did launch a stopgap show, *Thank Your Lucky Stars*, featuring such new kids on the block as the Rolling Stones, Britain had to wait until *Ready Steady Go* in 1964 for a true successor to Good's brilliant, energetic and, yes, vulgar exercises in unadulterated rock.

Had Cochran not died he would have returned to the UK on 27 April and resumed an extended tour in Hanley, Lewisham, Cheltenham, Salisbury, Guildford, Halifax, Chester, Wolverhampton and Romford. On his return Vincent picked up the threads at the Lewisham Gaumont (later renamed the Odeon), a regular rock'n'roll venue when not showing movies, now alas demolished in favour of a dual carriageway. He was still clearly feeling the effects of the crash, frequently massaging his collarbone. He told the audience. 'I want to sing for you Eddie's favourite song.' Although this preference is a little hard to believe, there could nevertheless have been no more appropriate tribute than Vincent's beautiful version of 'Over the Rainbow', and inevitably it brought tears to many in the audience.

In May 'Three Steps to Heaven' entered the British Top 20, climbing week by week to peak at No. 2 in the *Melody Maker* chart, but reaching the top spot in rival *New Musical Express*. In its own way, just like Buddy Holly's 'It Doesn't Matter Anymore', it was a death disc. And like Holly, memories of Cochran soon faded at home, where 'Three Steps to

Heaven' didn't even chart, while in the UK their posthumous fame was to remain bright for many years. A 1979 American book, *Too Young To Die* by Patricia Fox Sheinwold, did not include Cochran in the author's survey from Rudolph Valentino to Elvis Presley – unthinkable if such a book was to be written in Britain.

Among the future plans for Cochran's career, it seems, was a higher-profile film role in the 1960 western *The Alamo*, starring John Wayne, a part that after his death went to Frankie Avalon. This could well have proved a fruitful development had he lived. Such scant lines of dialogue as he had been given in his second movie *Untamed Youth*, though hardly Oscar material, had been handled with casual ease, and he undeniably had a photogenic charisma. Working in Hollywood would also have appealed to him as being less risky than life on the road.

Larry Parnes announced that he had booked Vincent, together with such stablemates as Billy Fury, Joe Brown, Lance Fortune and Georgie Fame, to tour in the *Eddie Cochran Tribute Show*, each performing a number associated with Cochran and with part of the proceeds going to his bereaved family. It was slated to start at the Glasgow Empire on 6 June and run for five weeks. Jerry Keller was then added to the bill, instead of Vince Taylor.

'The original tour was tiring,' remembers Billy Raymond, 'but considering that we were together and really a bit confined for weeks on end we got on very well. Only very occasionally did tempers get a little frayed. Maybe there was a little bit of competition between Billy Fury and Vince Eager. Vince perhaps was the better all-round entertainer as such but Billy had that amazing sex appeal that sent girls wild, and I think Vince was envious of this.

'There were a number of dodgy occasions, the main being during Eddie's tribute tour when, at the Glasgow Empire, the drunks in the "gods" starting throwing lead ashtrays and bottles at the stage. The fire curtain was brought down and this caused a riot, which had the mounted police in the theatre swinging their batons. We didn't get out of the theatre until three in the morning, and the "Rock'n'roll Riot" story was front-page headlines . . .'

And so Raymond had by now gone back on his vow never to work with Vincent again, out of loyalty to Cochran. After this Raymond broke back into television as compere of the popular game show *Spot the Tune*, and then went to Australia as tour compere of *The Vera Lynn Show*. He returned to Australia many times before emigrating from the UK to there, and he still works in Australian television, radio and theatre.

When the tour reached Liverpool Stadium on 3 May Parnes put a couple of local bands into the line-up. Although Gerry and the Pacemakers would, three years later, become the first-ever artists to reach the top of the charts with their first three singles, the big Scouse heroes on the bill were Rory Storm and the Hurricanes, who included Ringo Starr on drums.

Vincent went into EMI's Abbey Road Studios on 11 May with the Beat Boys. He and Cochran had planned a duet version of the Al Dexter country song 'Pistol Packin' Mama', which Vincent now cut alone, together with his own ballad, 'Weeping Willow'. 'Pistol Packin' Mama' found Vincent in spirited form, and although the song is somewhat folksy, with its repeated 'Lay that pistol down' lyric, the band (including Georgie Fame on piano) attack it with gusto and by June Vincent was rewarded with his biggest-ever UK hit when it reached No. 15.

On 18 June 1960 it was announced that Vincent had received the tragic news that his eighteen-month-old daughter Melody had died of pneumonia, and that he had cancelled all his commitments in order to fly back to the States. 'I am thinking now of retiring,' he said. 'I have been in this business for six years and I'm tired.'

In tears, he broke the news to the audience at the Theatre Royal in Nottingham during the Cochran tribute show. *Disc* reported it under the headline 'First It Was the Eddie Cochran Tragedy, Then Came the Death of his Daughter Melody, but his Fans Understood . . .' Writer Richard Adams described Vincent as 'moody, quiet, appears to be shy . . . He registers no change of expression when his name is mentioned and rarely smiles.' In the *Hit Parade* account of the Nottingham announcement some people in the audience laughed, thinking he was talking about his dog. So much for Britain's reputation as a dog-loving nation.

Reported the *NME*: 'Gene Vincent's British visit ended on Sunday when a limping figure, head bowed, walked slowly across the tarmac at London Airport . . . Death and illness have dogged Vincent while he was here.' His performance in Nottingham is described as 'what could be his last-ever professional appearance'.

'I've lost first my best friend, then my baby daughter,' he said, '[but] I don't believe Britain holds a jinx for me.' He was still toying with the idea of retiring from rock'n'roll and becoming a farmer. His onstage performance at Nottingham had been as wild and committed as ever, but his offstage demeanour was that of a man weighed down with wearying troubles.

A week later the *Melody Maker* splashed the headline: 'Vincent Death Gram Was a Hoax'. The paper said that Vincent, speaking from

Vancouver, admitted that 'the telegram [saying that his daughter had died] was a phoney'. But his agent Norm Riley, now back in Hollywood, was noncommittal. 'No comment. I only spoke to Gene briefly when he arrived. He seemed a bit incoherent. I put it down to the car crash.'

Vincent stated: 'Larry [Parnes] was very kind. He even arranged my ticket home for me. He could have insisted I return after a few days' rest – but he didn't.' Parnes gritted: 'I shall have to see my lawyer . . . Certainly the cancellation put us to a lot of trouble in rearranging acts.'

Vincent denied sending the telegram to himself . 'I'm sorry for all the upset I've caused in Britain,' he said. 'The wire was signed in my wife's name. But now I find she did not send it. Melody was quite well all the time.' Then who *did* send the telegram? 'I just don't know.' His daughter Sherri, however, thinks it 'very likely' that he did send the telegram. 'It's just the sort of stunt he would have pulled to get out of a difficult situation,' she says.

Adrian Owlett is even more certain. 'It was him,' he says simply. 'He was a consummate con artist. It was well within his capability to have rigged it, arranged for it to be sent to himself. He was not dim.' But he was certainly deeply troubled. Within days the story took another turn, when Vincent simply disappeared. A worried Norm Riley said: 'I honestly don't know where he is right now. I hope I can find him and help him. I could get him to have some psychiatric treatment. It could help him.'

Riley also denied telling a British newspaper that Vincent had invented the story of Melody's death to wriggle out of his British bookings. 'I told the papers I believed that Gene, under a great deal of pressure, and still shaken up badly from the auto accident . . . *could* have made up the story. Gene was acting oddly in England towards the end of his stay there, and I honestly think the experience of the accident could have hurt his mind. I understand that he went to a doctor in London who told him he might be on the verge of a nervous breakdown and that he should take a rest. If he did this thing [send the phoney telegram to himself], it was the only way he could figure to get out from the pressure he was under.'

Larry Parnes was now magnanimous. 'I am not taking any action. Any damage that has been done, Vincent has done to himself.' Compere Billy Raymond added: 'When he received the telegram he appeared to be heartbroken.' So the mystery remained – and if Vincent did send himself the wire, he was clearly a very good actor. Vincent's whereabouts after his sudden departure were a mystery. It was assumed by many that he had retreated to Vancouver, to hide out with Darlene's parents, and the press was soon on the trail. Darlene's brother Denny was protective towards him when quizzed by local paper *The Journal*, denying that he was there but off-guardedly admitting that 'he was in the neighbourhood'. But Vincent would be back . . .

3. GENE VINCENT: PROLOGUE

Norfolk, Virginia, sits at the southern end of Chesapeake Bay on the east coast of the United States. The bay is a huge, indented inlet running up beyond Baltimore. Just south of Norfolk, incidentally, is the candidly named Dismal Swamp. With neighbouring Portsmouth and Newport News, Norfolk forms the port of Hampton Roads, one of the finest natural harbours in the world. It has long been a major shipping and industrial centre, handling coal, grain, tobacco, seafood and farm products along a vast fifty-mile waterfront, as well as being an embarkation point for passenger ships.

Its geographical situation and its natural advantages also give it a huge strategic importance, and it is home to an important naval base. Norfolk was effectively destroyed by fire at the outset of the American Revolution in 1776 – only St Paul's Church survived – and in the Civil War it was a Confederate base until captured by the Unionists in 1862.

Mary Louise Cooper, known as Louise, and Ezekiah 'Kie' Craddock came from North Carolina, but their families moved into Norfolk in search of work and they grew up in the same district, Brambleton. They married in 1934. Eugene Vincent was their first child, and his birth certificate states that he was born on 11 February 1935. Although Louise later said that her handwritten application for a certificate was misread, and that the birth date was actually the 17th, Vincent's officially recorded birthday is the generally accepted one, accurate or not. The family was eventually completed by three sisters: Evelyn was born in 1938, Tina in 1948 and Donna in 1949. Kie and Louise moved for a while to Munden Point, a small town just outside Norfolk, trying to make a go of running a general store, but they soon moved back to the city and Kie found more secure work on the naval base.

As with his contemporaries Elvis Presley and Carl Perkins, the young Vincent was exposed both to hillbilly music on the radio and to the blues and gospel tunes of blacks in the neighbourhood, the vital ingredients for the synthesis of rock'n'roll in the mid-50s. Indeed, this cross-fertilisation was essential to the health of country music itself – from Jimmie Rodgers to Hank Williams to Johnny Cash, there is a sturdy backbone of the blues. And so, as with his future friend Eddie Cochran, Vincent grew out of a country-music environment imbued with black influences, which enabled him to embrace rock'n'roll.

The boy attended Roffner Junior High School and South Norfolk High School, but was not particularly studious. He was also conscious of being a lightweight, short and skinny, and as with Cochran when he moved to an area where he did not know anybody, he did not make friends easily and consoled himself by playing his guitar. He was bullied because of his size, and developed both a short emotional fuse and an ability to look after himself.

In 1959 Vincent recalled: 'My teacher in high school used to beg me to sing at the end-of-the-year concert, but the type of song they wanted me to sing was so way out that I just could not oblige. We compromised and I sang "Marching Through Georgia" to an upbeat tempo. Knocked them dead. Needless to say I was never again asked to sing at one of their concerts.' Still with no realistic thought of music as a career, and surrounded by strutting sailors with money to spend, the seventeen-year-old Eugene joined the navy early in 1952.

At the time America was obsessed with Communists, real and imagined. The witch-hunt of alleged Communist Party members and fellow travellers launched by Senator Joe McCarthy in 1950 rumbled on, and in 1952 McCarthy himself was under attack. Senator William Benton was seeking McCarthy's expulsion from the Senate on the grounds that he accepted an illegal payment from the Lustron Corporation, and that he had perjured himself by claiming that he had implicated 57, not the actual 205, alleged Communists in his original 1950 speech.

Meanwhile President Harry Truman submitted to Congress the biggest-ever peacetime budget, and in the chill and paranoia of the Cold War three-quarters of it was earmarked for national security. 'Peacetime' at home, maybe, but of course America was embroiled in the Korean War, partly explaining the security allocation.

Strictly speaking there had never been any declaration of war, and Korea was divided at the 38th parallel almost by accident. At the Potsdam Conference in July 1945 the Allies and Russia had agreed that independence should be restored to Korea, and when Japan was defeated the arrangement was for Russia to accept the surrender of Japanese troops in Korea north of the 38th parallel, and America to the south.

This led to a Communist north supported by Russia and an anti-Communist south financed by America, and when in June 1950 northern troops crossed into the south, a state of war existed in all but name. President Truman sent American forces into the country, led by General Douglas McArthur, and three bloody years of conflict began.

McArthur became critical of American policy and was dismissed by Truman in the following year. He is buried, coincidentally, in Vincent's home town of Norfolk.

Hawks in government and the military began to advocate the bombing of China, which would surely have precipitated a Third World War just years after the end of the Second. As it was, American casualties were vast and the expense was a constant drain on the economy, preventing recovery until the mid-50s. Although, by means of truce and conference, hostilities ended in 1953, the United Nations failed in their ambitions to reunite the country, which remains dangerously divided even today.

It was election year in 1952, and in July Dwight D. Eisenhower won the Republican nomination, to be opposed by the Democratic candidate Adlai Stevenson. Eisenhower's running mate was an enthusiastic anti-Communist, Richard Nixon. In September he went on television to deliver the infamous, cringe-making 'Checkers' speech. He had been called to explain a 'supplementary expense' fund amounting to $18, 235. Nixon, his voice breaking with feigned emotion, denied that he had ever made improper use of campaign money, but that he had accepted one gift – a dog called Checkers for his daughter Trisha. 'We're gonna keep it,' he said defiantly. Eisenhower stated that Nixon had been 'completely vindicated as a man of honour'.

Eisenhower won the election and as President elect he made a three-day visit to the strategically important territory of Korea in December. As the Korean War dragged on Eisenhower stated his opinion that it might need to be stepped up in order to ensure victory, and that Korea would require aid for the foreseeable future in its fight to withstand Communism. On 28 December, in the spirit of the season, Nixon taunted election loser Adlai Stevenson as an appeaser of Communists who had gained his PhD from 'Dean Acheson's College of Cowardly Communist Containment'.

It was in this atmosphere of ideological tension and warfare that the young Eugene Craddock donned his uniform for the first time. The situation in Korea must have been partly responsible for his mother's reluctance to approve of his ambition to serve in the Navy, but in the face of his determination she gave way. He completed his training and first went to sea late in 1952. In the next two and a half years he served on the USS *Chuckawan*, trained on a two-week course on USS *Amphion*, and then returned to the *Chuckawan*. He travelled to the Mediterranean, where on shore leave in Naples he bought a cheap guitar. It seems that he was committed to the Navy, but the love of country and blues music that had been with him since childhood, both on the radio and through listening to black street singers in Munden Point, remained strong.

The guitar cost about $10 (as high as $25 in some accounts), and in 1959 Vincent said: 'I still use the old guitar, although everyone says I should get a new one. This is the first guitar I ever had, and I will use it until I get out of show business.'

He had a new interest as well, motorbikes. He re-enlisted in the navy for a further term of six years and celebrated by buying a beast of a bike, a British Triumph racing model. By signing on again he qualified for a bonus of $600, with half as much again in 'mustering out' pay. So that he could enjoy his new toy all the more, he renegotiated a transfer of duty, and was now a despatch rider working on the base at Norfolk. He was crossing an intersection one day in July when a woman in a Chrysler drove through a red light on his left and hit him at speed. His left leg was so badly broken as to be almost severed above the ankle.

This is the accepted story of the accident. Intriguingly, though, Hal Carter has another version. 'Gene had problems, there's no doubt about that. He told me about how he came to hurt himself. It was that he'd gone out that night on his motorbike, drinking, and he'd come back to the naval base sozzled. They had a security barrier across the gate so you'd have to stop. But he tried to ride under it and the bike came down on his leg. Because he was late getting back to the base. That's what he told me.' This may have been a Vincent fantasy, because he also claimed that the case was settled out of court because he signed the papers while heavily sedated. If there was no woman in a Chrysler, there was presumably no case to settle.

Vincent was taken to the naval hospital where his entire leg was set in a plaster cast to immobilise it. He was in and out of hospital for the rest of 1955 while on sick leave, and the leg had to be reset several times. It seemed to be very resistant to healing. The damage was so severe that amputation would probably have been the best option, and this was certainly the advice of his doctors. But Vincent always fought against this, begging his mother to refuse permission for the operation. It seems equally likely, however, that Eugene became impatient with using crutches all the time, which hardly did much for the self-image of a twenty-year-old, and so he never actually gave the leg sufficient chance to get better. It deteriorated throughout his life, and by the mid-1960s osteomyelitis, which attacked the bone marrow and reduced his shin to a blackened stump, had set in.

'They rebuilt his leg with pins and put the iron on him,' says Carter, 'but the doctors told him he had to walk without the iron as much as he could to build up the muscle of his leg. But he got this great sympathy thing as he hobbled along, so he got so he didn't want to take the iron off. And so the leg withered from non-use. Everyone went out of their way for him and he didn't want to lose the sympathy.' This would have been later, once the plaster cast had been replaced by a metal splint. But in later life his dynamic onstage performances meant that the leg was frequently fracturing within the brace, and so he would be back in plaster for a time, sometimes walking with crutches.

The lasting legacy of his impatience, or if Carter is right his reluctance to lose the sympathy vote, was an open wound on his shin that never healed. It was a vicious circle – when the leg was originally confined within its cast it itched mercilessly. Vincent was regularly driven to straightening out a coat hanger and shoving it down inside the cast to scratch the intolerable discomfort. And so the wound was forever reopened, weeping and often infected. Whenever it broke and had to be replastered, the torture by itching would arise once more. His sister Evelyn once said: 'That leg of his wasn't nothin' but a big mess of pain for him. I imagine it would be like having one big bad toothache all your life.'

With so much time on his hands he now began to take playing the guitar more seriously, and he began writing songs while confined to his hospital bed. This was the year, 1955, when a new hybrid music began to enter the pop charts. Bill Haley's light, syncopated, hillbilly interpretation of rhythm 'n' blues, which had been making modest waves for a couple of years, now broke through when Haley's cover of 'Rock Around the Clock', released the previous year to little effect, was used behind the credits of the teen-rebellion movie *The Blackboard Jungle*, starring Glenn Ford. This sudden new exposure helped the record to the top of the charts, and Haley and his Comets were signed to make their own first movie, *Rock Around the Clock*, which prolonged the huge success of this proto-rock song when released in 1956. This double bull's-eye, hit record and box-office movie success, led to a follow-up movie, *Don't Knock the Rock*.

1955 was also the year when black artists became accepted by the mass market as never before – Little Richard with 'Tutti Frutti', Chuck Berry with 'Maybelline' and Fats Domino with 'Ain't That a Shame'. And there was also Elvis Presley, a month older than Vincent, whipping up a storm on travelling package bills, the television show *Louisiana Hayride* and on Sun Records. Those early recordings were popular fare on Norfolk radio station WCMS, and familiar to Vincent.

However, a glance at the list of records that reached the top of the American charts in 1955 – though they do indeed include 'Rock Around the Clock' in June – confirms that the rock'n'roll revolution had not yet arrived. They include Joan Weber's melodramatic 'Let Me Go Lover', the over-the-top cha cha 'Cherry Pink and Apple Blossom White' by the Perez Prado Orchestra, Mitch Miller's redneck 'The Yellow Rose of Texas' and Dean Martin's somnambulistic 'Memories Are Made of This'.

In October Dave Bartholomew's slab of New Orleans R&B 'I Hear You Knocking' did reach No. 2, but not in the Smiley Lewis original. As was still the general rule, it was the white cover version, in this case a polite reading by Gale Storm, that got the sufficient airplay and efficient distribution to score. Similarly, earlier in the year 'Sincerely' made it to the top, but by the McGuire Sisters, not the wonderful Moonglows.

After months of convalescence Vincent was discharged from the navy hospital, his leg still in plaster, supporting himself on the hated crutches, and in receipt of naval sick benefit. In September WCMS promoted the Norfolk leg of a touring show starring Hank Snow, with Cowboy Copas, the Louvin Brothers and Jimmy Rogers. Down among the supporting acts was Elvis Presley. When Vincent saw Presley perform, a career plan began to take shape. It was to be the same with Eddie Cochran, when he first witnessed the Tupelo Flash.

Vincent's first exposure to a wider audience than the captive one in the hospital ward came late in 1955, when he started to perform on the Saturday afternoon show of local disc jockey Teddy Crutchfield, later to become a Blue Cap for a brief while. His voice, though soft in volume, was distinctive, capable of breathing life into hackneyed material, flexible and expressive. It soon came to the notice of two important players – WCMS disc jockey Bill 'Sheriff Tex' Davis and Capitol Records A&R man Ken Nelson.

Vincent's personal life was changing, too. At about the time he first started singing on the radio he began seeing a fifteen-year-old schoolgirl, Ruth Ann Hand, and they were soon engaged. In spite of his parents' objections – they thought *he* was too young to commit himself to marriage, let alone Ruth Ann – they were married on his 21st birthday, 11 February 1956.

Ken Nelson was to play a significant role in the first, successful stage of Vincent's career. He knew what he was looking for – Capitol Records' answer to Elvis – and as someone who had tried to sign Elvis himself to a management deal before being gazumped by 'Colonel' Tom Parker, he was presumably qualified to guide Elvis's rival.

However, his varied, middle-of-the-road experience is surely exposed by some of the titles he required Vincent to record in his early sessions. Although he brought 'Woman Love' with him to the 'Be Bop a Lula' session, a mark in his favour, it was Nelson who then insisted on 'Jezebel', Frankie Laine's 1951 melodrama, 'Peg O' My Heart, 'Wedding Bells', 'Waltz of the Wind', 'Lazy River' and 'Ain't She Sweet', all of them tackled during Vincent's second and third Capitol sessions. Vincent's talent was such that he could make a decent fist of all of them, but they were not really what we remember him for. It took until the fourth 1956 recording date for Nelson to order a strict rock'n'roll diet. Nevertheless, it was he who fought a lone battle with other Capitol executives, insisting that they would be left behind in the music business if they did not invest in a little rock'n'roll.

Nelson, born in Minnesota in 1911 into a family who soon relocated to Chicago, was an announcer on classical-music radio in the 1930s, rising to be station director on WJJH. In the late 1940s he began to moonlight part-time for Capitol in their Chicago offices and in 1948 he moved to California to take over their transcription department. By 1950 he was an A&R man in the country division, which is when he went after Elvis and when he met WCMS's Bill 'Sheriff Tex' Davis at a disc-jockey convention in Nashville.

Nelson recalls only 'Be Bop a Lula' on the demo tape sent to him by Davis, but by every other credible account Vincent and Davis's hurriedly assembled band also did 'Race with the Devil' and 'I Sure Miss You'. It was Nelson who shortened 'Eugene' and lopped off 'Craddock' to give Vincent his stage name, and fifteen-year-old drummer Dickie Harrell who christened the band 'the Blue Caps' in honour of an item of stage gear they soon took to wearing. The unlikely inspiration was said to be the golfing caps worn by President Eisenhower.

It might indeed be questioned whether or not Nelson was the right man to get the best out of the wildest singer since Elvis, and one who – although he presented a humble, polite front to the world – was to prove a sometimes difficult customer. But Nelson was later to recall: 'The recording sessions with Gene and the Blue Caps were never difficult. They had everything rehearsed and came off smoothly. I don't recall ever having a problem in the studio.' And he can claim to have supervised the recordings that, whatever happened later, represent Vincent's lasting legacy.

In 1991, Bill Davis recalled his dealings with Nelson. But first he remembered his initial meeting with Vincent. 'We started a [talent] show every Friday night . . . and this one day, I guess it was about in November of '55 . . . this kid came in . . . he had a broken leg, it was in a cast, but he didn't want to wear crutches . . . He says, "Mr Davis, my name is Eugene Craddock. I can sing." . . . At that time Elvis was just getting started so he sang "Blue Moon" for me . . . He tore me up. I said, "You're on the show this week." Everybody did just one song and . . . he did "Blue Moon" and the people in the audience . . . they ate him up . . . We used him every week as a headliner.'

Disc jockey Joe Hoppel recalls it slightly differently: 'I was in the control room the day Gene Vincent auditioned for a live stage show we produced [Country Showtime] – he sang "Heartbreak Hotel". Later I cut the acetate disc we sent to Ken Nelson, "Be Bop a Lula".'

Before long Vincent was performing with the WCMS house band the Virginians, led by another twenty-year-old, Willie Williams. 'All the chicks went berserk,' is Williams's recollection of Vincent's debut. They played the live Friday-night Country Showtime, broadcast from a club called the Carnival Room, and Eugene kept on turning up, singing 'Be Bop a Lula' and Elvis songs. 'He had something special,' said WCMS's Joe Hoppel. Vincent and his acquired group were hired to play at the local Chevrolet dealership on Saturday afternoons and, partly because of his popularity, Country Showtime had to move to a larger venue, Gates Theater.

Vincent's local success immediately attracted the attention of a talent agency run by the owner and station manager at WCMS, Cy Blumenthal and Roy Lamear. This spin-off from the radio station booked their artists into concerts and used WCMS to promote the shows. And so Vincent signed with L&B Talent Management.

Davis soon got the call from Nelson, who was phoning round every disc jockey he knew. 'I need a guy that sounds like that kid they got at RCA, Elvis Presley.' Davis's reaction was, 'I got one!' He told Vincent that he would need an original song, not an Elvis cover, to impress Nelson.

Davis's claim is that he was the co-composer of 'Be Bop a Lula'. The generally accepted story, however, is that Vincent and fellow patient Donald Graves had put the song together while lying in the Portsmouth Naval Hospital, Vincent strumming on his Neapolitan guitar, and the shrewd Davis now bought out Graves's interest for a reputed $25, seeing the potential of both Vincent and the song. In this story, the inspiration was a comic-strip character called Little Lulu. It has also been said that Graves wrote the song by himself, and sold it to Vincent for $50.

In 1971 Vincent confirmed the first version, although some sixteen years after one of the most celebrated motorcycle accidents in history he was still pretending that he had been wounded in Korea. 'I was in the naval hospital, actually I was crippled up. I just had a hit in Korea. My mother said to me, "Son, why don't you enter this contest?" I said, "What bloody contest, what are you talking about?" She said, "Why don't you record something?" So I recorded a thing that I wrote. I come in dead drunk and stumbled over the bed. And me and Don Graves were looking at this bloody book – it was called *Little Lulu*. And I said, "Hell, man, it's bebopalulu." And he said, "Yeah, man, swinging." And we wrote this song. And some man came to hear it named Sherriff Tex Davis, and he bought the song from Donald Graves for $25!' By this time, note, Vincent's years in England had made 'bloody' his polite expletive of choice.

However, by 1991 Davis's version was: 'I put on a record by a guy called Tiny Hill . . . "You Can Bring Pearl with a Turned-Up Nose but Don't Bring Lulu" . . . I said to [Vincent], "You know this Bop stuff that you're doin', this real Be-Bop stuff. How about a girl named Lulu who likes to Bop . . . you put her in a store and put her in blue jeans . . . No, everybody's in blue jeans . . . let's put her in *red* blue jeans.'

As the Davis version unfolds one begins to feel that Vincent was lucky to retain even half a song credit, and that perhaps Davis is about to claim that it was in fact him singing on the record. Vincent apparently suggested the title 'Bopping Lulu' but to Davis it sounded like 'Bop a Lula'! This all sounds like a rewriting of history, possibly unconsciously. 'I said, "You go over there into the studio . . . and play around with this thing and call the guys and tell them to come on in here tonight and we'll fool around with it after I get off the air." ' Davis still had not told Vincent why he needed the song – to submit to Nelson.

He claims that when he finished his afternoon slot he crossed the building to the studio. Apparently the band thought that the song was 'Garbage! Lousy! Terrible!' but they came round to his way of thinking. This is in direct conflict with later recollections by the musicians, who were aware that, potentially at least, they were on to something. The strutting guitar lines and excited screams on the eventual recording are not born out of indifference.

Davis also claims that the other two songs on the first demo were two of the Elvis numbers that Vincent was featuring on *Country Showtime*, 'Blue Moon' and 'Mystery Train', which of course conflicts directly with the advice he says he gave Vincent, that original songs were necessary. Another account, in local paper the *Virginian Pilot* in 1984, insists that the demo included 'Heartbreak Hotel', which seems highly unlikely for the same reason.

As might be expected with such a volatile and driven employer as Gene Vincent, musicians were to pass through the ranks of the Blue Caps at a fair clip. There were to be twenty of them at least in the two and a half years between recording 'Be Bop a Lula' and November 1958 when Vincent, unable to pay his band, did a runner and left them stranded in Los Angeles.

Davis called up some local musicians to accompany Vincent, and they became the original Blue Caps line-up – plumber Cliff Gallup, schoolboy drummer Dickie Harrell, who used to haunt the radio station looking for chances to play, Willie Williams of the Virginians on rhythm guitar and bass player Jack Neal.

Harrell recalls their first meeting before *Country Showtime*: 'I went down to the station and a guy comes up on the elevator with his crutches . . . he had a white cast and his pants were split on the side so he could put them on . . . All these bands would get up and play and sing, different ones, and it was time for Gene to come on. So he was real nervous sitting there – I think he smoked three packs of cigarettes before he got out there. But Bill came out and said, "Are you ready?" and Gene said, "Yes, sir." . . . So they introduced Gene and he wobbled out there on stage and you could'a heard a pin drop. I think he did "That's All Right, Mama". He played about four bars of it and that was it. From then on they just loved every minute of it – I think he did about six songs. He weren't supposed to do but two. And that was the beginning of Vincent Eugene Craddock.'

Cliff Gallup was to play on just 35 Vincent tracks during three extended sessions before returning to life as a semi-professional musician in Norfolk, yet this was sufficient to establish him at the very top of the pantheon of rock'n'roll guitarists. His instrumental breaks and guitar fills shape the songs as distinctively as does Vincent's voice. His style was based on the technique of the country music virtuosos like Chet Atkins and Merle Travis, and before becoming a Blue Cap he was frequently hired to back country artists when they came to Norfolk to appear on WCMS, and he also appeared on a handful of local recordings. Before joining Vincent he was playing with Ricky and the Dixie Serenaders. When the call came he somehow transmuted his deft country picking into pure rockabilly. Like Atkins, Gallup played with a plectrum held between first finger and thumb, with picks on the other fingers that simultaneously plucked at the top strings, and he favoured a Gretsch Black Duo Jet model.

What Harrell brought to the band above all was his sheer youthful enthusiasm, an abandoned, extrovert style that may have caused the tempo of songs to gradually increase as he got carried away, but which added greatly to the visual appeal of the act.

Neal, born in 1930, had been playing upright bass since he was a teenager, performing in local bands while holding down a day job at the local Ford car plant. When Elvis Presley first appeared in Norfolk, Neal was also on the bill. Late in 1955 he joined a group led by Garland Abbot, playing a weekly spot on *Hometown Hoedown* on WCMS. When 'Be Bop a Lula' broke out nationally he took a chance on going professional, and stuck it until December 1956.

The demo session, on 9 April 1956, produced versions of 'Be Bop a Lula', another Vincent original, 'Race with the Devil', and a ballad, 'I Sure Miss You', written by Norfolk songwriter Evelyn Bryan. Photographs of the band, including one of Vincent used on the cover of his first album, *Bluejean Bop*, were also taken as part of the demo package. As Harrell recalls it, the demo version of 'Be Bop a Lula' was taken at a slower tempo that the hit.

'The guy's the greatest,' was Nelson's reported reaction, and he acted quickly, offering a round trip to Nashville for Vincent, Davis and the four soon-to-be Blue Caps. They flew with a small local outfit, Piedmont Airlines, and it involved a roundabout trip changing planes at Richmond, northwest of Norfolk, before heading southwest for Nashville. Capitol's signing of Vincent coincided with the opening of their new offices in Hollywood. The huge Capitol Tower, built to represent a pile of discs, was an impressive statement of confidence in the future and became an instant landmark.

Nelson had booked the band into Bradley's, the Nashville studio run by Owen Bradley, for a debut session on 4 May. This was one of the first recording studios in the city, and had been used by the young Buddy Holly just prior to Vincent, a year before he scored his first hit with 'That'll Be the Day', which was a tougher remake of one of his Nashville sides. Rockabilly artist Johnny Carroll had also recorded there, and it was at his suggestion that the Vincent cuts were drenched in so much echo.

Carroll stayed close to Vincent, and after the latter's death he recorded a tribute, 'Black Leather Rebel': 'The black leather rebel is now in the ground/But his spirit goes around and around and around/The deejay leeches are still cutting him down/But Gene keeps a rocking to the Wild Cat sound'.

The studio was known as the Quonset Hut – in England these relics of the war were called Nissen Huts, cheap and temporary troop accommodation made of corrugated iron. As his business flourished Bradley was able to relocate to what became the most celebrated studio in Nashville, Bradley's Barn.

As an insurance against the young semiprofessional musicians being unable to produce the goods, Nelson had hired some of Nashville's finest session players on standby, including Grady Martin, Buddy Harman, Hank Garland and Bob Moore. But it only took Gallup's nimble, thrilling introduction to 'Race with the Devil' to convince him that they were redundant. The band recut their three demo numbers plus one from an acetate that Nelson had brought to the session, the lascivious 'Woman Love', written by Jack Rhodes, which had previously been cut by a Starday artist called Jimmy Johnson. This was named as the first A side, but most disc jockeys preferred to play the flip, 'Be Bop a Lula'.

The Davis account of the session accords with the familiar story in one respect, that it was Nelson who came up with 'Woman Love' – though Davis says that it had already been sent over, presumably as a publisher's acetate, for the band to practise. But in his 1991 conversation he couldn't remember the name of the song – 'What was the one on the other side of "Be Bop a Lula"?' – which of course calls into question the accuracy of his recollections as a whole. Nor could he recall the names of the other two songs cut at the first Nashville session.

Davis does, however, capture the excitement of the moment they cut 'Be Bop a Lula', with just fifteen minutes of the session remaining. 'They said, "Shit, we'll do it in one take . . . c'mon, let's go." Vincent was . . . so excited. We all were but he was more so and he started the song and Dickie got so excited he screamed on the record . . . and Nelson said, "What's that? What's that?" I said, "Leave it alone . . . let them do what they want to do." . . . Mort Thomasson [the engineer] was going crazy on the dials with all the screaming . . . He said, "Let's just cover ourselves and do it one more time." So they had two cuts on the thing but they went back to the first cut . . .' Harrell's story, as told to Rob Finnis and others, has always been that 'I want my family to know I'm on the record so I screamed.'

Thomasson divided his time between the local Nashville radio station WSM and Bradley's studio, and worked on all the early Blue Caps recordings. His main claim to fame is that in 1961 he engineered three million-sellers on the same day – Joe Dowell's cover of 'Wooden Heart', which reached the top of the Hot Hundred, Leroy Van Dyke's reverb-heavy moral tale 'Walk On By' (No. 5) and Ray Stevens's novelty number 'Ahab the Arab' (also No. 5). As with Ral Donner's version of 'Girl of My Best Friend' in the same year, Dowell was able to have a huge hit with an Elvis number because Presley's versions remained as album tracks in the US, and so were hardly heard on the radio.

Thomasson was impressed by Vincent's behaviour in these early days. 'Gene was very likeable. He put you at ease and appreciated everything you did. He was an easy guy to work with and he knew what he wanted.'

One immediately noticeable quality of 'Be Bop a Lula' and 'Woman Love' is the clarity of the sound. This arose initially because Vincent had such a quiet singing voice. With Gallup's guitar cranked up high and the excitable young Harrell bashing away he would have been inaudible, and so he and his microphone were put into another room. He wore headphones giving him a feed from the band.

The musicians were also isolated from each other in the main studio itself. This was the first out-and-out rock'n'roll session that Bradley's had handled, and no doubt Nelson and Thomasson were a little apprehensive about being associated with a harsh cacophony of sound, and so the four Blue Caps each sat in their own temporary booth surrounded by baffle boards.

The record was put out in June 1956, and Capitol dubbed Vincent 'The Screaming End' in their trade advertisements. In some cases the apparent preference for 'Be Bop a Lula' was because the lascivious nature of 'Woman Love' was considered too strong for the airwaves, although 'Lula' itself is hardly an innocent tale of young love. In the UK, where the BBC claims never to ban records but rather to hand out guidance, 'Woman Love' was decreed to be way beyond the pale. As was often the way in an industry made up of hundreds of local radio stations, the success of the record began in one particular area – in this case Baltimore, after an anxious couple of weeks – and spread swiftly until it was recognised by the *Billboard* chart as a national smash – from Baltimore to Atlanta and Pittsburgh, then Minneapolis-St Paul, Cleveland and Boston, Milwaukee, and out in ever-wider circles.

Often small, independent labels could sell hundreds of thousands of a record but be denied hit status, because they only had the resources to 'work' one area at a time. They might even distribute the records from the boot of the boss's car, as in the case of Chess. Capitol, however, had a slick machine in place, and soon claimed 'Be Bop a Lula' as the fastest seller in the history of the company. They immediately increased Vincent's one-year contract to five years. The record sold across the board, and achieved the rare distinction of appearing in *Billboard*'s pop, R&W and C&W top-ten listings.

Vincent, now invalided out of the navy with a small service pension, was suddenly a star. It happened so quickly that he, a shy, semi-cripple, was completely unprepared for it. He just loved making music, as simple as that. These days, it seems, that process has often been reversed. The driving motivation is a desire to be a star, and as so many artists from

Madonna onwards have proved, musical ability is an optional and often absent extra. Throughout his chaotic career Vincent showed that the only thing he could do well, the only thing he wanted to do, was sing. He was pretty hopeless at everything else.

However, it was an easy decision for him to go out on the road – there was nothing to stop him. He did not regard marriage as a restriction, and with career options severely limited by his injury, and a hit record in the charts, it was the obvious choice to make. The four musicians were faced with a harder decision, but in the euphoria of such overwhelming success they decided to give it a go. Harrell quit school, Williams took leave from his WCMS gig, and Gallup and Neal left their jobs. Davis, who was now acting as Vincent's booking agent as well as manager, having seemingly eased out the L&B agency, arranged a three-week tour and an appearance on the top-rated *Perry Como* television show.

The dispute over who 'owned' Vincent inevitably came to a head. It is possible that Vincent signed management contracts with Lamear and Blumenthal on the one hand, Davis on the other. Since they were all among the senior staff at WCMS he could have assumed it was simply the same deal, or that one was for agency and the other for management. L&B did not see it that way, sued Davis for compensation and dismissed him from the radio station. They also took out a suit against Vincent that was to come to a head early in 1957. It was the start of a lifetime of litigation.

But Davis, though keen to keep his hands on as much of the band's sudden earning power as possible, was out of his league as a nationwide booking agent. Williams recalls one gig at a Polish club in Philadelphia, where the crowd demanded polkas and complained that they were too noisy. Davis signed the band to a New York company, General Artists Corporation (GAC), and during the summer of 1956 the band played at a series of open-air shows and county fairs in and around New York, as well as appearing on the *Perry Como* show. They were assigned a driver, former docker Red Gwynn, who kept the band under control but later recalled that Vincent was already in the habit of popping pills. Vincent did not react well to being chaperoned.

If anyone needed scrupulous, experienced management it was Gene Vincent. With rock'n'roll still in its infancy there were no blueprints, however, only 'Colonel' Tom Parker assiduously ripping off Elvis Presley down in Memphis. The best that could be said about Bill 'Tex' Davis is that he was a seasoned radio man, not a rock manager. Rhythm guitarist Williams observed the situation shrewdly: 'I think [Gene] found it very difficult to make a personal, emotional transition from the have-nots to the haves, and I think this . . . caused him not to watch his money. He was just a kid, a sailor . . . If his manager had taken the time to be concerned with Gene's personal wellbeing, he would have sat him down and said, "Look, this may be your only record, let's reach a figure and bank that much first . . ." '

It was Williams's opinion that neither Lamear and Blumenthal nor Davis systematically ripped Vincent off, it was just that they were out of their depth, they were bunglers. 'There was tragic mishandling.' Williams noticed a trait in Vincent that remained with him throughout his life, and is surely a vital key to his ultimately tragic character. He had a low sense of self-esteem, a feeling that he was unworthy of adulation. What he needed was someone to guide him through this bewildering world of stardom and easy money, but there was no such person. Unused to money, indifferent to its value, Vincent simply spent it, on others as much as himself. 'I never meant to make money. I never wanted it. I'm a singer,' he said later.

Nor was there any sort of Fame Academy for aspiring rock'n'roll stars. The rules had not been written yet. The Blue Caps were the first real rock'n'roll band, establishing the template for the Crickets and the Beatles alike. Carl Perkins wrote some of the greatest rockabilly songs ever, but he was not a rocker onstage – his image was that of an old-fashioned country performer, even while his fingers were ripping out those marvellous rock'n'roll solos. Presley and Vincent, two polite, 'yes sir, no sir' southern boys, were the originals, and their stagecraft had to be instinctive.

If there were any models for onstage movement they would have come from black R&B singers, but what was new was the hysteria that Presley and Vincent caused. They fed off the audience, teasing the screaming girls, showing off to the boys. And yet Vincent's stage posturing, the characteristic crouching stance, the upturned eyes, seems to have come as much from his shyness and the limitations of his plaster cast – regularly broken and replaced at doctors' surgeries along the way – almost as if he was trying to make himself small.

Whereas Elvis flaunted his sexuality, Vincent on stage always seemed wrapped up in himself and the music. And, of course, when he did explode into movement, high-kicking over the microphone stand or swirling it around his head, the effect was that much more dramatic. What is for sure is that he never analysed it or preplanned it for a moment. As a stage performer Vincent was a complete natural.

In June the second recording session was arranged, again at Bradley's Studios in Nashville. The studio was booked for four days, as an album was needed as well as a follow-up single. For some reason, the successful experiment of isolating each player was abandoned, and so the sound lacks that pristine quality of six weeks earlier.

Nelson had no time to plan carefully, so instant had Vincent's success been, and he was short of material. A Nashville session player, the singer/guitarist Jerry Reed, whose 'US Male' and 'Guitar Man' were later huge Presley hits, was recruited to write an instant rock'n'roll classic, and came up with 'Crazy Legs'. As a rush job it turned out well, echoing the sentiments of 'Be Bop a Lula': 'I got a little woman called Crazy Legs, she's the queen of the teenage crowd.'

There were other rock songs available – Vincent's own 'Who Slapped John?' and 'Jumps, Giggles and Shouts', 'Gonna Back Up Baby' by Danny Wolfe, the wonderful 'Bluejean Bop' (written by Hal Levy but quintessential Vincent, with the singer claiming a co-credit), Cliff Gallup's hurriedly written 'Bop Street' and 'You Told a Fib', 'Jump Back Honey' by boogie pianist Hadda Brooks, and Bobby Carrol's 'I Flipped' and 'Well I Knocked, Bim, Bam'. Nelson should then have taken a leaf out of Elvis's book – his first RCA album was completed by his re-readings of such classics as Carl Perkins's 'Blue Suede Shoes' and Ray Charles's 'I Got a Woman'. Instead, alas, Nelson gave such material as 'Jezebel' and 'Peg O' My Heart' to Vincent.

'Race with the Devil' and 'Gonna Back Up Baby' made a strong follow-up, released in August when 'Be Bop a Lula' was still in the Top Ten, but incredibly it barely limped into the Hot Hundred – just one week at No. 96. Maybe the timing was wrong, with 'Lula' still getting airplay, maybe the world was not ready for a song with the Devil in the title. There was also the problem of the almost indecipherable lyrics, so urgently and abstractedly does Vincent deliver them in service of the galloping momentum of the song.

In addition, there is a suggestion that the shy Vincent was already beginning to alienate disc jockeys by cancelling planned interviews – he was uncomfortable doing them, and was unable to grasp the public-relations implications of avoiding them. He was a singer, pure and somewhat simple.

The third single, hurried out in September along with the *Bluejean Bop* album, was a third double-sided classic, and yet 'Bluejean Bop' and 'Who Slapped John?' did even worse than its predecessor, without even a token week in the chart. Nelson may have been limited in his grasp of rock'n'roll but he cannot be faulted on his choice of singles, artistically at least. Capitol were beginning to think that Vincent's career was over almost as soon as it had begun, and that rock'n'roll was indeed just the latest evanescent craze. The album, however, did better, reaching No. 16 in the charts.

In the UK, the country where he is still a hero, the first three singles were all hits. 'Be Bop a Lula' dodged in and out of the charts and peaked at No. 16, 'Race with the Devil' reached No. 28 and 'Bluejean Bop' also made it to No. 16. Although there were to be no more hits until the tour, Vincent was established as an original rock'n'roll star, not as a one-hit wonder.

After playing the fairs around New York in the summer of 1956 Vincent and the band were teamed up with Lillian Briggs and the Johnny Burnette Trio for a six-week tour. The Trio – Johnny, his brother Dorsey on slap bass and guitarist Paul Burlison – were one of the finest of the pioneering rockabilly bands, and yet they never had a hit. Ironically they could have signed with Capitol when Nelson was urgently seeking rock'n'rollers, but chose Coral instead.

Earlier, they had been rejected by Sun in their home town of Memphis, because label-owner Sam Phillips thought that Johnny sounded too much like Presley. Nowadays such tracks as 'The Train Kept a Rollin' ', 'Rockabilly Boogie', 'Lonesome Train' and 'Honey Hush' can be seen as among the most exciting rockabilly sides ever recorded, with Burnette's frantic, echo-drenched singing and Burlison's urgent, stuttering guitar lines, but in 1956 they were ahead of their time. Before he drowned in a boating accident in 1964 Johnny Burnette did break through with such songs as 'Dreamin' ', 'You're Sixteen' and 'Little Boy Sad', as did Dorsey with 'Tall Oak Tree' and 'Hey Little One', but there are no echoes left of their trailblazing work with Burlison. Instead, under the guidance of producer Snuff Garrett, who also worked with Eddie Cochran towards the end of the singer's life, Johnny Burnette was turned into a mainstream but mightily effective pop singer.

A display advertisement for the tour, after the come-ons 'On Stage! In Person! Rock'n'roll Show', contains the remarkable assurance that this is an 'All White Revue'. At the top of the list was 'human dynamo' Lillian Briggs, the 'hottest item to hit the disc business'. But during her career she never did manage to 'hit' the Hot Hundred. As was the custom the show also included the screening of a new drive-in movie, in this case *Storm Fear* starring Cornel Wilde, Ann Wallace and Dan Duryea, and the musicians performed three shows a day.

Burlison remembered Vincent with affection: 'He seemed pretty serious until he got on stage, then he got wild. He had to limp to the mike sometimes, but I didn't feel sorry for him at all 'cause he went over so well. But because of his leg he couldn't express himself as well as he wanted.'

Burlison said that Jack Neal played bass by ear – he did not know the correct fingering for each note, based on the relevant chord, and yet always hit them with perfect intuition. He indicated that Williams was a showman on stage, and that Gallup was already pining for home. Gallup and Burlison on the same tour – what a tutorial in rock'n'roll guitar.

In mid-September Willie Williams, with a foot in both camps – WCMS and the Blue Caps – tired of life on the road and decided to return to the radio station. 'I was looking at a picture of my wife in a bathing suit. Then I looked around the room at all those hairy-legged guitar pickers and I said to myself, "Man, I must be crazy!" ' Another factor was that income from 'Be Bop a Lula' was beginning to shrink, and he was asked to take a pay cut. He declined, and played his last gig as a Blue Cap in Fredericksburg, Virginia.

Many years later, Williams had only fond memories of Vincent. 'He was easy to work with and knew exactly what he was doing. From the minute I met him I found him to be agreeable. There was no arrogance or egotism.'

The band moved on to a two-week residency at the Casino Royale in Washington. They were now short of a rhythm guitarist but the problem was immediately and fortuitously solved. Steel guitarist Paul Peek was playing in a country and western band, the Tunetoppers, in a bar opposite the Casino when the Blue Caps arrived in town. He was a fan of 'Be Bop a Lula' and dropped in to hear the band rehearsing on the day before starting their residency. He invited them to come and see the Tunetoppers across the street, and in conversation afterwards discovered that they were looking for a rhythm guitarist. Although he had never played the instrument before he decided to bluff it. He proved to be a quick learner, and mastered the repertoire that night.

Peek also proved to be a dynamic presence on stage. He had been playing in another country band called Country Earl and the Circle E Ranch Boys back in Greenville, South Carolina, and the Ranch Boys were to prove a regular source of musicians for the Blue Caps as the turnover continued. Future Blue Cap bass player Bill Mack was, like Peek, playing both in the Tunetoppers and the Ranch Boys. When Peek joined the Blue Caps, Mack said: 'Get me into this. If you don't, I'll kill you.' Three months later he got the call.

Cliff Gallup was the next to decide that he had had enough, and after serving two weeks' notice he returned to his day job and family in Norfolk. He was almost of a different generation, and so the appeal of life in the fast lane soon faded. 'I left Gene because of the pressures of the road which were all so new then, and my family life was being neglected.' Another local musician, guitarist Russell Willaford, was co-opted in time for the group's cameo appearance in *The Girl Can't Help It* but this and one gig were his only contributions to the Blue Caps – he never appeared on record.

Gallup, in fact, agreed to play on the next session, though he refused to change his mind about going on the road, even though Ken Nelson offered him a lucrative job as soon as he learned that he had quit. When he left, the band moved on to Los Angeles. Rick Rare, a fan living in Georgia, remembers one of the last Blue Caps performances with Gallup on board. 'Gene had his leg in a cast . . . but that didn't stop him from rolling around on stage like nothing we had ever seen before. This was also one of the last times that Cliff Gallup would tour with them and his crystal-clear guitar riffs sent shivers up your back.'

The Girl Can't Help It was distinctly different from the rash of rock'n'roll movies that appeared in the second half of the decade. Not only was it in colour and boasted stereophonic sound, and enjoyed a far more generous budget than the quickies rushed out to capitalise on what the industry expected to be a short-lived phenomenon, it was also a comic satire. Its sardonic attitude to the music it celebrates so gloriously enables it to be watched with pleasure today, whereas the others – usually showing how the kids and their wild jungle music win over the staid town dignitaries or school authorities, with the head-master jiving awkwardly but enthusiastically in the final scene – are of interest only for the performances they have preserved.

The plot involves gangster 'Fats' Marty, played by Edmund O'Brien, who hires a show-business agent (Tom Ewell) to turn his girlfriend Jerri Jordan into a rock'n'roll star. Since the girl, played by Jayne Mansfield, has a vast chest but no voice, this is a challenge. Her debut record is a deliberately amateurish Marty composition, 'Rock Around the Rockpile', with O'Brien singing uncomfortably and his protégée simply letting out a squeal at seemingly appropriate moments.

Helping her are cabaret performances by Little Richard ('Ready Teddy', 'She's Got It' and the title song), Fats Domino ('Blue Monday'), the Platters ('You'll Never Know'), and cameo appearances by Vincent and Eddie Cochran. One perceptive reviewer referred to Little Richard as 'a diminutive South Sea Islander who plays the piano standing up'. Inevitably the satire element in what remains a wonderful comedy becomes confused: if the dire 'Rock Around the Rockpile' is indeed indicative of this rubbishy new music, then Fox should not have hired four of the greatest rock'n'rollers to help out.

The Blue Caps were only on the set of *The Girl Can't Help It* for a day, miming to 'Be Bop a Lula' over and over again, before flying to Nashville for their next recording session, booked for 15–18 October. Gallup joined them for his last tracks as a Blue Cap. Again the recording technique was changed – this time, Vincent and the band performed together as they did on stage to achieve a rougher, tougher 'live' sound, and Vincent's voice was much stronger, seasoned by a summer on the road. In support of this, most of the material this time played to Vincent's strength as a rocker, although 'Unchained Melody' did slip in. Apart from that and the Delmore Brothers' standard 'Blues Stay Away From Me' the songs were originals. For a few of the numbers Ken Nelson borrowed the Jordanaires from Elvis Presley to augment the sound. This was surely a tactical mistake – Vincent was his own man, and the use of the vocal group so intimately associated with Presley risked unwanted comparisons.

Together with 'I Sure Miss You' from his very first session, the repertoire and brash performance made for a very strong album when released the following March as *Gene Vincent and the Blue Caps*. As well as the two standards the band cut Mel Tillis's 'Five Feet of Lovin' ', Vincent's own 'Teenage Partner' (both omitted from the album), the classic 'Cat Man', 'Hold Me, Hug Me, Rock Me' and 'Cruisin' ', also by Vincent, Paul Peek's 'Pink Thunderbird', a bragging song in Chuck Berry style, 'Double Talkin' Baby' and 'Pretty, Pretty Baby' by Danny Wolfe, Vincent's ballad 'Important Words' (also held back from the album), Cliff Gallup's 'You Better Believe' and three Jack Rhodes songs, 'B-I-Bickey-Bi-Bo-Bo-Go', 'Red Blue Jeans and a Ponytail', and 'Five Days, Five Days'. Bill Davis continued to slip his name on to the Vincent compositions, and he gave himself a share of Peek's 'Pink Thunderbird' as well.

In November the band played for a week in Toronto (their first booking outside the States) headlining with doo-wop group the Flamingos, followed by a long engagement at the Sands Hotel in Las Vegas. The Flamingos, although they had to wait until 1959 to score in the pop charts, had had a recent R&B smash with 'I'll Be Home'. The disc jockey Teddy Crutchfield, who had given Vincent his first radio break, was briefly engaged as lead guitarist for the Blue Caps. They went down a storm in Canada but a Las Vegas casino was hardly suited to a wild rockabilly act. They were required to perform a twenty-minute set every hour from midnight to six in the morning, sharing an awkward bill with the Mary Kaye Trio and the Four Lads. As Paul Peek remembers it, the booking was eventually cancelled a few days early because Vincent rebroke his leg when he slipped over on stage, completing the set with blood seeping from his plaster cast.

Bill Davis had different memories of the Las Vegas stint, however, saying that stars like Liberace, Gene Krupa and Lena Horne would come in, curious to see the new rock'n'roll sensation, and that the management were in fact annoyed that Vincent was going down *too* well – gamblers were watching the show instead of donating their money to the gaming tables and the fruit machines.

Although Vincent was uncomfortable with the booking and glad to get out of it, Dickie Harrell tends to confirm Davis's version. 'When you go to a lounge show it's real quiet . . . The first night we set up and we busted open and started playing, the manager came over and raised holy Cain . . . people in the casino had stopped playing to see where this noise and this vibration was coming from. And he told Bill, "You got to do something. We're losing money. People don't wanna play, they wanna come over here and watch."

'So after the first show he said, "Gene, I want you to tone it down." Well, that just made Gene mad. So the rest of the night we went out there and did three times as much. I told Jack to put the bass up in the air . . . and the bridge came off and almost knocked some guy out at the bar . . . By that time you couldn't even get in the lounge!'

There were now two significant changes in personnel. Jack Neal, like Williams and Gallup before him, went back to his wife and children in Norfolk, leaving only Dickie Harrell of the original band. Neal expressed some dissatisfaction at the way the business was being handled by Bill Davis, who he felt was too fond of the racetrack and was therefore not around when he was needed to sort something out. But then Davis also quit – it is unclear whether he was sacked, if indeed Vincent was in a position to do so, or whether he too was tired of the constant travelling.

'We agreed to disagree,' commented Davis, who was also annoyed at the early pull-out from Las Vegas. Maybe after one hit and two flops he did not see Vincent and the Blue Caps as a long-term investment, and without hits they were condemned to an exhausting nonstop life on the road. One thing was certain, that they had all spent 1956 learning the rock'n'roll rulebook as they went along. In fact they were writing it – there *were* no rules. It hadn't happened before.

When the New Year arrived Vincent was off the road for two reasons. After staying with his parents over Christmas he returned to the Navy hospital for further treatment to his leg, and he was advised that the wound would never heal if he remained out on the rock'n'roll road. But he was also ordered by a judge in Norfolk County Court to stop work for three months. L&B Talent Management had taken Bill Davis to court, claiming that they had a legal contract with Vincent but that he had been lured away by Davis.

Vincent was the innocent party in this, but he was the one to suffer. L&B claimed lost commission, 25% of Vincent's earnings since he had begun performing in the previous summer. He was forced to hire lawyers of his own, counterclaiming that the contract with L&B was void – basically because they had done nothing for him. His reasoning was that GAC got the gigs for the band, and Davis attended them on the road. The case dragged on into early summer, when in a compromise settlement Vincent was ordered to pay $13,000 in return for freedom from L&B.

Meanwhile Capitol released 'Crazy Legs', backed by the ballad 'Important Words', in early January. Worryingly, it did little – one of the most dynamic stage acts in the country, playing to capacity halls, was still trading in the glow of 'Be Bop a Lula'. Without another hit that glow would inevitably soon dim, and indeed the paydays got smaller until the 'new' Blue Caps scored the next summer with 'Lotta Lovin' '. The second album *Gene Vincent and the Blue Caps*, largely recorded during those October sessions, came out in March and the fifth single followed – 'B-I-Bickey-Bi-Bo-Bo-Go' plus 'Five Days, Five Days'. It was another failure.

And so early in 1957, during this period of enforced idleness, Vincent took the opportunity to reorganise the band. He came up with the idea of two 'clapper boys' to add to the onstage excitement, men who could provide hand-clapping, dancing and backing vocals. This idea must have come from the choreographed style of the black harmony groups he had seen – notably the Flamingos, with whom the band had shared the Toronto bill. Peek, who had been successfully bluffing as a guitarist but brought an exuberant image to the group, became one of them and a school friend of Harrell's, seventeen-year-old Tommy 'Bubba' Facenda, was also hired.

'Elvis had the Jordanaires at that time,' says Facenda, 'and Gene wanted some background singers and he asked me how I'd like to do it . . . Gene was looking for a showband this time. He wanted everybody to be like Dickie. Paul Peek was already playing rhythm guitar and he was wild and crazy. Paul was singing background with me until we could find somebody else . . . We weren't just background vocalists, we were also performers, dancers – we kind of thought of ourselves as Gene's leg that he could never use. We went out on the road and knocked 'em cold 'cos we were doing things that no white band was doing at that time.' The commitment to the show was all-important – Vincent once told Facenda that 'the applause was his paycheck'.

Facenda had somewhat painful memories of his life as a Blue Cap. 'At the bridge he [Gene] used to shout "Rock!" and one night he busted my mouth open with his mike. The blood was flowing . . . but he grabbed my hand and said, "They love that." I thought, "I'm going to have to do this every night." '

Peek had a very strong voice, and had occasionally sung a few numbers of his own during Blue Caps sets the previous autumn. Facenda went on to have a hit of his own, 'High School USA', which reached a creditable No. 28 in the Hot Hundred in 1959, but two years later he left the music business for the comparative sanity of the fire service.

Performing 'High School USA' live was a feat of memory, since the selling point of the song was that it mentioned all the high schools in a particular area. Facenda recorded 28 variations of the song, and had to work out first where he was and second the list of relevant schools. This made it the biggest-ever exercise in tailoring a song to suit regional audiences. Recently the Norfolk, Virginia record label Legrand has released a CD of all the versions, although it is hard to imagine sitting down to listen to it all the way through. Facenda directed the song at Virginia, New York, Nashville, the Carolinas, Los Angeles, Indiana, Washington DC and Baltimore, Philadelphia, San Francisco, Chicago, Detroit, New Orleans, Texas, Pittsburgh, Minneapolis-St Paul, St Louis, Florida, Newark, Alabama and Georgia, Boston, Cleveland, Cincinnati, Memphis, Buffalo, Seattle, Hartford, Denver and Oklahoma. There was also an all-purpose 'national' edition.

Gallup's most lasting replacement as lead guitarist was Johnny Meeks, who was in the Circle E Ranch Boys with Peek. Like Gallup, he made a seemingly effortless transition from country picking to its rude bastard son rockabilly. And he made it in his own way, rather than trying to copy the inimitable original. This suited Vincent fine – he had the musical nous to realise that what he needed was the first Meeks, not the second Gallup.

Neal was replaced by Bill Mack, who played an electric bass rather than a stand-up bull fiddle, but in spite of his enthusiasm to land a job with the band he resigned after one tour and another Circle E Ranch Boy, Bobby Lee Jones, joined the group. Meeks was nineteen years old, and the band had been doing well enough for him to have taken the chance and left school. The Ranch Boys were led by the top disc jockey in the Greenville area, Country Earl, who also had a local television show, and the resulting publicity ensured full houses wherever they played.

Country Earl must have had a very relaxed attitude to losing musicians to the Blue Caps, since each one of the band at this time would, sooner or later, make the move. The fact was that Earl was the star, and he never had any difficulty in recruiting keen young replacements. 'I wasn't sore at all,' he insisted. 'In fact I was a bit flattered that a big star like Gene wanted one of my boys.' Vincent and Peek travelled to Greenville to see the Ranch Boys and the gig was effectively an audition for Meeks, which terrified him. Vincent was struck by his three-necked guitar as well as his picking, and hired him immediately.

Not only was Vincent living back with his parents and his three sisters, but Meeks, Peek and Mack moved in as well – the two babies of the group, Harrell and Facenda, were still living with *their* parents. In spite of the crowd, they managed to turn one room into a rehearsal studio, preparing for the time when Vincent was allowed to go back on the road. Somehow, their pride in their son's achievement enabled Louise and Kie to put up with the noisy, cramped chaos.

In fact, as Meeks later recalled, Vincent anticipated his freedom and the band joined a six-date tour of Ohio, a 'Rockabilly Spectacular', while he was still under the court restriction. 'I think Sanford Clark was on it, Perkins was on it [and] Roy Orbison . . . I was playing that ol' three-necked guitar. It was awkward and heavy, it was a home-made thing.' One neck was short, like a mandolin, giving a high-pitched sound, the middle one was a standard guitar and the bottom one was a 12-string. Vincent liked it so much that he took it over and used it for a while as a gimmick, and Meeks was happy to return to a conventional lightweight guitar.

Clark, who deserves at very least a footnote in rock'n'roll history for his dark, driving top-ten hit 'The Fool', was indeed on the bill, and later recalled that by now Vincent was drinking fairly heavily as well as popping pills. 'Yeh, we tipped a few,' he said.

Mack left after the Ohio trip and Jones replaced him. This line-up was to remain stable until Harrell left late in 1958. Vincent returned to hospital yet again, this time to have the plaster cast replaced by a leg iron. They then travelled to Philadelphia for a week's engagement in a vast package show, 'The Rock'n'roll Jubilee of Stars'. Eddie Cochran, with his first hit 'Sittin' in the Balcony', was also on the bill and this is when he and Vincent met for the first time – Cochran and the Blue Caps filmed their numbers for *The Girl Can't Help It* on different days. They then played in Chicago and the audience rioted, breaking through the police cordon to mob the band.

As soon as he was freed from his L&B contract Vincent, on the advice of Ken Nelson, signed with Dallas agency Artist Service Bureau, owned by Ed McLemore. The band were assigned a road manager, Larry Thacker, who was to be responsible for handling the gig money, expenses and wages. Thacker, it was reasoned, was a middle-aged minder who would not stand for any nonsense. As the band hurled their blue caps into the screaming audience, Thacker would solemnly take an inventory.

They were provided with a huge Chrysler sedan and an equipment trailer, and kitted out with new stage suits – black trousers plus red jackets for the musicians, green for the clapper boys, and anything for Vincent that made him stand out – often a billowing satin shirt above black trousers – he usually wore black to disguise first his plaster cast, covered in a black sock, and now the metal leg brace.

Of course, these things would have to be paid for, but it seemed that business was at last being put on a firmer base than Bill Davis's somewhat opaque, ad hoc methods. Vincent was earning all right – one report of his declared income for 1956 put it at $330,000, so there is no suggestion that anyone was seriously screwing him – but his career needed to be put on solid ground. This was something he was incapable of doing for himself. It also helped that Jones was a little older and more sensible than the rest, and could help take care of business on the road. Vincent's optimism about the new management set-up is indicated by the fact that he now bought a large house, his first, near the agency in Dallas.

McLemore sent the band out on some southern dates while, at Capitol, Nelson was assembling material for an overdue recording session, fixed for 19 and 20 June. Understandably, the label's sessions were now all to be held at the bright new offices in Hollywood. A cold, clattering, orchestra-sized studio is not best suited to a rockabilly combo, although Capitol were to produce some rock'n'roll masterworks like Wanda Jackson's belting 'Let's Have a Party' and the tongue-in-cheek instrumentals of the Piltdown Men.

The Blue Caps, and their house engineer John Kraus, did well in retaining the vibrancy of the band, and Capitol Tower was the venue for all future Blue Caps recordings. It must be wondered, though, if the Blue Caps could not have sounded even better in some relaxed, down-home studio – Johnny Otis, for one, refused to use the Tower studio after one experience there, and there was clearly a degree of ignorance of rock'n'roll requirements at the label more accustomed to Frank Sinatra.

With Bakersfield country-rocker Buck Owens playing rhythm guitar, the first day produced a classic in Dallas writer Bernice Bedwell's 'Lotta Lovin' ', driven along by an urgent, choppy rhythm and with Vincent's clapper-boy innovation gloriously vindicated in the syncopated interplay of the voices. Owens was there for the same reason that session players were hired for 'Be Bop a Lula' before being stood down – Nelson had not heard Meeks play, and wanted some insurance. 'I Got It' and 'Rollin' Danny' were also up to par, although Nelson hedged his bets with the ballad 'Wear My Ring'. Vincent, however, had the voice to winkle out whatever there was to be found in such pleasant but routine fare.

It was written by Bobby Darin, soon to emerge as the chameleon of pop – from rock'n'roller to hip, finger-snapping cabaret artist to the 'serious', moustachioed Bob Darin (almost 'Dylan') of the *Commitment* album – and Don Kirshner, who became a major-league player in the music business. Above all, he assembled the Monkees, and also rode the crest of the bubble-gum wave with a series of shorter-lived confections.

On the following day, by which time Nelson was satisfied that Owens was superfluous, the band cut a grade-one track, 'Dance to the Bop', along with 'True to You', 'In My Dreams' (also by Bedwell) and 'Time Will Bring You Everything'. 'Lotta Lovin' ', backed by 'Wear My Ring', was the chosen first single from the session, released in July. Disc-jockey indifference to Vincent's post-'Lula' offerings was replaced by enthusiasm, helping the record into the Hot Hundred and on to reach No. 14. Some of them preferred 'Wear My Ring', in fact, making it a double-sided hit. As a result, the gig situation began to look healthy once more.

'Bubba' Facenda conveyed the varied nature of these gigs, which typified the experience of white rock'n'roll acts at the time. 'One week we might be playing the *Ozark Jubilee* in Springfield, Missouri or the *Louisiana Hayride* with all the C&W artists, the next week we might be playing nightclubs, the next week we might be playing rock'n'roll shows or R&B shows.'

Facenda confirms that Vincent had indeed learned from watching black groups when he introduced the choreography element to the act. 'We used to work on routines like a lot of the coloured groups had back in the '50s. Gene would make all of us go through routines and we had a few numbers where we really had a lot of good precision work down and we practised hard at it.'

At rock'n'roll dance dates, while the Blue Caps warmed up the audience with a brief set including current instrumental hits and maybe a couple of songs from Johnny Meeks, Vincent would keep Peek and

Facenda back with him in the wings. This was a shrewd piece of stagecraft – the 'star time' element of the show was given extra charge when Vincent came on with a dancing clapper boy on either side of him. Suddenly the stage was full, the preliminaries were over, and Vincent's wonderful voice would tear into his first number. But sometimes Vincent would annoy them by not including enough numbers in the set that they sang on, leaving them clapping, jigging about and feeling rather foolish.

The success of 'Lotta Lovin' ' sustained the band through the summer of 1957 and in September they went abroad for the only time as Gene Vincent and the Blue Caps, to Hawaii, Fiji and on to Australia. This was one of the great package tours – Vincent, his new friend Eddie Cochran, their hero Little Richard, 'the female Elvis' Alis Lesley and, in Australia, home-grown rocker Johnny O'Keefe, whose local hit 'Real Wild Child' was covered by Jerry 'Ivan' Allison when Buddy Holly and the Crickets visited Australia. It reached No. 68 in the following year. The tour was a huge success, selling out halls in all the big cities circling around the southeast rim of the country.

This was when Little Richard made the most celebrated of several retirements from rock'n'roll in favour of the church. As Paul Peek remembered it: 'We were on a school-type bus on a ferry and Little Richard got in an argument with his half-brother who played sax in his band and his brother said: "If you really had religion you wouldn't wear those flashy rings and clothes and be showin' off." And Richard said: "Well, I'll show you." And he rolled the window down and threw the rings into the water . . . He gave Gene some of his flashy suits. And he gave me some really expensive shoes . . .' Richard returned to the States and enrolled in a bible college in Alabama.

When the Blue Caps got home it was clear that the success of 'Lotta Lovin' ' had given the band a new lease of life, and they found themselves whipping up more hysteria than ever among the crowds. They were also apparently creating the blueprint for bad behaviour on the road – noisy parties, trashed motels, groupies, drink and drugs and all the other accoutrements so enthusiastically taken up by the groups of ten years later.

In early November 'Dance to the Bop' was released with 'I Got It' on the flip. This time the band managed a follow-up hit, and the record made respectable progress as far as No. 43. They were booked on to the prestigious *Ed Sullivan Show* to promote it – the same programme that had banned Elvis from the waist down and was to introduce the Beatles to America. By this time Vincent was seeing a fan of the band, Darlene

Hicks, who first met Vincent when hired by a promoter in Oregon to check the tickets at the door. The promoter was Pat Mason, who ran a club called the Wagon Wheel, and would later briefly manage Vincent.

Although they were never to marry, the relationship between Vincent and Darlene lasted several years. At this time, though, Vincent was still married to Ruth Ann – though not for long. Tired of being tied to an absentee husband, Ruth Ann sued for divorce, and Vincent happily accepted his freedom in return for a modest settlement. At the time they met Darlene was a divorcee with a one-year-old daughter, Debbie.

And now, just at the height of their popularity, there was another personnel shuffle, ending the era of the 'second' Blue Caps. Dickie Harrell, the only remaining original, was going out with 'Bubba' Facenda's sister and was pining for a more settled life. The agency sent out the drummer from the Sonny James band, Dude Kahn, and another Dallas musician, Max Lipscomb, also joined the Blue Caps. Lipscomb was a seventeen-year-old, not by his own admission a virtuoso, and he was hired as a backing singer and rhythm guitarist before becoming the band's first pianist. 'I was able to learn to fake it. I used to play Chopin stuff when I was a little kid.'

He joined in time for the Ed Sullivan appearance, playing live as was the tradition of the show, but by this time Harrell was already back in harness. Kahn returned to Dallas having only played a few gigs. Capitol called another four-day recording session to commence on 5 December. By now Ken Nelson was ready to admit that the vast Capitol Tower studio was not best suited to a small rock'n'roll combo. 'The Hollywood studio . . . would just dwarf his group. We used to shove them all in a corner where they could be closer to their music but it hardly made any difference, the sound would just spread all over the place.' But the company accountants could hardly see the logic of hiring an independent studio when they had spent a fortune on their own.

Although the sessions would produce one of the finest of all Blue Caps tracks, 'Baby Blue', the repertoire suggests new uncertainty in Nelson's mind as to how to maintain the band's appeal. 'By the Light of the Silvery Moon' made for a raucous rocker when sung by Little Richard, but was not ideal Vincent material. But there were other bonuses from the four days – the frenetic, jittery ensemble singing of 'Yes, I Love You Baby' and the rocking 'I Got a Baby' among them. They also cut 'Right Now', 'You'll Never Walk Alone', 'Your Cheating Heart', 'Walkin' Home from School', 'It's No Lie', 'Should I Ever Love Again', 'Flea Brain', 'Brand New Beat' and 'Frankie and Johnny', an impressive work rate. Lipscomb was by now on piano, credited with the name under which he would later have some solo releases, Scotty McKay. Peek has said that 'Yes, I Love You Baby' was written by the whole band in the corner of the studio, and that it took about fifteen minutes.

After an appearance at New York's Paramount Theater on an Alan Freed bill, the band split up for Christmas, although Vincent alone mimed 'Dance to the Bop' on Dick Clark's *American Bandstand*, Philadelphia-based but by now networked, and in January 1958 'I Got a Baby', backed with 'Walkin' Home from School', was the chosen follow-up record, but it failed to register. Lipscomb decided to go back to school, although he would return briefly to the band. Back on the road, Paul Peek and 'Bubba' Facenda also decided that they had had enough. Vincent was now drinking heavily, subject to mood swings and toying with guns, and the thrill of being a bunch of young rock'n'rollers taking on the world had faded.

There were new recruits as well, however. Another of the Circle E Ranch Boys, Clifton Simmons, joined on piano in January, while Vincent's brother-in-law Ed Butler, married to his sister Evelyn, became Vincent's personal driver. Vincent and Butler had met aboard the *Chuckawan*, and were close friends as well as relatives. Also, Vincent missed the extra solidity to the sound provided by a second guitar, and so a further Dallas musician, Grady Owen, was dispatched in January to catch up with the band in Omaha, Nebraska. He was struck by the continuing hysteria shown by the fans. 'They rioted and 'bout tore the place down!' he said of one gig in Milwaukee.

The relentless touring continued well into 1958, and while they were as successful as ever as a live attraction, Vincent's behaviour was becoming ever more erratic and unreliable. It was a wholly unnatural way of life, and after two years of it the strain was beginning to show in his deteriorating mental state. But he could still inspire affection. As Owen put it: 'We all loved Vincent, we all hated Vincent at the same time. He'd get a little bit drunk occasionally and fire us all after the show, or he'd pass out before a show was over and we'd have to go and collect his money for him, but we loved him!'

In the meantime Capitol released their third album in March, *Gene Vincent Rocks and the Blue Caps Roll*, and the McLemore agency signed them up for their second movie, to be called *Hot Rod Gang*. Harrell proved no less homesick during his brief second stint with the band and finally left, being replaced in mid-March by a Mexican fifteen-year-old, Juvey Gomez, a Dallas schoolboy whom Vincent had seen playing on the same Fort Worth bill as the Blue Caps. Gomez secured the permission of his mother and his teachers, in return for a planned series of school-work assignments. He rehearsed with the band and travelled with them to Hollywood for the next recording session. Peek and Facenda were persuaded to return to provide the backing vocals, and the studio was booked for five days.

On four of those days Eddie Cochran was present. The first session only produced two tracks but they were classics, 'Dance in the Street' and 'Git It'. The former is a piano-led rocker while the four-part harmony singing and stop-start rhythm of 'Git It', written by Dallas disc jockey Bob Kelly, make it one of the most original Vincent tracks, predating the Beach Boys sound by five years. It owed a huge amount to Cochran who – as with the other sides he appeared on in these sessions – moonlighted from Liberty Records to sing the bass part, and probably played a substantial role in plotting the distinctive arrangement. Meeks's guitar spits out of the meshing voices to complete the effect.

On the following days another fourteen tracks were cut, including two Hank Williams standards, 'I Can't Help It' and 'Hey, Good Lookin'', George Gershwin's 'Summertime', echo-drenched and set to a pattering rhythm, 'The Wayward Wind' and 'Now Is the Hour'. More typical Vincent fare was provided in 'Teenage Partner', 'Lovely Loretta', 'Little Lover', a dynamic rock arrangement of the bluegrass tune 'Rocky Road Blues', 'Somebody Help Me', 'Five Feet of Loving' and 'Look What You Gone and Done To Me', with 'I Love You' and 'Peace of Mind' completing a solid week's work.

Most of the tracks made up the fourth album, *A Gene Vincent Record Date*, and the band immediately moved over to the film studios of American-International to perform their segments for the quickie movie *Hot Rod Gang* (it was retitled *Fury Unleashed* when released the following January in the UK: 'Crazy Kids – Living to a Crazy Beat!'). They filmed 'Dance in the Street' and 'Baby Blue', and 'Dance to the Bop' and 'Lovely Loretta' are also heard on the soundtrack. Vincent also had a few lines of dialogue. Cochran's then-current group the Kelly Four appear in the movie, with his manager Jerry Capehart credited as musical director. When the movie was released in July it was on a juvenile-delinquent double bill with *High School Hellcats*. Meanwhile the next single was 'Rocky Road Blues' and 'Yes, I Love You Baby'.

The four movie songs were released as an EP, *Hot Rod Gang*. As soon as their work was done Gomez returned to school to sit his final exams, Peek and Facenda retired from the group for a second and last time, and the rest of the band took a break awaiting the return of their young drummer.

In May one of Vincent's stand-out numbers, the dramatic, bluesy 'Baby Blue', was released as the next single backed by 'True to You'. It bombed. Meanwhile the band was back out on the road, travelling up the West Coast. After a motel-wrecking night Vincent was dragged off stage by the police and thrown into jail. He was bailed just in time for the next gig, which ended in chaos when the audience began fighting. 'I decided that it was a little too much,' said Gomez in measured tones, 'so I came back to Dallas.' He joined another McLemore band, the Texan outfit Buddy Knox and the Rhythm Orchids. Although Knox never equalled the success of his debut hit in 1957, 'Party Doll', which reached No. 2 and made the British Top Thirty, he continued to nudge into the charts into the 1960s and remained a popular performer on rockabilly revival tours.

There was worse to come for Vincent in terms of defections. The 'second' Blue Caps had been pinned around Johnny Meeks's guitar and Bobby Lee Jones's bass, and now they too had had enough. Meeks would be back, though Jones returned to Greenville permanently, but in the meantime a hole had been knocked through the middle of the band – three musicians leaving and more than a month of work in Canada booked, on a bill that included Cochran.

However, there was an ever-growing number of ex-Caps who could by now have recharged their batteries and be willing to provide a pool of potential players, and so it proved. Max Lipscomb returned to play rhythm guitar, with Grady Owen moving to bass, while newcomer Butch White took over the drum stool. Auditions in Dallas turned up their next lead guitarist, Howard Reed, and they were off once more. 'Rocky Road Blues' and 'Yes, I Love You Baby', meanwhile, proved yet another artistic triumph and commercial turkey.

White did not last long, however, and an emergency phone call was placed to Elvis's drummer D.J. Fontana, who joined at one day's notice. Then Vincent tinkered with the personnel yet again, going back to the 'clapper boy' idea with Owen and Lipscomb, and rehiring Bill Mack on bass. But no sooner was the Canadian tour over than Vincent changed his mind, virtually disbanding the group. Owen joined Juvey Gomez in Buddy Knox's band, Fontana and Reed went home, and for the remainder of summer 1958 the Blue Caps, with a nucleus of Simmons and Mack, varied from gig to gig. Vincent's indecision went hand-in-hand with ever greater dependence on alcohol, pills and painkillers, more impulsive, irrational behaviour, fits of violence and baffling, unsettling mood swings.

But in September Johnny Meeks decided to rejoin. 'I missed it . . . the screaming, the hollering, the good money and all that.' He brought with him another Circle E Ranch Boy, drummer Clyde Pennington. The new recruit later recalled: 'Gene would get to drinking so we'd do things like raise the key on "Be Bop a Lula" without telling him!' Finally, Owen returned on bass to replace Mack, and the last recognisable Blue Caps line-up was in place. A wonderful single combined 'Git It' with the rocker 'Little Lover', but again it was a baffling failure.

In the Norfolk *Morning Star* published on 10 January 1998, Bill Mack, who now confines his musicianship to the local church, told staff writer Lee Roberts about his bruising time with Vincent. 'He didn't like people,' he says of his former employer. 'He was rotten. He didn't get along with nobody.'

Writes Roberts: 'In their short, violent time together, Mr Mack and Vincent got into fisticuffs numerous times, squabbling over money, women, even cars. One time Vincent put a gun to Mr Mack's head and told him to get out of his house . . . Everywhere Vincent went, a trail of busted equipment, trashed hotel rooms and deflowered schoolgirls followed.'

As Mack recalled it, the Blue Caps in the late 50s were indeed laying down the blueprint for Keith Moon and the next generation of wild rockers: 'That's all it was, just pills, parties and poker games. We were kids out on the road. We'd throw bottles across hotel rooms, toss furniture into swimming pools, get into fights all the time. Anything we wanted to. We just didn't have no discipline.

'In New Mexico one night we were backing up a one-way street. This woman came over to us and said, "You crazy SOBs, this is a one-way street!" So Gene told me, "Waste her," and he put a gun in my hand. So I pointed it at her and she went running down the street screaming. That's how lost I was.'

Mack described the circumstances of his quitting the band for the second time. He had been accused of locking a thirteen-year-old girl in a hotel room, and Vincent fired him. Mack, however, insists that she was seventeen, got herself somehow into Vincent's room and got wasted on pills and drink. In fact, he says, it was money – or lack of it – that was the final straw.

'After that problem with the girl in the hotel room, he got mad and went up to every member of the band and said, "Do you like me? Do you like your job?" When he got to me I said, "I don't like you and I don't like your job either." He wouldn't pay me money he owed me.'

It is said that yet another fight ensued and when the police were called they forced Vincent to stump up the money he owed to Mack. Vincent, in desperation, later asked Mack to rejoin him for a tour of

Germany. 'That's the last I ever saw of him,' says Mack. 'I probably would have killed him if I'd went . . . This man had a lot of troubles with his leg and he was hurting. Man, he was hurting.' In spite of his bitter feelings about Vincent, undimmed forty years on, Mack's trailer home at the time of the interview was decorated with pictures of Vincent and album sleeves, while his car registration plate read 'Be Bop a Lula'.

The band went out on the road for a few weeks before heading for Hollywood and a marathon recording session – 7 days commencing on 13 October, producing 23 tracks. On four of the days they were augmented by a tenor saxophonist borrowed from Johnny Otis, Jackie Kelso, and the great baritone player Plas Johnson, an innovation that successfully – artistically if not, alas, commercially – pushed Vincent's rockabilly sound towards R&B.

Together with 'Now is the Hour', recorded the previous March with Cochran present, eleven of the tracks made up the next album *Sounds Like Gene Vincent*: 'My Baby Don't 'Low', two Little Richard covers, 'I Can't Believe You Wanna Leave' and 'Ready Teddy', 'I Might Have Known', 'In Love Again', 'You are the One', 'I Got to Get to You Yet', 'Vincent's Blues', 'Maybe', Johnny Burnette's 'My Heart' and Chuck Berry's 'Maybelline'. The other titles were 'Lonesome Boy', 'The Night is So Lonely', Huey Smith's 'High Blood Pressure', another Little Richard song, 'Rip It Up', 'Beautiful Brown Eyes', one of his lasting classics 'Say Mama', 'Be Bop Boogie Boy', 'Who's Pushing Your Swing', a second attempt at 'Important Words', 'Anna-Annabelle', 'Gone, Gone, Gone' and Vincent's beautiful reading of 'Over the Rainbow', with Cliff Simmons switching from piano to celeste.

Some of the held-over tracks were released in France in 1963. 'Say Mama' was the chosen single, backed with 'Be Bop Boogie Boy', and again, incredibly, the American public ignored this excellent pairing.

One reason for Vincent's demise as a chart artist, in America at least, must be that, in an industry awash with payola, bribes and freebies, Capitol Records took the high moral ground and refused to join in. Then there was the malign influence of Dick Clark, who used the unrivalled influence of *American Bandstand* to usher in the era of 'the Frankies and the Bobbys', polite, anodyne, pretend rockers in tight Italian suits, in whose records Clark often had a financial interest.

To help round off the year for Vincent and the now-pregnant Darlene, the Internal Revenue Service seized their house in lieu of unpaid taxes, condemning the couple and daughter Debbie to a vagrant life of rented flats, hotels and the generosity of a dwindling number of friends.

The band began gigging again, for what proved to be the last time. Money was getting tight now, and Vincent failed to pay the band for several weeks. They were booked to play on a Los Angeles television show *Country America*, and Vincent promised to pay them from the television-company cheque. Instead, with the band holed up in a hotel, he did a runner to Anchorage, Alaska, leaving them high and dry. It was here that, on 27 April 1959, Darlene gave birth to Melody Jean. Eight months later he still had not paid the band.

Three of the abandoned Blue Caps, Simmons, Meeks and Pennington, immediately picked up session work in Los Angeles with, among others, Eddie Cochran and Johnny Burnette. They then worked together in a short-lived band called the Tunetoppers. After this Simmons and Pennington went home to Greenville and Meeks went on to various bands, notably the Champs ('Tequila'), Louisiana singer Jimmy Clanton ('Venus in Blue Jeans' was one of his many hits), the ex-Monkee Mike Nesmith ('Joanne') and country giant Merle Haggard. Owen returned to Dallas and later formed a band to back Vincent's friend, rockabilly singer Johnny Carroll.

The break-up of the band meant that Vincent could no longer work, his contract with the McLemore agency in Dallas became void, and no further recording sessions were planned. Vincent's career was in free fall, although rockabilly artist Whitey Pullen became his new manager at this time. Forced to work abroad with just one permanent band member, new guitarist Jerry Lee Merritt, Vincent toured Japan and the Far East in the spring of 1959.

Merritt had been leading a band called Jerry Lee and the Pacers, working mainly around Washington state, and had bumped into Vincent on the road. He then became Bobby Darin's guitarist and they met once more. Once the Darin tour was over Merritt accepted Vincent's offer of work. They worked as a duo using local rhythm sections, wherever jobs were to be had.

And then, on 3 February 1959, 'the music died'. Buddy Holly was not the first popular artist to die prematurely – country music had lost Hank Williams, Hollywood James Dean and black music Johnny Ace, for example – but Holly, Ritchie Valens and The Big Bopper were the first pop stars of the rock'n'roll era to fall out of the sky, marking a symbolic end to the heyday of the music. And as far as many resentful, cigar-chomping veterans of Tin Pan Alley were concerned, it could not come too soon.

News of Vincent's dissolute ways and debts had not travelled as far as Japan, where he was still a rock'n'roll hero. By now, according to Merritt, Vincent was washing down handfuls of painkillers with beer and whisky. After the termination of his relationship with the McLemore agency and his brief arrangement with Whitey Pullen, Vincent was now being managed by Pat Mason, the owner of the club in Oregon where he had often played and where he had met Darlene. 'I had worked with [Gene] in the North West,' recalls Merritt. 'An agent called Pat Mason called and asked me if I wanted to go to Tokyo, out of a clear blue sky. Sure, I'll do it . . .'

The tour was later recalled by Merritt: 'Gene would say it was probably the biggest thing that happened to him in his career. I met Gene at Anchorage and we flew to Japan from there. There were ten thousand people to meet us.' Later Merritt added to the story the fact that an American senator and his wife were on the same plane, deluding himself that the greeting was intended for him. 'We didn't even have to clear customs – it was all cleared for us. Then we had a parade all the way up town to our hotel . . . We had bodyguards and limousines . . . We had to eat in our rooms because there were so many girls in the hallway trying to get in . . . We broke all records in the theatre. It held twenty thousand people and there were three shows a day. It was packed every day . . . We had to sign autographs for a solid two or three hours . . .'

The unlikely suggestion that the band cowered in their rooms while sex-crazed girls tried unsuccessfully to get in suggests that perhaps Mrs Merritt was a keen reader of fanzines at the time. Briefly, Vincent was earning big money once more, and as he was pining for Darlene and Melody he, for one, probably *was* behaving himself sexually. Indeed, in a typical moment of impetuous, irresponsible, emotional brainstorm, he disappeared from Japan with four days of the tour to go, and flew home to be with his family, without any warning. Merritt was ordered to impersonate Vincent, and he got away with it. It is easy to see how, at least so far from home. They are about the same height, both sported black, tousled, greasy hair and Merritt had sharply defined cheekbones just like Vincent.

In spite of his pledge to stay faithful to his $10 Neapolitan guitar, Vincent is shown in press photographs to be strumming a semi-acoustic Gibson alongside Merritt's Fender. For most numbers, however, the guitar was abandoned and the crouching, kneeling, splay-legged microphone technique that found its finest expression a few months later in Jack Good's biker creation takes over. The pictures of the tour suggest great empathy between Vincent and Merritt, cavorting on stage as an intuitive unit in front of ecstatic crowds. This and the reception Vincent was to receive in the UK contrasted sharply with the low-key gigs that had been his American diet for the past months.

Soon Vincent was to stop playing the guitar on stage, although he always had one handy in rehearsals to demonstrate what he wanted. 'If I can carry on making a go of it as a singer I'll be more than happy,' he said. 'I suppose it was my belief in this idea that made me stop playing guitar.' Vincent claimed that he wanted to avoid being compared to Elvis, even though Presley had long abandoned his guitar as a prop. Vincent defined the difference between their musical approaches: 'His is more of a race-and-rhythm style, while I favour the bop approach.'

On 30 May 1959 *Disc* ran a piece by Gerry Myers, 'the famous Canadian dj'. Here Vincent seems at one point to claim sole authorship of 'Be Bop a Lula', writing the song 'while I was in the Navy, and on my final trip back to the US. We had been in Naples, and I had gotten the idea from a jukebox which was blaring out some sort of Italian song.

'All the people kept asking about be-bop, and someone said something to the effect of be-bop being a lulu. Well, we kicked it about on board ship,' – does the 'we' admit to additional help? – 'and when I arrived home I had a song, a guitar, but I knew no one.'

In this 1959 version of the story Vincent was playing a gig in Dallas, Texas, 'at a local night spot, when Ed McLemore, of Capitol Records, arrived with a party. He heard me sing "Be Bop a Lula" and said I should come down next day to see him.'

In June, Vincent and Merritt were reunited, the singer's sudden departure from Japan apparently forgiven, and on 3 August the two of them went into the Capitol Tower studio for a four-day session. Kelso was present once more, together with drummer Sandy Nelson ('Teen Beat', 'Let There Be Drums'), bassist Red Callender and pianist Jimmy Johnson. There was also a vocal backing from the Eligibles.

The stand-out track, cut on the first day, was the insidious Jerry Merritt composition 'She-She-Little Sheila', co-written with Whitey Pullen, and the day's work was completed with a rather bitter blues message to his partner, 'Darlene', the standard 'Accentuate the Positive' and 'Pretty Pearly'. The second day provided the title track for Vincent's next album, 'Crazy Times', together with 'Why Don't You People Learn To Drive' and the Kingston Trio's 'Greenback Dollar'. Then came 'Big Fat Saturday Night', 'Wild Cat', the single released in the UK to coincide with his visit, 'Hot Dollar', 'Right Here On Earth', Fred Rose's 'Blue Eyes Crying in the Rain', later a hit for Willie Nelson, 'Everybody's Got a Date But Me' and a nod to his recent tour, 'Mitchiko from Tokyo'. Meanwhile, 'Right Now' and 'The Night Is So Lonely' became the latest Vincent single to fail.

Vincent was now based in Los Angeles, and spent the rest of 1959 touring along the West Coast, either with Merritt and a pick-up band, with San Francisco band the Heartbeats or with a group run by local musician Clayton Watson, the Silhouettes. Other posters from this period name his backing band as the Big Beats and the Frantics, local groups flattered to be hired at short notice by such a star.

The growing scandal of payola came to a head at this time. It began with the revelation that some television quiz shows were fixed, with a predetermined winner being fed the answers and the unlucky loser being paid off. When the investigation spread inevitably to the music industry, Alan Freed was the selected scapegoat. He, more than any other disc jockey, was tarred with the rock'n'roll brush – after all, he had popularised the term, and so among those who saw in the music only subversion – Communist agitation, the advancement of black causes, the questioning of authority – Freed was public enemy number one. He refused to testify that he had never accepted payola, was sacked for this from his radio and television shows, and was eventually convicted of minor bribery charges. With a tax evasion charge also hanging over him his career was over, and he died prematurely of the effects of alcoholism in 1965.

Dick Clark, in spite of having a finger in so many musical pies and using *American Bandstand* to benefit from them, escaped. In 1960 the network transmitting the show, ABC, ordered Clark either to resign or to sell his shares in music publishers, record labels and other related businesses. He sold out, and testified that he had never accepted payola.

In April of that year he appeared before the subcommittee investigating the scandal, and baffled them with mathematics. Yes, he admitted through a statistician, he had a financial interest in 27% of the records played on *American Bandstand*, but it was claimed that this was matched by the 'popularity index' of those records, whatever that might mean, and that he was therefore simply following public taste. He said that he had given up his financial interest in 33 companies since the scandal broke, and that though he owned the rights to 160 songs he had never knowingly plugged any of them. Somehow, he got away with it.

Meanwhile Vincent, the fallen rock'n'roll star without a hit or a permanent band, got a new manager in Los Angeles agent Norm Riley and prepared to visit Britain for his *Boy Meets Girls* booking in December. Speaking of the visit Merritt said: 'He wanted me to go on that tour, but I was having domestic problems at the time.' Vincent later recorded two more Merritt songs, 'Hurtin' For You Baby' and 'Born to be a Rolling Stone', and, after parting from Vincent late in 1959, Merritt formed a new band, Jerry Merritt and the Crowns. Now Vincent was truly on his own.

4. EDDIE COCHRAN: PROLOGUE

Albert Lea lies in Freeborn County, south Minnesota, just north of the border with Iowa and due south of Minneapolis-St Paul. The city is an important railroad junction and agricultural centre, and it stands at the west end of Albert Lea Lake, seven miles long and a mile broad. It was here in Albert Lea that Eddie Cochran was born, on 3 October 1938.

Cochran's paternal grandparents Joseph and Corda lived at 1012 West 1st Street in Oklahoma City, with their four children Frank, LaVerne, Flo and Trella Faye. Joseph ran a business on North Western Avenue, J.T. Cochran and Son Auto Repair, in partnership with Frank, who worked as a mechanic. In 1923 the family moved twice, both within the same street, to 1200 and 1228, by which time Frank had married sixteen-year-old Alice Whitley and left home.

With the Depression on the horizon the family firm folded in 1925, forcing both father and son to seek out whatever work they could as motor mechanics. While still in Oklahoma City Alice gave birth to three children, Gloria in 1924, Bill in 1925 and Bob three years later.

Frank's sister Flo, meanwhile, was working for a meat-processing company in Oklahoma City, Wilson & Co. Inc., but by 1928 she had been transferred to their premises in Albert Lea, a community of some 12,000 people 600 miles to the north. She secured a job for Frank in the processing plant and, around 1930, he moved his family north to Albert Lea, renting a house at 108 Shell Rock.

The fourth child, Patty, was born in 1932 and in 1938 the family moved to 909 Marshall, where Edward Raymond Cochran was born. When he was three, by which time Bill was serving in the Navy, they moved yet again, to 230 Charles Street. In 1944 Frank changed jobs, moving to the Olsen Manufacturing Company as a machinist, and in 1946 he became a mechanic at the South Broadway Garage.

So, when Eddie became of school age – first Ramsey Elementary School, then Albert Lea Central Junior High – brother Bill was overseas, but he left behind an acoustic guitar. Eddie took to it, and also to that vital aid to so many budding rock guitarists, the *Chord and Harmony Manual* compiled by Nick Manaloff. The equivalent for the first generation of British rockers was Bert Weedon's *Play in a Day*, a title that surely should have attracted the attention of the Trades Description people.

It was perhaps inevitable that Eddie would graduate to the guitar, although his first fancy was to be a drummer – indeed, he later showed considerable expertise behind the drums. As we have heard, he taught Brian Bennett how to add syncopated patterns to the basic rock'n'roll beat. He then decided to play trombone in the school band but was advised by the music teacher that he would not be able to manage the necessary embouchure. Eddie turned down the proffered alternative, the clarinet, as being too cissy, and so Bill's old Kay guitar it was.

During the 1940s Gloria, Bill and Bob got married in turn, and Frank moved back to Oklahoma City. The state capital had grown up in the middle of an oilfield, surrounded by derricks, and was Oklahoma's most important financial, industrial and livestock centre. Its growth had begun in 1889 when this part of the Union was opened up to settlers, and it spread to become one of the most extensive cities in America.

Central to its economy was the Tinker Air Force Base, one of the biggest distribution depots serving the armed forces anywhere in the world. It was here that Frank got a job on his return. The move back to his home town did not work out, though. Alice missed the rest of the family – of the children only Eddie had moved with them, while Patty lodged with Gloria – and so they were soon back in Albert Lea.

Almost immediately, however, they were on the move again. Bill, who had left the Navy in 1946 at the end of the war, married and settled in California, where he had served out his last naval posting. With nothing much to lose Frank decided to try his luck there, and moved with Alice and Eddie to the Los Angeles suburb of Bell Gardens to be near his eldest son.

California, the destination of so many hopeful 'Okies' during the dust-bowl years of the Depression – and Eddie always claimed to be one in spite of his short stay in Oklahoma City – was still a powerful magnet. It had oil and oranges, Hollywood and aircraft factories, car plants and sunshine. The population of Los Angeles nearly doubled in the 1940s with the influx of people like Frank, seeking a better life. He soon found work, once again as a machine operator.

The family graduated from a trailer in an empty lot to an apartment, and then to a house on Priory Street, and Eddie began the academic year starting in September 1951 at his new school, Bell Gardens Junior High. His interest in playing the guitar strengthened when he formed a friendship with schoolmate Connie 'Guybo' Smith, born in LA in 1939, who played stand-up bass in the school band.

When he was fourteen Eddie formed his first group with Guybo and another school friend, Al Garcia, called the Melody Boys. It became steadily apparent to older local musicians, notably steel guitarist Chuck Foreman, who was to play an important part in Eddie's early career and was five years his senior, that the youngster had a prodigious ability to absorb musical knowledge, to improve rapidly, and to be able to reproduce on his guitar what he heard on record or radio. Eddie was by now more guitarist than schoolboy, inseparable from his instrument. During the long trek west from Albert Lea, the family possessions piled into and on top of two cars, he had held on to it all the time, and called it his 'best friend'.

He and Foreman began playing into a tape recorder, and when Foreman bought a second machine they experimented with overdubbing, building up a performance bit by bit. The master of this technique was Les Paul, but otherwise Eddie and Chuck were young pioneers in something that was yet to become standard practice in recording studios. Almost all commercial recordings still consisted of a 'live' performance, retaken as often as necessary to eliminate fluffed notes and cracked voices.

In spite of their youth, and with no previous examples to go on, the pair's tapes were precociously professional, as evidenced by those that have surfaced on Tony Barrett's Rockstar label in the UK. Just fourteen years old, Eddie was already on the road to becoming a serious, inventive and technically proficient musician. And even when he became a pop star, that is essentially what he remained. This would give his later musical relationship with Gene Vincent a lot of its dynamism – the virtuoso and the force of nature, the 'intellectual' musician and the instinctive animal performer.

Cochran's teenage musical education was nurtured at a local music store run by a friendly man called Bert Kiefer, the Bell Gardens Music Center, which was a meeting place for local musicians. Out of this grew the Bell Gardens Ranch Gang, a group of country-playing teenagers who had met at the store – Cochran, guitarist Warren Flock, bass player Dave Kohrman, violinist Forest Lee Bibbie and singer-guitarist Clete Stewart – who gigged locally and even appeared on local radio and television.

Flock was one of those who shared Cochran's youthful passion for guns. This had been nurtured in the countryside around Albert Lea, and now in the desert beyond the Los Angeles city limits. Cochran's particular favourite, one that he was proudly photographed with on more than one occasion, was a Buntline Special .45, a fearsome looking phallic weapon with a very long barrel. Cochran also became a quick-draw specialist, never to be beaten. As Phil Everly later described it: 'Eddie was an extraordinarily fast draw. A man can make a move on a gun and it takes the brain 17/100th of a second to register that his hand has moved. Cochran's reaction time was about half of that.'

Cochran's gun-toting pal Flock died on 14 April 2003 – after his flirtation with music he got a 'proper job' with Coca-Cola, and worked there for 38 years.

Cochran's interest in guns was fostered by his older brothers, and it survived a childhood accident when he was accidentally shot in the leg when a gun went off unexpectedly. Fortunately the wound was more painful than life-threatening.

On his British visit, still claiming to have been born in Oklahoma City, Cochran recalled the incident. 'I grew up in the wonderful natural scenery of that state [Minnesota, after the move back to Albert Lea], which is a paradise for fishing and shooting. I remember going on many hunting trips and developing a great love for all kinds of outdoor sports. In fact it was on one of these trips that I nearly lost the chance of becoming a singer – or anything else for that matter.

'I was out with my brother searching for frogs one day. He had a .22 automatic, which got jammed. As he was trying to work it free, the gun went off accidentally and shot me in the leg. That kept me in bed for several months and gave me plenty of time for thought and contemplation. It occurred to me that I might become a singer . . .' This seems unlikely, but no doubt as he lay there his guitar playing began to look like a safer option.

Cochran was still playing and experimenting musically with Chuck Foreman when the Ranch Gang fell apart late in 1953. In the following year the duo sat in with a hillbilly band called the Shamrock Valley Boys, led by Richard Rae, and Cochran was to become particularly friendly with the group's singer and guitarist Bob Denton, real name Robert Bull, with whom he would later make records. Denton was another of those who enjoyed going off into the desert to shoot game. More significantly as far as the next stage in Cochran's career is concerned, the Shamrock outfit sometimes had another singer-guitarist sit in with them, Hank Cochran.

Hank, christened Garland Perry, was born in Mississippi but orphaned very young. He ran away from his orphanage and grew up in New Mexico, where an uncle's family lived, and he arrived in California in 1951. Within two years he had become a radio and television regular and he was now, at the precocious age of seventeen, looking to form a country duo to play locally. Fifteen-year-old Eddie Cochran was recommended to him by Denton and, struck by the coincidence of the name, Hank sought him out. Eddie, always ready for a jam session, mightily impressed Hank with his dexterity on guitar, and so they became the Cochran Brothers, working the West Coast dance halls.

Above Swinging: an Eddie Cochran publicity shot taken in Hollywood, April or May 1957. (Redferns)

Right A moody Cochran publicity picture from 1959, in Hollywood. (Redferns)

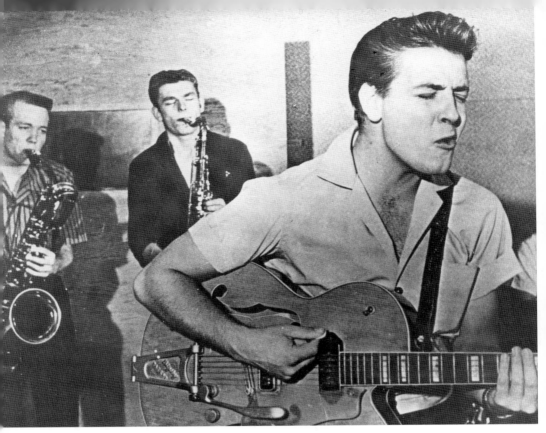

Above Cochran at Goldstar Studios in Hollywood, 1959. (John Collis Collection)

Right Cochran live on stage in Nebraska, 1959. (Redferns)

Above Cochran rehearses in Soho for *Boy Meets Girls*, 1960. (Redferns)

Right Cochran hams it up at the press reception welcoming him to England, 1960. (John Collis Collection)

Daily Mirror

MON APR. 18 1960

No. 17,522

2

'ROCK' STAR DIES IN CRASH

● PICTURED ABOVE: Singer Eddie Cochran. LEFT: The wreckage of the car after the crash which killed him

AMERICAN rock 'n' roll singing star Eddie Cochran died yesterday after a car taking him to London Airport crashed.

The crash happened late on Saturday night at Chippenham, Wilts.

Cochran, 21, was travelling to the airport by hire-car from Bristol, where he topped the bill last week in a stage variety show.

With him were three other passengers.

One was American girl songwriter Sharon Sheeley, 20.

Song Girl

Another was American girl songwriter Sharon Sheeley, 20. The third was theatrical agent Patrick Thompkins, 29, of Camberwell, London.

As the car went through Chippenham it suddenly spun in the road and crashed backwards into a concrete lamp-post.

Cochran was flung into the road.

● GENE VINCENT

Flung out as car is wrecked

People living near it heard the crash. They ran out in their nightclothes to help him and the others in the crash.

Cochran had severe head injuries.

Vincent was badly bruised, and had slight head injuries. Miss Sheeley had a fractured pelvis.

By NED GRANT

and back injuries. Thompkins was bruised and cut.

The car-driver—George Martin, of Blackthorneroad, Hartcliffe, Bristol—was unhurt.

The four injured passengers were taken to hospital at Bath.

And there, just after four o'clock yesterday afternoon, Cochran died.

Thompkins said in hospital last night : "The crash happened so suddenly that I don't think any of us knew much about it.

Cochran, whose records have included "Summertime Blues" and "C'mon Everybody," had been in Britain since January doing stage and TV work.

He was due to fly back to America yesterday, to do some filming.

Vincent—his first big hit was "Be-Bop-a-Lula" —was flying with Cochran to take a holiday.

So was British "rock" singer Vince Eager, 19.

He did not know of the crash until he called to collect his plane ticket at London Airport yesterday.

Then Eager was given a message from Bath about the crash.

He cancelled his flight and drove to Bath. There he saw the three injured people.

With Body

Last night a spokesman for Eager's manager—agent Larry Parnes—said the British singer would fly to America with Cochran's body after the inquest.

And Cochran's last record, called "Three Steps to Heaven," will be issued on schedule in Britain within a few days.

The toll: 30 dead 628 injured so far

AT least thirty people have been killed and 628 injured on the roads since the Easter Holiday started on Good Friday.

First reports of YESTERDAY'S ACCIDENTS showed that nine people were killed and 12 injured.

Provisional figures for GOOD FRI. DAY and SATURDAY announced by the Automobile Association were: Twenty-one dead and 616 injured.

Last year's figures for the same two days were: Fifteen dead and 460 injured.

Last night the Automobile Asso-

ciation made this urgent Bank Holiday appeal:

An all-out effort will be required by everyone if the toll on the roads is not to be greater than last Easter.

Bank Holiday motoring conditions call for every bit of concentration on the part of drivers, cyclists and pedestrians.

A second's carelessness could mean another lost life.

The Margin of error allowed by congested roads and heavy traffic is so small that no one can afford the slightest mistake.

● See: Bumper "Parade" to the Sea—Back Page.

Above The *Daily Mirror* front page recorded a grim Easter weekend on the roads. (Mirrorpix)

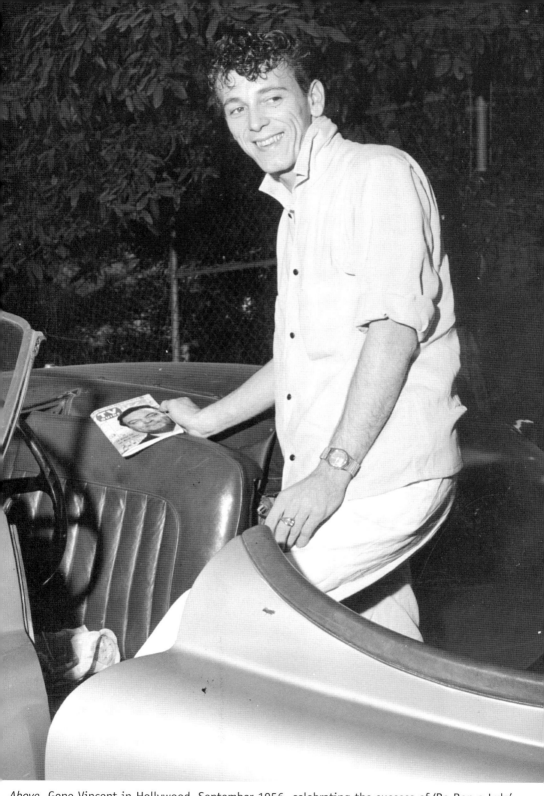

Above Gene Vincent in Hollywood, September 1956, celebrating the success of 'Be Bop a Lula'. (Redferns)

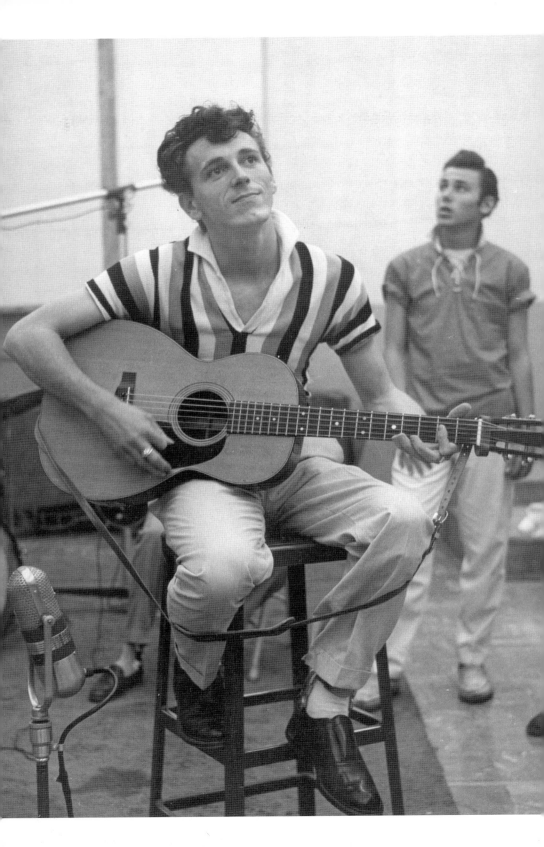

Above The Blue Caps show off their new white Stratocasters in a December 1957 publicity shoot for Capitol Records. From left: Max Lipscomb, Dickie Harrell, 'Bubba' Facenda, Johnny Meeks (partly obscured by Vincent), Paul Peek, Bobby Jones. (Redferns)

Left Vincent in Capitol Records Studios, Hollywood, June 1957, with 'Bubba' Facenda in the background. (Redferns)

Right Vincent rehearses for *Boy Meets Girls* in Manchester, December 1959. (Redferns)

Above Vincent's pavement star on Hollywood Boulevard. (© Sherri Vincent courtesy of Gene Vincent Music Ltd)

Above Vincent's grave in the Eternal Valley Memorial Park, California. Note that the more usual 'Eugene Vincent' is reversed, and that the musical notation for 'Be Bop a Lula' is inaccurate. (© Sherri Vincent courtesy of Gene Vincent Music Ltd)

Eddie's age limited the venues they could work in, but there was a thriving circuit outside the bars and licensed clubs.

In January 1955, aged 16, Cochran left school to concentrate on music and in April the duo were taken on by a booking agency that dominated country music on the West Coast, Americana Music, which guaranteed appearances on the most prestigious local television shows like *Hometown Jamboree* and *Town Hall Party*. The former, presented by Cliffie Stone, came from the Legion Stadium in El Monte and was broadcast live each Sunday on television station KLAC, while the latter was broadcast from Compton, south of Los Angeles. Rockstar has recently released both CD and video of appearances by Cochran on *Town Hall Party*. The duo also made appearances on another local TV show, *Country Barn Dance*.

Stone was part-owner of Americana, along with such country stars as Merle Travis and Tennessee Ernie Ford. Agency boss Steve Stebbins pointed the Cochran Brothers towards the independent record label Ekko, which, though based in Memphis, had an office in Los Angeles to scout for West Coast talent. They were signed up by the company's A&R man Charles 'Red' Matthews.

The recordings the duo made for Ekko in 1955 and 1956 show a fascinating tension between two talented performers. Hank was, and remained, a country purist, while Eddie can be heard turning from hillbilly picker and harmony singer into a rock'n'roller. The progress from the nasal tribute to Hank Williams and Jimmie Rodgers, 'Two Blue Singing Stars', to Eddie's first chaotic attempt at 'Pink Pegged Slacks', an out-and-out rocker, took less than a year, from May 1955 to April 1956. The label released three Cochran Brothers singles. The first, 'Mr Fiddle', is actually a jaunty showcase for violinist Harold Hensley, with Eddie plunking along on his bass strings in the background, with 'Two Blue Singing Stars' on the flip. The second release was the up-tempo 'Guilty Conscience', again with nimble bass-string work by Eddie, and the sentimental 'Your Tomorrows Never Come'.

It is the third single that shows the split beginning to form between the musical ambitions of the partners. 'Tired and Sleepy' opens with a brilliant guitar figure from Eddie and, while Hank still takes the lead vocal, Eddie's guitar break is pure rock'n'roll . Hank copes gamely with the lyric but it is Eddie's 'response' lines that come over stronger, and his youthful enthusiasm actually unbalances the song – it doesn't know if it is an up-tempo country shuffle or a rocker. And on the other side of the record, 'Fool's Paradise' shows them even further out of kilter. Clearly it would not be long before they would go their own ways, although it would prove to be an amicable parting of two musicians who simply happened to have different ambitions.

Having first seen Elvis Presley perform in Memphis, Cochran finally met his hero in May 1955 in Dallas, Texas, backstage at the *Big D Jamboree*, a show broadcast on radio station KRLD. Presley's dynamic, overtly sexual stage presence and driving rockabilly rhythm had already made a deep impression on Cochran, easing him subconsciously away from Hank Cochran's purist approach to country music.

Two months later, on 23 July, again at the *Big D Jamboree*, Cochran and Presley met again. In October, when the Cochrans were promoting 'Guilty Conscience', they bumped into Presley at Memphis radio station WMPS. They had financed this trip themselves and once they reached Memphis they ran out of money. Cochran pawned his amplifier to feed them and they hitchhiked back to Los Angeles. On 8 June 1956 Cochran was backstage when Presley made his Los Angeles debut at the Shrine Auditorium. Presley returned the compliment later the same evening, watching Cochran play guitar behind rockabilly artist Glen Glenn.

The young Cochran and Glenn often shared a bill in those days. In 1981 Glenn recalled: 'Eddie just mainly played guitar. In fact, for a long time I didn't realise that Eddie sang that much. Hank carried most all the leads, and Eddie would just play. Once in a while, like on a chorus, Eddie would sing harmony at the mike with Hank.'

In the meantime, Jerry Capehart had appeared on the scene, and was introduced to Eddie by Bert Kiefer at the Bell Gardens Music Center in October 1955. He is the link between Eddie the junior partner in a country act and Eddie the rock'n'roll star. Hank and Eddie cut several tracks with Capehart on vocals, although only one surfaced as a single at the time, on the Cash label, and it is easy to see why. 'Walkin' Stick Boogie' has a rollicking piano introduction by Ernie Freeman and an ambitious guitar solo from Eddie, but they are out of keeping with Capehart's lacklustre singing voice and corny delivery. The other side, 'Rollin'', does show Capehart taking a step away from the nasal harmonising of the early Brothers material, but again his voice is too lightweight to be convincing.

'I was born on 22 August 1928,' said Capehart in 1978, 'in Goodman, Missouri, a rural community of 250 people. My background was that of the average Midwest farming family of the Depression era, which accounted for my father picking up and moving. However, he was also a fiddle player, and this provided our livelihood on numerous occasions. He was at one time hired by Bob Wills, but never played with him because my mother insisted he didn't go on the road. We made the trek to California in a Model T with the mattress on top. After a year we decided to return to Missouri, stayed for a couple of years and then went to Arizona, where my father had a job. When I was twelve we moved again, to Bell Gardens, California.

'I'd completed one year at college when I enlisted in the US Air Force, and I stayed until I was 25. I'd decided on a career in law, but economics forced me to take a job at North American Aviation. I would work the graveyard shift and try to go to school in the daytime, but that didn't work too well. I pursued the music side, because I'd had a little success with local bands. So I worked the graveyard and hustled my music all day. Within six months I'd got myself established at North American Music.

'About this time I met Eddie Cochran, when I was performing as a singer. Earlier I'd written some songs in Korea, and they'd taken two or three of them. Then I went to Japan and recorded the Wagon Masters, who were the top country & western group there. This would be early 1954. They didn't speak English, but by listening you could tell which artist they were copying for a particular song!

'I met Eddie for the first time in a music store in Bell Gardens. In the back was a small demonstration studio. Eddie introduced me to his partner Hank Cochran. We started recording. Our first experience was, I believe, with the Cash label. I recorded "Walking Stick Boogie" and "Rollin' ". Very amateurish recording. Also we made some demonstration records in the back of the store.'

The Cash label was based over in Watts. Its tiny studio was in the back room of a record store, like many other shoestring outfits, including the celebrated Chicago blues label Cobra, home of Magic Sam, Otis Rush and Buddy Guy. Cash was owned by a black entrepreneur, John Dolphin. He employed a disc jockey, Huggy Boy, who operated from the window of the record shop to attract customers. Acetates made in the studio at the back could be heard on the street almost instantly, to test reaction. The experiment of combining R&B musicians like Ernie Freeman with hillbillies could have worked as an exciting variation on rockabilly were it not for Capehart's vocal limitations.

The same was true of another Cash attempt, this time without Hank but with the considerable bonus of Joe Maphis, fighting out the guitar solos with Eddie. However, 'Rockin' and Flyin' ' is once again brought down to earth by Capehart's vocals. Far more successful was 'I'm Ready', with Hank singing, but Dolphin had already decided that this fusion music had no commercial future, and pulled the plug on the experiment.

Cochran, still only seventeen, was already becoming a seasoned studio musician, much in demand for the touch of class that his prodigious guitar playing could bring to a record. The Brothers played on a Cash single by singer-guitarist Don Deal, 'Cryin' in One Eye', and Eddie appeared on pianist Ernie Freeman's 'Fast Jivin''. A session involving Eddie and another guitarist, Gary Lambert, apparently produced 39 instrumentals, or parts of them, but to date nothing has surfaced.

Deal met Cochran because he worked for Bert Kiefer at Bell Gardens. 'The first time I met Eddie was at that music store. [We] became good friends . . . we would play music, sing each other new songs we had written. Eddie was a very clean-cut boy.' Interestingly, Deal detected an ambition in the young Cochran that contrasts with the more familiar image of him as a dedicated guitarist but reluctant rock'n'roll star. 'He had what you call "star-itis" . . . because he was very ambitious. He wanted to be a star.'

Deal played amateur shows with Bob Denton before turning profes-sional. He played on the same country dance circuit as the Cochran Brothers, their paths crisscrossing. When a would-be songwriter, Tom Reeves, came into the store with half a song – 'Cryin' in One Eye' – Deal helped complete it and took it to John Dolphin at Cash. Confirming that both Cochrans played on the record he said: 'Eddie could play so many different styles . . . if he had lived he would have been one of the greatest guitarists ever.

'The booking agency wanted me to form my own band. It was called Don Deal and the Moontars. Hank Cochran played and sang in the band after he and Eddie went their separate ways.' Deal signed with the Era label and had a local hit with his own song 'Unfaithful Diane'. Eddie Cochran played on a number of his other records including 'Don't Push' and 'My Blind Date', co-written with Hank. Later Deal toured with Johnny Cash and Carl Perkins, and remains active in the music business today.

Even after Cochran was beginning to establish his solo career, he was always happy to get back into the studio in support of one or other of the loose fraternity of Bell Gardens musicians, and at other times he was hired directly by the record label involved. He is on the Crest single 'Butterscotch Candy and Strawberry Pie' by Jack Lewis and the Americans, for example. Meanwhile the Cochran Brothers had been kept busy as a live act, working along the coast – San Francisco, Oregon, Washington – and they were briefly based in Stockton, up in the hills due east of San Francisco, while appearing as regulars on the local television show *California Hayride* during the early part of 1956.

Capitol Records hired Cochran and Guybo – who were to become musically inseparable and joint architects of Cochran's mature style – for a split session shared by two of their country artists, Wynn Stewart with 'Slowly But Surely' and Skeets McDonald with 'You Oughta See Grandma Rock'. In autumn 1956 Cochran played on Crest singles by Jack Lewis and Lynn Marshall, and late in the year both he and Guybo played on a Ray Stanley session at Goldstar Studio. Given that pianist Stanley was no more a singer than was Capehart, the most successful result was the moody instrumental 'Pushin'', with a twanging, treble-heavy Cochran guitar break, which is certainly as impressive as many basic twelve-bar instrumentals that did manage to break into the charts. After cutting his first hit, 'Sittin' in the Balcony', Cochran could still be heard behind other singers, above all his friend Bob Denton.

Glen Glenn later recalled: 'When Eddie died, his best friend at the time was Bob Denton. In fact, every time you saw Eddie you saw Bob Denton too. Eddie always liked to go hunting, and the two of them went to the desert a lot. Bob was with Eddie just before he made that last tour to England.'

Little record companies were mushrooming on the West Coast at this time, sometimes imploding after one failed single, and often they were not too scrupulous about paperwork. Cash in hand and a chance to play were all that Cochran needed, though, and he was constantly in demand, returning at dawn to his parents' house. It may never be known how many records he actually played on, and how many sessions remain in rusty cans. He continued this aspect of his career until his fateful departure for Britain.

The fact that we now know so much about his activity at this time is less due to officially documented records, much more to the inspired detective work of such dogged enthusiasts as Tony Barrett of Rockstar Records. When one such expert tracks down an obscure single from the right place and time, perhaps hears a familiar guitar style or backing voice, and ideally receives confirmation from a surviving witness, another piece of the Cochran jigsaw is dropped into place. This process is dealt with in more detail in the epilogue to Cochran's career. The huge and detailed discography compiled by Derek Glenister for the 1988 box set *The Eddie Cochran Story* provides the benchmark, and it has been added to and modified ever since.

In 1983 Cochran's youthful reputation as a guitarist remained intact, 23 years after his death. A lengthy article in *Guitar Player* magazine by William J. Bush analysed his distinctive and influential style. Bush referred to Cochran's 'driving rhythm guitar, his impeccably executed double- and triple-string lead breaks . . . Rockabilly is *cat* music and, to some, Cochran was the coolest of them all – a perfect blend of street savvy and technical prowess.'

Of all the pop stars of the 1950s, as opposed to the great backing guitarists like Scotty Moore, Cliff Gallup, Joe Maphis or Cochran's particular hero Chet Atkins, he was the one most qualified to stand in their company. Buddy Holly had an immediately identifiable, innovative and hugely influential style, but it was firmly rooted in the discipline of the rhythm guitarist, with his lead lines sketched out by the shape of the chords. This technique, married to Jerry Allison's imaginative drum patterns, gives Holly's tracks their rhythmic drive. Cochran could play an immensely powerful rhythm, his guitar meshing with Connie 'Guybo' Smith's rumbling bass, but he could also take off with the single-note dexterity of a great bluesman. No – he *was* a great bluesman, going far beyond white-boy pastiche.

As a teenager he listened to jazz records, and could quickly figure out how to reproduce the virtuoso effects he heard. When the family moved to California he came under the influence of country musicians, Atkins among them. He studied the records of Andres Segovia and became adept at the classical style of guitar playing. Later he used to take a gut-stringed classical model on the road with him to play at night, as an ineffective sop to those musicians who preferred to get some sleep rather than indulge in his obsessive music-making.

By the time he became a rock'n'roll star, therefore, he was vastly overqualified technically to play the music. As he once told Chuck Foreman: 'This stuff is simple, man. I can play it without even trying.' Such was his skill that this sounds more like a simple statement of fact than a boast. Sharon Sheeley once said: 'Eddie really thought of himself as a musician, not a rock'n'roll star.' She was also convinced that he saw his long-term future in the studio, like Chet Atkins, as guitarist and producer, rather than out on the road. This feeling intensified when Buddy Holly died, of course.

A more arrogant musician than Cochran would have completely missed the spirit of rock'n'roll in his determination to show off. One thinks of Alvin Lee's blues playing with Ten Years After – technically staggering, but arguably at the expense of feeling. Cochran, by contrast, kept all that power in reserve for the right moment. He could play a fast jazz tune by defining each note as a different chord shape, or he could pick as nimbly as Nashville's finest. But when he came to play rock'n'roll such skill was put entirely at the service of the music, and played in its spirit. As Phil Everly put it: 'Eddie was able to mix it all together into the perfect soup ... Rock'n'roll or rockabilly had a lot of technical distortion to it, but Eddie's playing always cut through it.'

Although Cochran had unusually small hands for a skilled guitar player, he compensated for this with a seemingly boneless suppleness. Mike Deasy, guitarist and saxophone player in his 1959 backing band, the Kelly Four, said he would 'get his wrist right under the neck, with his thumb in the middle for support, and really stretch out'. Deasy said that, although a twelve-bar instrumental like Bill Doggett's 1956 smash 'Honky Tonk' would naturally be played in the key of E, Cochran would deliberately make it difficult for himself by moving up a tone to F.

The Kelly Four's bass player Dave Shrieber noted that 'Eddie was one of the few guys I've ever seen who actually played the guitar with *all* his fingers.' He learned this by copying Atkins, who could use a pick on the bass strings and his fingers on the higher ones to give a chiming, syncopated double effect – a skill he shared with Cliff Gallup – and he was already familiar with the overdub techniques of pioneering electric guitarist Les Paul that he and Chuck Foreman had played around with at home.

Atkins, although best known as a Nashville producer, session player and ultimately a top RCA executive, also made the hit parade in his own right, with 'The Poor People of Paris' in 1956, the slithery, reverberating 'Boo Boo Stick Beat' backed with the virtuoso piece 'Django's Castle' (a nod to Django Reinhardt) in 1959 and, while Cochran was in the UK, with the double-sided 'One Mint Julep' and 'Teensville'. Les Paul and his wife Mary Ford were best known for their 1951 smash 'How High the Moon', a bravura piece of technical trickery taken at a breakneck pace, but they went on to a further string of mid-'50s hits.

Cochran was such a good pupil of Atkins and Paul on record that, according to Shrieber, he could play 'Arkansas Traveller' and 'Yankee Doodle' at the same time. He could also switch from thumb-pick to plectrum in an instant, sticking the pick between his teeth without missing a note.

The *Guitar Player* profile traces a development in Cochran's technique as a prodigious teenager, from an imitation of Sun rockabilly playing to the teen ballads like 'Sittin' in the Balcony', where his guitar break transforms a lightweight smoocher, to Chuck Berry-styled rock'n'roll, and finally to his own, mature sound heard in 'Summertime Blues' and 'C'mon Everybody', based on a dominant bass guitar figure and a metallic acoustic drive, judiciously bolstered with tape echo – rather than with the echo chamber that was a celebrated feature of the Goldstar Studios, a vital component of Phil Spector's 'Wall of Sound'.

The studio was situated on Santa Monica and Vine and Cochran used Studio B, equipped with a mono machine and a second one to provide the tape-delay echo effect. The underlying track of bass, drums and acoustic guitar was created first, with the electric guitar decorations laid on top. Nothing was ever dubbed a second time, to retain the clarity that is a feature of his records, a characteristic strengthened by Cochran's hard, dynamic guitar sound.

His acoustic technique was indeed so 'hard' as to turn his guitar into a percussion instrument – usually the only one required. Sharon Sheeley has said that he once wove a strip of paper between the strings to increase the percussive effect. The end result is that some of the finest rock'n'roll ever recorded was created with minimal equipment – even with a miked-up cardboard box for a drum.

Without there being an officially appointed producer in the studio the precocious Cochran was almost totally in charge, giving instructions to everyone including the studio's co-owner and regular engineer Stan Ross, who worked on most of his sessions. Ideas would be bounced back and forth but Cochran was always very clear about what he wanted. Although it is Guybo playing bass on both 'Summertime Blues' and 'C'mon Everybody', it was Cochran who devised the riffs, and advised on the use of an extra-heavy pick to help create that distinctive rumbling effect.

Goldstar had been opened in 1950 by Ross and his partner Dave Gold, who installed the machinery, and in 1956 the second studio was brought into operation when the store next door went out of business. While Cochran was happy with the intimacy of the little, modestly equipped Studio B, its big brother Studio A was to be where Phil Spector worked in the early '60s.

Cochran's biting acoustic sound was achieved with a Martin D-18 guitar, while the electric model he played throughout his career, the co-star of many an album cover and publicity shot, was a Gretsch 6120 Chet Atkins Hollow Body model, bought at the Bell Gardens Music Center. Johnny Meeks of the Blue Caps began with a similar model, but when Leo Fender presented him with the lighter, slicker Stratocaster he gratefully swapped allegiances.

Cochran, however, remained faithful to his heavyweight Gretsch. The only modifications he made over the years were to replace the front DeArmond pick-up with a Gibson one, to achieve a less brittle sound, and to add a Bigsby tailpiece. Guybo, meantime, played upright bass on the early sides, graduating to a Fender Precision when they became rock'n'roll stars.

Cochran experimented with string gauges, though he always used the same brand, Squier. As we have heard, he showed Big Jim Sullivan one secret of the bent, bluesy notes he could achieve – he used light strings in the first place, made even lighter by using a B string instead of the G and a banjo string for Top E. His nephew Bobby Cochran told *Guitar Player* that another Bell Gardens music shop, The Academy of Music, kept a chart of his requirements, built up from different sets, so that they could even post them on to him while he was on the road.

Cochran favoured the Fender Bassman amplifier, although as his fame spread and he graduated to bigger and bigger halls, this 'beat group' favourite proved inadequate. Rather than go on the road with more cumbersome equipment the band simply cranked them up and replaced them when the speakers blew. It was a disposable technology.

Cochran's first session in Goldstar's Studio B was on 4 April 1956, a Cochran Brothers date that included Capehart. It was significant in two ways – Eddie now sang lead on three of the songs, and one of them was his first undiluted, uncompromised rock'n'roll song, 'Pink Pegged Slacks'. It was pretty ramshackle at this stage, but it was nonetheless a giant step forward – Eddie had energy and enthusiasm to burn, and it is already clear that with a little reorganisation there is a rock'n'roll classic in waiting here.

No longer is the song about the country-music concerns of love lost and found, or eager anticipation of the Saturday night hoedown with your best girl. 'Pink Pegged Slacks' moves into the area of consumer fetishism that is a feature of rock'n'roll – designed, after all, for newly affluent youth – cars, movies, blue suede shoes and, in this case, a 'cra-a-azy pair of pink pegged slacks'.

Cochran's other two songs from this session are interesting in that they show the first moves towards his secondary, smoochy, 'teen idol' image that reached fruition with 'Sittin' in the Balcony'. However, 'Yesterday's Heartbreak' and 'My Love to Remember', on this evidence, are very much works in progress – even as demos, they are too tentative. Capehart, inevitably, had a song to sing, 'Heart of a Fool', but far more impressive is Hank Cochran's 'Latch On', which moves along at a fair clip even if the dynamic vulgarity of 'Pink Pegged Slacks' suddenly makes the style seem a little staid. There can be no doubt that Hank could have continued to restyle himself as a rockabilly artist, but his heart was not in it.

Although solo stardom was still far from Eddie's mind, these tracks were the passport to all the session work outlined above and more – American Music booked demo sessions at Goldstar every Wednesday to see what new material they had, with Eddie and Guybo as regulars. Stan Ross noted a development in Eddie's confidence. 'He was not a performer when he started out – he was a recording artist or a studio artist . . . he could do anything in the studio. He didn't know if he was good or not, but when he went on the road and started appearing . . . with other people, he realised they were important and [so] he must be important too. That helped his ego and that helped his sound. Eddie was more interested in his guitar work than thinking of himself as a star.'

In autumn 1956 the Cochran Brothers cut their final Ekko session at Sunset Recorders in Hollywood, which resulted in their third and last single, 'Tired and Sleepy' and 'Fool's Paradise'. They were augmented by Guybo, drummer Roy Harte and pianist Les Taylor. Two other tracks remained in the can until Rockstar's *The Young Eddie Cochran* was released in 1982 – 'Slow Down' and 'Open the Door' proved to be two more spirited ensemble rockers that again foreshadowed the end of the partnership.

In Capehart's recollection the dates had become a little hazy, but he evoked the busy activity of the time. 'The Cochrans performed as an individual act and also backed me on my performances. Shortly after that, 1954, Eddie and Hank had an opportunity to record for Ekko. "Mr Fiddle" and "Two Blue Singing Stars" might have been released under a different name, but they were on the session. Also "Guilty Conscience", "Fool's Paradise", "Tomorrows Never Come", "Yesterday's Heartbreak". I was managing them by then. "Pink Pegged Slacks" was done at Goldstar. "Latch On" and "I'm Ready", these were both recorded by Eddie, and I believe they were done looking for a solo record for Hank. We also did a version of "Latch On", with my vocals in Bill Haley style, at Master Records. Out of this whole group of sessions the only thing that came out at the time was Eddie's "Skinny Jim".'

There was inevitably a degree of tension between Hank Cochran and Jerry Capehart, and in a tug of war over Eddie the greater rock'n'roll sensibilities of Capehart were always going to win. Although, above all, Eddie just wanted to play his guitar, it was turning more and more into a rock'n'roll instrument. As Capehart came to recognise his limitations as a vocalist he began to see himself as a songwriter and manager rather than a performer, with Eddie as his meal ticket. He was a hustler at heart, and was carefully driving a wedge between the Cochrans.

Also, it was beginning to look as if the Cochran Brothers would never come up with a hit single, though they remained popular in the West Coast dance halls. Maybe potential buyers could detect the creative uncertainty in the music – if they even heard the records, that is. A company like Ekko could hardly afford payola, and anyway tiny regional labels relied on a local 'break-out' to excite the interest of bigger radio stations. This meant that the duo could only earn a living by staying out on the road, which was beginning to interfere with Eddie's burgeoning career as a session guitarist. And, anyway, things were beginning to move for Eddie as a solo artist as well, under Capehart's energetic guidance, while Hank felt that his future lay as songwriter.

One of Hank and Eddie's last engagements together was almost their last of all. Prior to a week in Hawaii on a bill with Lefty Frizzell, who by that time had already scored eleven hits in the country charts, they drove over to Hollywood where the star was recording. They gave some strumming support, once they had put the spare tyre on to Hank's car after picking up a puncture. When the same misfortune was repeated on the journey home they had no further replacement, and so they telephoned Eddie's brother Bill, the nearest potential rescuer, to come and help them. It was bitterly cold and so they left the engine running while they waited. Fumes from the exhaust seeped into the cabin, and by the time help arrived Hank and Eddie had slipped first into drowsiness, then into sleep, and finally into unconsciousness. Bill arrived just in time to pull them out into the fresh air.

'Nothing against rock'n'roll, but I would rather be in the country end of it,' said Hank. He moved to Nashville, now beginning to assert itself as the country music capital, and in the most competitive musical city in the world established himself as one of its leading songwriters. With Harland Howard he wrote the Patsy Cline hit 'I Fall to Pieces', which in 1961 revived her career four years after 'Walkin' After Midnight' and topped the country chart, reaching No. 12 on the Hot Hundred as well. Cline's next and follow-up hit was 'Crazy' by Willie Nelson, whom Cochran is credited with discovering. Cochran also wrote 'She's Got You', the follow-up to 'Crazy', which again reached No. 1.

In 1962 actor-singer Burl Ives scored twice with Cochran compositions – both 'A Little Bitty Tear' and 'Funny Way of Laughin'' made the pop and country Top Ten listings. In 1963 Ray Price took Cochran's 'Make the World Go Away' to No. 2 in the country charts, and Timi Yuro reached No. 24 in the Hot Hundred. Two years later Eddy Arnold topped the country charts and made No. 6 in the pop list with the same song, and followed up with Cochran's 'I Want to Go with You', another chart-topper and a decent pop hit as well.

Cochran married Jeannie Seely and presented her with her first hit, 'Don't Touch Me', another No. 2. In the meantime his singing career flourished, and he did respectably with 'Sally Was a Good Old Girl' and 'I'd Fight the World' in 1962, and 'A Good Country Song' a year later. In 1967 'All of Me Belongs to You' was a minor hit.

Into the 1970s, and Cochran was supplying songs and duetting with such as Willie Nelson and Merle Haggard – 'It's Not Love (But It's Not Bad)' – and the later generation of country stars like George Strait also turned to his songbook ('The Chair' and 'Ocean Front Property', both No. 1s, were co-written by Cochran with Dean Dillon). So the reluctant rockabilly was right all along: he was indeed happier – and far more successful – 'at the country end of it'.

In July 1956 Capehart secured a one-single solo deal for Eddie with Crest, surely not a struggle since he was such a valuable player in their game, and they went into Master Recorders studio where, earlier that year, Little Richard had cut his follow-up to 'Tutti Frutti', 'Long Tall Sally'. Richard had reached the Top Twenty in March, making the record the most successful uncompromisingly black rock'n'roll record to date.

The band for Cochran's studio date, who were also to back another new Crest signing, Gene Davis, on a split session at the same time, were Guybo, drummer Jesse Sailes and Ray Stanley on piano. Stanley co-wrote one of the Cochran cuts 'Half Loved', a tremulous ballad that, while a distinct improvement on 'Yesterday's Heartbreak', is still not playing to the singer's vocal strengths and virtually ignores his skill as a guitarist.

The other track, however, is a rock'n'roll classic, the next step forward from 'Pink Pegged Slacks', even though Cochran stumbles vocally when trying to turn 'Be Bop a Lula' into a repetitive chorus line. 'Skinny Jim' is bursting with musical energy, and the lyric seethes with teenage frustration. The title character, built like a male 'Bony Moronie', is a vexing success with the girls in spite of being nothing but 'bone and skin'.

Cochran spits out the lyric – 'My baby came with me but she left with him' – against a frantic, scudding rhythm that constantly threatens to run out of control. He whistles, grunts and whoops, carving out a guitar solo of metallic brilliance, and at the end the song collapses into an exhausted heap. Although most of Cochran's lingering fame now rests with some of the most perfectly crafted of all rock songs, notably 'Summertime Blues', he showed on 'Skinny Jim' that he also had a mean streak of musical anarchy, rocking to the brink of disintegration.

Cochran then played on the Gene Davis cuts, both decent-quality rockabilly, 'Drowning All My Sorrows' and 'Let's Coast Awhile', released under the name Bo Davis. 'Drowning' could have been from Buddy Holly's Nashville sessions if Davis had more of Holly's echo-soaked vocal charisma, while on 'Let's Coast Awhile' Cochran injects extra interest by slightly dragging his guitar figures, more rock'n'roll than purist rockabilly. They also recorded a new, dynamic version of Hank Cochran's earlier demo 'Latch On', although Crest did not release it – Rockstar put it out in 1982 on *Eddie Cochran Words and Music*.

At around this time – the Derek Glenister discography actually places it just before 'Pink Pegged Slacks', although it is impossible to pin down everything during this frenetic summer with total confidence, and no precise date is known – Cochran, Guybo and Capehart (slapping a cardboard box to achieve the drum effect) recorded four established songs to demonstrate Cochran's versatility. He deliberately chose two rockers in Carl Perkins's 'Blue Suede Shoes' and Little Richard's 'Long Tall Sally' and two ballads – Ivory Joe Hunter's stately blues 'I Almost Lost My Mind' and the smoochy standard 'That's My Desire', a tune that also attracted Buddy Holly's attention. These were intended as calling cards, bolstering an attempt by Capehart to move Cochran on from his one-off Crest deal to something more substantial.

'To get the Liberty contract for Eddie,' said Capehart, 'I used the demos of "Long Tall Sally", "Blue Suede Shoes" and "Twenty Flight Rock", all with me playing on a cardboard box. Eddie wanted to go solo, that's why we did the demos. Also "Dark Lonely Street", "Half Loved", "Skinny Jim". By this time Eddie had also started working sessions. Everyone knew he played fine guitar. They were really demo dates, basically for American Music, plus one or two for Liberty, and some doo-wop with the Four Dots. We'd produce these sessions. "Skinny Jim" and "Half Loved" were eventually recorded for Crest. I took the demos to Liberty – they didn't have an act like Eddie so we got a contract.'

But before that, the next break in Cochran's career came from a totally unexpected direction. Boris Petroff, a B-movie director, dropped by the recording studio one day – he knew Capehart slightly – and was struck by Cochran's photogenic good looks. Petroff in turn knew an ex-Warner Brothers animation director, Bugs Bunny veteran Frank Tashlin, who was then filming the rock'n'roll comedy provisionally titled *Do-Re-Mi*. Out of the blue, Petroff offered Cochran a cameo part in the movie, and confirmed it with a phone call the next day.

Once Cochran and Capehart realised that the deal was on, they went to American Music in search of a song. Among the demos they were provided with was 'Twenty Flight Rock', written by Nelda Fairchild – a pseudonym for the unlikely-named Nelda Bingo.

This is how Jerry Capehart recalled this period: 'Si Waronker, the founder of the label, knew that Fox were producing *The Girl Can't Help It* and were looking for young talent to go with their established stars. We took them the demo of "Twenty Flight Rock". Eddie was only seventeen at the time so we had to get a work permit. Liberty then offered us "Sitting in the Balcony" by Johnny D, who was John D. Loudermilk. We had the Johnny Mann Singers on that session. Three-track recording had just come into existence, and this was our first experience of it. We went in about eight in the evening and stayed till six.'

Capehart, quoted earlier, said that 'Twenty Flight Rock' was among the demos they took to Liberty, but it fits more neatly to assume that his second version is more accurate – they took it to Fox as a candidate for the movie, and hence to Liberty.

It was happening so fast for Cochran now, from the spring promise of 'Pink Pegged Slacks' to his first rock'n'roll masterpiece 'Skinny Jim' and now the chance of the biggest publicity boost ever to be offered to an unknown – a spot in a Hollywood movie alongside Little Richard, Fats Domino and current chart star Gene Vincent. Cochran and Capehart took Guybo and the cardboard box into Goldstar and created the first Cochran pop classic. With its slippery rhythm, Guybo's inspired slap-bass playing, amusing storyline and Cochran's spitting, staccato guitar solo, 'Twenty Flight Rock' could surely not fail.

The session also produced a pleasant but slighter song along similar rhythmic lines, 'Completely Sweet', and Cochran's first convincing stab at a slow, moody number, the husky 'Dark Lonely Street', with its chiming, repetitive guitar figure. Coincidentally, one of Gene Vincent's most affecting slow songs is the brooding, careworn 'Lonely Street'. Both men adopted the persona later used – and deemed to fail – in the UK television commercial campaign for a new brand of cigarette, in which a Bogart-like figure on the London Embankment on a rainy night is 'never alone with a Strand'.

'Eddie Cochran, one of America's top rock'n'rollers', as he was introduced in the movie, filmed his cameo in August, shoehorned into the plot as performer on a television show – just him, his Gretsch and a tiny amplifier, jigging about in front of a backdrop of stage curtains, a perfect impersonation of a 'top rock'n'roller', Elvis-style. From session player to film star in one leap – the movie, retitled *The Girl Can't Help It* after one of the Little Richard numbers featured, was the perfect showcase.

Interviewed for *New Musical Express* during the UK tour, Cochran was clear that this was the big break in his career. 'I wasn't even a singer before I made the movie,' he claimed. 'One day I was playing guitar on a session when up comes a guy, and asks, "How would you like to make a picture?" Well, the next day he called and asked if I could sing. I went along with the gag, said I could. Then he asked me to make a demonstration disc of a tune called "Twenty Flight Rock". I still thought it was a joke – let's face it, I didn't know if I could sing. Anyways, I made the record, he liked it, signed me for the film, and that was the start of everything!'

Even allowing for the journalistic licence involved in tickling up an interview like this – would Cochran really have said 'demonstration disc', for example? – the quote is revealing. We know perfectly well that he had been a singer ever since he began to play with Hank Cochran, but he still cast himself in his own mind as a session guitarist.

Years later, Nelda Fairchild recalled the premiere of the film. 'Bobby Troup and Julie London signing autographs in the spotlight. Full houses, it turned out to be a smash hit. It was the greatest thrill of my life to see and hear Eddie Cochran sing my song . . . I was walking on air.'

After filming his segment for the movie Cochran went back to his day job, playing on Goldstar sessions behind Jack Lewis, Lynn Marshall, Ray Stanley, Lee Denson and the Holly Twins. The last act was signed to Liberty, and Cochran contributed guitar and an Elvis impersonation to their squeaky novelty 'I Want Elvis for Christmas'. By this time, Cochran was also a Liberty artist.

At around this time Cochran met an aspiring actor, Johnny Rook, billed as Johnny Rho. In later years Rook was to become one of the leading figures in the American radio business. Their friendship was to last for the rest of Cochran's life. Rook had seen Cochran on the Twentieth Century Fox lot and sent him a note, thinking that maybe he was another young hopeful and that they might have something in common. To his surprise he received a telephone call from Cochran's mother, Alice, inviting him over to Bell Gardens, but not before eleven in the morning, as her son worked late and slept late.

Cochran was indeed still in bed when Rook arrived, but Alice and Cochran's sister Gloria, politely filling in time, found out Rook's entire life history in a few minutes of questioning. Eventually Cochran appeared, wearing a white bathrobe and drinking coffee. 'He was several inches shorter than me and his voice sounded as though he was just getting over a bad cold. Clearing it, he blamed the hoarseness on many hours in recent studio work,' recalls Rook, who later noted that Cochran sipped at a mixture of whisky and honey in the studio, to keep his throat lubricated.

There was quite a houseful at the Bell Gardens property in those days – Frank and Alice, Gloria, her husband Red and their son 'little Eddie' as well as Eddie senior, who never moved out of Frank's house and pined for home comforts whenever he was on the road. It was clear to Rook that the women of the house doted on Cochran as he began to make his way in the music business, spoiling him and handling his growing volume of fan mail, and this caused a little friction sometimes with Frank and Red, who could not afford to spend half the day in bed being waited on.

Cochran invited Rook to come to the Liberty studios for his next session. Liberty, though hardly a major force in the record business, was a sizeable leap up from Ekko. It was started in 1955 by former Twentieth Century Fox soundtrack violinist Simon Waronker, a 1930s refugee from Hitler's Germany, in partnership with Al Bennett, and hit big with Julie London's 'Cry Me a River' – another highlight, however out of context, of *The Girl Can't Help It*. Waronker had been trying to sign Bobby Troup, composer of 'Route 66', and got his girlfriend instead.

According to Waronker, however, the film had nothing to do with signing Cochran – he claimed never to have heard of it, which seems strange as London was not the only Liberty artist featured, and there were solid ties between the record label and the movie. Rather, he insists, Cochran came and sat in his outer office until Waronker relented and auditioned him. He was immediately convinced, and on 8 September 1956 Cochran signed with the label. The Waronker version simply does not add up, and is in direct conflict with Capehart's recollections, but either way Cochran had a contract in his pocket. Surely it would have been Capehart staging the sit-in. Cochran was not a natural salesman for his talent, even though it was plain to see and hear. Indeed, in Capehart's version of the story it *was* him in the outer office, with a fistful of demo discs. He was not always a reliable witness, but rings true this time.

A further signature forged a further link with Gene Vincent, when Cochran signed with the same agency for live appearances, General Artists Corporation, and he was booked for a more substantial role in his second movie, *Untamed Youth*. Aimed at the drive-ins rather than the Oscars, and directed by Howard W. Koch (the 'W' distinguishes him from the co-writer of *Casablanca*), the film is set on a cotton-producing prison farm for delinquent teenagers led by Mamie Van Doren, an actress who had a couple of things in common with the star of *The Girl Can't Help It*, Jayne Mansfield. *Untamed Youth* had a two-week filming schedule on land near Bakersfield, close to Los Angeles, home of Buck Owens and the West Coast country scene.

Cochran's featured song is the pleasant – nothing more – novelty 'Cotton Picker', and he is given a few lines of fairly painful, supposedly hip dialogue, which he delivers in trouper spirit. He also backed Van Doren on her four songs in the movie: 'Salamander', his and Capehart's 'Oo Ba La Baby', 'Rollin' Stone' and 'Go Go Calypso', released as an EP, although for the film soundtrack itself musical director Les Baxter for some reason wiped the Cochran takes and re-recorded the backing tracks without him.

Meanwhile Cochran was still busy in the studio – and still without a first Liberty single. He cut the lively 'Sweetie Pie' and 'Teenage Cutie', and at last 'Twenty Flight Rock' backed with 'Dark Lonely Street' was slated for pre-Christmas release. Before this could happen, however, Waronker decided that the John D. Loudermilk composition 'Sittin' in the Balcony' would make a better debut, and 'Twenty Flight Rock' was put on hold.

Whether Waronker's decision was made on artistic grounds seems very doubtful. He had been thwarted in his attempt to pick up the original version, cut by Loudermilk under the name Johnny D, from the small southern independent label Colonial. It was instead assigned to ABC-Paramount for national distribution, and so Waronker's insistence that Cochran cut a hurried cover version was presumably prompted by sour grapes.

It was recorded in January 1957 at the new Liberty Custom Recorders studio in Hollywood, with Guybo as ever on bass and additional sweetening by the Johnny Mann Singers. It was, Waronker admits, as precise a copy of the original as they could manage and, as Capehart confirmed, it needed a long night's work to get it right. The icing on the cake, giving this blatant cover its own distinctiveness, was Cochran's perfect guitar solo, a gem of imaginative precision. Although such confections have not stood the test of time as well as Cochran's classic rockers, this attractive little smooch number was certainly right for the 1957 market. 'Well, dad, I think it's a hit,' was Cochran's verdict. Later, however, when interviewed by NME, he had a different story. The biggest disappointment of his career to date, he said, was 'hearing the playbacks after my first recording session. I cut "Sittin' in the Balcony" and didn't like it at all. But it went on to sell a million, and I was the most surprised of all.'

With 'Dark Lonely Street' retained as the B side, pressing and distribution were hurriedly carried out in an attempt to swamp the original version, and the strategy worked – it pipped Johnny D in the race for the racks. But it was a risky tactic. Not only was Cochran slugging it out in the market place with Loudermilk, but *The Girl Can't Help It* was released at the same time, confusingly promoting the surely stronger 'Twenty Flight Rock'. No matter – a double dose of Cochran did the trick, and as he had predicted the record was a hit. It climbed to No. 18 in March, while Johnny D only got to No. 38.

'It was a hit,' said Capehart, 'and Eddie went on the road promoting it. In Philadelphia he did the Dick Clark and Mike Douglas shows, and he met Alan Freed in New York. Eddie travelled to New York two years in succession to do the Alan Freed show, and several times to do Dick Clark. And I remember once he lent his clothes to Jackie Wilson, who had lost his somewhere on the road.' Meanwhile, back in Bell Gardens Cochran's family were even busier organising their ad hoc fan club in response to all the mail that was beginning to flow in.

His agency, GAC, booked Cochran and Guybo on to a huge package playing for a week in Philadelphia at the Mastbaum Theater, starring Gene Vincent and billed as the *Rock'n'roll Jubilee of Stars*. It was here that their unlikely friendship began. GAC kept Cochran busy for much of the year, and like all new faces in the charts he also did the rounds of the radio stations for in-person interviews.

The poster for the Mastbaum Theater week screamed 'Big Time Rock'n'roll Comes to the Big Mastbaum!' in a 'Jubilee of Stars'. The only artists pictured were local radio DJs and comperes Cal Milner and Larry Brown, and Vincent and the Blue Caps were billed as being in the 'musical battle of the century' versus Bobby Boyd and his Jazz Bombers. Among such forgotten names as Maureen Cannon, Gene Nash, the Harvey Boys, the Willows and 'extra added attraction' Lloyd Thomas and the Calypso Troubadours are the blind jazz crooner Al Hibbler, formerly of the Duke Ellington Orchestra, country star George Hamilton IV and R&B artists Nappy Brown and Bullmoose Jackson.

Local paper the *Inquirer*, in its review, concentrated mainly on top-of-the-bill Hibbler, but did refer to Cochran's 'blaring electric guitar' and mentioned that 'Vincent and his boys' won the so-called battle with Bobby Boyd.

When Cochran appeared in Chicago with Chuck Berry and the Everly Brothers, on a bill promoted by local disc jockey Howard Miller, *Billboard*'s reviewer swallowed a dictionary before filing his copy. 'The interpretation of Southern Negro and whitefolk idioms within the framework of today's pop market was particularly evident in contrasting the hillbilly harmonies flying out of Berry's guitar against the leadbelly-type [lower case] harmonic runs that young Eddie Cochran employed so liberally.'

It was on the Chicago bill that Cochran first met Charlie Gracie, who scored three hits in 1957 with 'Butterfly', 'Fabulous' and 'I Love You So Much It Hurts'. In 2002 Gracie recalled: 'Eddie and I seemed to hit it off right away. We sat backstage and switched guitars – he played around on my Guild and I on his Gretsch . . . I don't believe any of us really understood our popularity or how long rock'n'roll might last. I believe that Eddie felt at home with my parents, especially my mother, who prepared big Italian meals for them [Cochran and Capehart] during their visits. My mum would make pasta and red sauce with meatballs, sausage and pork. Eddie and Jerry just loved it.

'He [Eddie] asked my mom if he could consider her his "mother" away from home. Of course she was honoured and still talks about it to this day . . . Eddie was genuine, a very warm fellow . . . It's still difficult for me to accept Eddie may be gone, but I shall never forget him, neither will rock'n'roll . . . I am so grateful to have known Eddie Cochran.'

What is most noticeable in this affectionate memoir is the confirmation that, like Elvis Presley, Cochran was indeed a 'mommy's boy' – so much so that he needed a surrogate mother as well as a real one.

Now there was the urgent matter of a follow-up single, and so in March Cochran and Guybo returned to Goldstar. 'One Kiss' was a disappointment from such a versatile artist, simply replicating the adolescent feel of 'Sittin' in the Balcony', although the B side's 'Mean When I'm Mad' had more muscle. Worryingly, and in spite of being promoted in one of the first-ever picture sleeves, it made no headway in the charts.

Remarkably, Cochran continued his session work throughout this busy year of 1957 when he was off the road. A couple of dates with his pal Bob Denton produced two Dot singles, 'On My Mind Again' and 'Love Me So I'll Know', Darla Daret's 'Honey Honey' was issued on the Crest sister label Silver, he played on a bunch of country tracks by Gary Williams in Washington, on Pamela Morgan's Demon single 'Only a Fool' and 'Someone to Love Me', Liberty rockabilly Al Casey's 'Willa Mae' and Don Deal's Era release 'Even Then'. This was clearly important and therapeutic work for Cochran, the pop star who was happiest in the studio among friends like Denton, Deal and Guybo.

In the summer Waronker took Cochran back into Goldstar to cut tracks for his debut album, which would be called *Singin' to My Baby*. It proved to be a polite mixture, more heart-throb than rocker, but this was in keeping with the time – like the preference for 'Balcony' over 'Twenty Flight Rock'. Businessmen like Waronker never had much faith in the lasting appeal of rock'n'roll, but felt that young girls would always swoon at a good-looking pop star, who might in time mature into a middle-of-the-road balladeer just right for Las Vegas. This would surely not have been Cochran's fate. More likely, like Chet Atkins and Duane Eddy he would have retreated back to his natural habitat, the recording studio, though probably bypassing Atkins's other life as a company executive. Rob Finnis has referred to 'Waronker's perception of Eddie as a cross between Elvis and Pat Boone', knowing that no such animal has ever been discovered.

Nowadays, a song like 'Drive-In Show' is easily dismissed for the gossamer-thin confection it is, whereas an utterly uncommercial Cochran indulgence like, say, his blistering attack on 'Milk Cow Blues', which would never have been considered for single release at the time, is evidence of his genius.

The aforesaid 'Drive-In Show', which alas failed to make the ukulele sexy even when plunked by Cochran, was kept back from the album session as the next single, confirming that Waronker saw Cochran as appealing only to girls. But the flip side, 'Am I Blue', allowed him and Guybo an opportunity to really rock, transforming a polite old standard into prime rockabilly. The single did little to revive Cochran's career, stalling at No. 82 in the *Billboard* chart. Like 'Milk Cow Blues' and 'Hallelujah I Love Her So', just two examples, 'Am I Blue' is stunning evidence of Cochran's ability to get under the skin of an unfamiliar genre and make it his own.

The album, the only one released during Cochran's lifetime, included 'Balcony' plus an energetic remake of a song from the 'Twenty Flight Rock' session, 'Completely Sweet'. The rest of the album, though, however professionally achieved and carefully targeted, is at best lightweight, at worst embarrassing. There's the sub-Elvis crooning of 'I'm Alone Because I Love You', the throwaway, walking-pace 'Undying Love' and another ukulele exercise, 'Lovin' Time', which is one of the dreariest songs he attempted, though he gamely does his best. 'Proud of You' is only a slight improvement.

'Mean When I'm Mad' lifts the mood somewhat, and 'Stockin's 'n' Shoes' is lively and confident. 'Have I Told You Lately That I Love You', which repeats the guitar figure from 'Dark Lonely Street', is the strongest ballad on the set, but the extraordinary 'Tell Me Why' is worse than any throwaway Elvis B side. Cochran is forced to intone such philosophical conundrums as 'Tell me why the ivy twines'. Who cares? To cling to the twig, perhaps. 'Cradle Baby' is politely paedophile and 'One Kiss' is just one pleasant chord change away from 'Sittin' in the Balcony'.

Along with the ordinary 'Pocketful of Hearts' the best results of the session were held back – a revisit to 'Twenty Flight Rock' and the finger-popping, echo-laden, two-speed 'Never', one of Cochran's most successful attempts to act like a real smoothie.

A further Goldstar date in September produced 32 attempts at 'Ah, Pretty Girl', a frustrating night's work, before in October Cochran was reunited with Vincent for their Australian tour. He was backed by the Deejays, Australian rocker Johnny O'Keefe's band. One photograph of the pair striding across airport tarmac shows a confident, muscular Cochran taking the lead, trailed by the finely chiselled, broomstick Vincent.

As Johnny Rook recalls, the reluctant traveller Cochran did not relish the prospect of the trip. The flight, in an old-fashioned propeller plane, took some twenty uncomfortable hours. Rook noticed what many others had, that Cochran was a home-loving boy whose natural environment was the recording studio rather than the stage. To cheer himself up before the trip, Cochran went hunting with Rook and Bob Denton. While relieving himself behind a rock Cochran was startled by a young steer, and shot it. Most of the carcase was eventually buried in brother Bob's yard, but it had to be dug up again when the summer heat made the stench intolerable.

A review in a New South Wales paper, unearthed by Rob Finnis, was written with nose wrinkled in distaste. Note in particular the use of quotation marks to imply 'so-called'. 'Screaming teenage admirers of an American negro rock'n'roll exponent, Little Richard, dragged him across the footlights and trampled him in a mob on the floor of Newcastle stadium . . . A grand piano was badly damaged when the drummer in a "musical" combination known as Gene Vincent and his Bluecaps stomped over the top of it and leaped off stage, over the footlights, beating a side drum under one arm . . . Footlight protection plates were pulled down when teenagers rushed forward to catch handkerchiefs thrown out by a "singer" called Eddie Cochran . . .' In trying to dismiss the concert as a vulgar cultural aberration all the writer succeeds in doing is to convey the rumbustious excitement of the occasion.

The poster for that date, at the Sydney Stadium, contained an 'Important Announcement!' This indicates how uneasy the authorities were becoming about the subversive power of rock'n'roll . It warned that 'the NSW Police Dept. have notified the Stadium they will NOT permit dancing on today's concerts as previously advertised. Anyone who does not wish to view the concerts from a sitting position may obtain a refund at the Stadium. We apologise for your inconvenience.' As the above review confirms, the audience simply rioted instead.

Back home, Cochran toured with *The Biggest Show of Stars* for '57, becoming particularly friendly with Buddy Holly, the Crickets and the

Everly Brothers, with whom he was immediately reunited on a Christmas bill in New York. The second version of 'Twenty Flight Rock', a year after the song was originally slated for release, became Cochran's fourth single, with the album track 'Cradle Baby' on the flip. Once again – and unbelievably – he failed to make the charts.

In 1998 Jerry Allison, the Crickets' drummer, recalled this tour with Cochran. 'We got a lot of "bus time" with Eddie on that tour,' he said. 'On a lot of those tours . . . performers got hung up about who went on first and who closed the show – the stardom thing. Eddie . . . really had no ego problem at all. He was far more of a musician than a star type . . . He was a musician first and foremost and he just wanted to play.'

Allison also referred to Cochran's no-nonsense habit of walking from the hotel, when it was conveniently booked nearby, picking up his guitar from the dressing room and strolling out on stage, just a professional doing his job. One night in New York they went out after the gig to jazz club Birdland and listened to a celebrated jazz guitarist performing. Either genuinely or diplomatically, Allison did not remember his name. 'Man, he's not hitting all the notes,' observed Cochran, and back in the hotel he demonstrated what he meant, improving on the jazzman's licks.

Disc jockey Freeman B. Hover caught up with the tour in Denver. He had a radio show in Chadron, Nebraska, a town just south of the South Dakota border. 'I had driven the three hundred miles to Denver from KCSR in Chadron for the performance and to finally meet Eddie in person. There seemed to be a parade of recording artists coming and going in Eddie's room. Some hung around the entire time I was there. They were just visiting, relaxing, and having a good time goofing around after their evening's performance . . . Buddy and Eddie were close friends. The afternoon of the Denver performance they went clothes shopping. Maybe you have seen the individual pictures of them both wearing the identical white pullover sweater . . . It was about three in the morning before I left the Albany Hotel. The troupe had to be on the road the next morning for their next one-nighter. They didn't get much sleep – slept on the bus, I guess. Those road shows were gruelling.'

During the interview Cochran rehearsed the story so far. 'I've been in the business just about five years. I was a guitar player playing record dates in Hollywood. I moved out there from Oklahoma City.' He described how a man walked in and asked him if he'd like to be in a movie, saying it was 'in between takes so I was just picking on my guitar for my own amazement.' Cochran plugged the imminent release of 'Twenty Flight Rock'. During the interview the telephone rang – it was 'one of the Crickets' – and Cochran said that Buddy Holly and Jimmy Bowen were in the next room and that they had stolen his ukulele. Eventually the disc jockey was rewarded with informal interviews with Bowen, Holly and Jerry Allison as well as Cochran.

At this time Liberty, a victim of falsified accounts and sluggish cash flow, almost went out of business. It was saved from an unlikely quarter – early in 1958 David Seville's rather tiresome novelty 'Witch Doctor' was a vast hit, reaching the top and spending sixteen weeks on the charts, just in time to prevent Liberty from drowning in debts. Seville had two further hits that year, 'The Bird on My Head' and 'Little Brass Band', and another in 1959, 'Judy'. Meanwhile he had devised the infuriating, tape-speeded Chipmunks in time for 1958's big Christmas hit, 'The Chipmunk Song'. It returned to the charts for the next four Christmases, and Seville presented Waronker with further smashes in 'Alvin's Harmonica', 'Ragtime Cowboy Joe', 'Alvin's Orchestra', 'Alvin For President', 'Rudolph the Red-Nosed Reindeer' (Christmas 1960, '61 and '62) and 'The Alvin Twist'. Meanwhile Cochran was struggling.

His first job in the New Year of 1958 was to cut the next in his line of great out-and-out rockers, an antidote to the heart-throb fare preferred by Waronker. 'Jeannie Jeannie Jeannie' (the lady is 'Jeanie' on some record labels) was written by fellow Liberty artiste Ricki Page as 'Johnny Johnny Johnny'. Cochran's version has a hard, urgent riff, a far more confident vocal attack than he had previously displayed, and it is driven along not just by Guybo but by the great session drummer Earl Palmer, a tougher proposition than Capehart's cardboard box. The session also produced another grade-one up-tempo number in Cochran and Capehart's sexy 'Pretty Girl'.

Waronker, however, was not prepared to risk a double-sided rocker, and hedged his bets by backing 'Jeannie Jeannie Jeannie' with 'Pocketful of Hearts' from the *Singin' to My Baby* sessions. Any hit is better than none, but one week in the Hot Hundred early in March at an almost invisible No. 94 was poor reward for one of Cochran's most exuberant numbers. Meanwhile, he worked on two more songs in the studio – 'Ah, Pretty Girl', first attempted the previous September, which still failed to gel (it is a different song to 'Pretty Girl'), and 'Little Lou'. The latter, a Jerry Capehart number later recorded by another of his artists, John Ashley, is driven along by Cochran's acoustic Martin and it is an attractive twelve-bar reminiscent in its structure of a Chuck Berry number.

In March Liberty tried again with the excellent 'Pretty Girl', but perversely made it the B side to a song in Cochran's other style, the heavy-lidded, husky-voiced romantic crooner. 'Teresa' has a pleasing melody but it is a lightweight piece of work, intentionally so – and it was another commercial failure. This probably worried Waronker more than it did Cochran, though by now the 'Witch Doctor' receipts were beginning to turn the company around. At the end of March Cochran returned to the studio, but now in anonymous support of his new friend Gene Vincent, notably on the harmony masterpiece 'Git It'.

Waronker may have misjudged the root of Cochran's appeal and strengths to some extent – he did exuberance better than smooching – but there could be no doubting the faith he showed in his artist. Now that Cochran is securely positioned in the pantheon of 1950s rock'n'roll greats it is easy to overlook the fact that his American chart career was both modest and halting.

Early in April Cochran bit the bullet and tackled 'Ah, Pretty Girl' yet again. It is a pleasant enough song taken at a sprightly tempo, with the Johnny Mann Singers to the fore, but hardly worth three sessions over six months, and it was not released at the time. After playing on a couple of Bob Denton sessions, however, Cochran returned to Goldstar in May. The frustrating wait for a decent hit would soon be over.

In 1978 Jerry Capehart recalled the moment. ' "Summertime Blues" was a spontaneous thing. We'd had "Sittin' in the Balcony", "Mean When I'm Mad", which was a terrible failure, and "Drive-In Show", which had been a hit in some areas. We had a recording session scheduled, and we realised the importance of the session because we badly needed a hit. Eddie came to my apartment on the previous evening, and after we'd run over the material I told him candidly that I didn't think we had one. He agreed with me.

'But Eddie said that he had a riff, and I liked it very much. I suggested that there hadn't been a blues about the summertime, about teenage problems during the vacation. We wrote it in half an hour and recorded it the following day. BMI tell me it was the biggest song of summer 1958. It established Eddie, and the songs that followed had that "teenage rebel" flavour that became his trademark.'

Capehart's memory was slightly faulty, even if we do allow him to claim most of the song apart from the riff. 'Summertime Blues' was a hit in August, but since it peaked at No. 18 and spent a total of six weeks in the Hot Hundred, it cannot have been such a huge number. It reached exactly the same position on the British charts. Summer smashes in America included 'All I Have To Do Is Dream' by the Everly Brothers, 'Yakety Yak' from the Coasters and Ricky Nelson's 'Poor Little Fool', written by Sharon Sheeley, compared to which 'Summertime

Blues' was simply a respectable autumnal success. Its lasting influence, however, totally overshadows those bigger hits. It has become a rock anthem as titanic as 'Blue Suede Shoes' and 'Johnny B Goode', and it has spoken to every successive generation.

By this time Sheeley had come into Cochran's life. She was born in Los Angeles on 4 April 1940, and as an attractive teenager in Hollywood in the mid-50s became what was later known as a groupie, although solo singers (and half of the Everly Brothers) were her targets. Among her dates were Don Everly, Ricky Nelson and P.J. Proby, she met a 'drunk and obnoxious' Gene Vincent and even insinuated herself into the crowd of hangers-on surrounding Elvis Presley.

'Poor Little Fool' was a poem, charmingly naïve, set to the ever-familiar C-Am-F-G chord sequence that, along with variations on the twelve-bar blues, fuelled so many hits of the 1950s. According to legend Sheeley found out where Ricky Nelson lived and pitched the song to him, saying that her godfather had written it for Elvis Presley but that she thought it would suit him better. By this time Nelson had had five big hits, four of them double-sided, but was finding the top spot in the charts to be elusive.

'I didn't really care for the song to begin with,' he admitted. 'It was a different kind of song, real uptown.' But Sheeley was persuasive and Nelson relented, still seeing the song as no more than an album filler. Disc jockeys and Imperial Records thought differently, and it climbed to the summit of the Hot Hundred in June 1958. Meanwhile the relentlessly networking Sheeley had met Jerry Capehart, who asked if she had a song for Cochran. She did not, but soon came up with 'Love Again'. It was recorded at Cochran's next session after 'Summertime Blues', along with another newly minted Sheeley offering, 'Lonely'.

She once claimed that she had been determined to date Cochran ever since she saw his photograph on the montage poster for *The Girl Can't Help It*. She had already met him briefly, when she was backstage with Don Everly, and now Capehart – impressed by 'Poor Little Fool' and her two made-to-order songs for Cochran – offered to be her manager. She sang 'Love Again' to Cochran and, like Nelson with 'Poor Little Fool', he was reportedly underwhelmed. And, again like Nelson, he cut it anyway. Sheeley must have attracted Cochran, as she had done Nelson and the others, because his opinion of 'Love Again' was accurate – it is a listless piece of work.

Cochran had been in a long-term relationship with a girl named Johnnie Berry since his mid-teens, and after his first hit he had been linked with other names such as actress-singer Connie Stevens. But now he had broken up with Johnnie and was not seriously involved with anyone else. The field seemed clear for Sharon, although Cochran would continue to live the rock'n'roll lifestyle – Johnny Rook remembers frequent games of strip poker, for example, during which young female fans seemed eager to lose every hand, while Cochran rarely lost more than his boots.

Remarkably, 'Love Again' was originally seen as Cochran's next A side, with 'Summertime Blues' in support. Although Liberty executive Al Bennett was now more in day-to-day charge of Cochran than Waronker, there was still a corporate nervousness regarding rock'n'roll , in spite of the fact that 'Jeannie, Jeannie, Jeannie' had sold rather better than most of his ballads. Once again, disc jockeys soon pointed out the error.

'Summertime Blues' is built of the simplest musical ingredients, assembled with genius. Cochran elects to stress the chord structure (there are as many as three of them) by preferring his Martin to the Gretsch. Guybo is plugged in, however, pinning the song to his snarling bass line, and Earl Palmer drives it along with rifle-shot precision. The chosen tempo is perfect – fast enough to let it rock, slow enough to allow the tale of teenage frustration time to brew in the listener's mind.

Even though the early, frantic rockers provided the most exhilarating evidence of young Cochran's prodigious talent, it was 'Twenty Flight Rock' that first hinted at a possibly fruitful area of individuality in which he could make his mark. Although that song failed commercially, the Cochran–Capehart masterwork 'Summertime Blues' confirmed that it had been heading in the right direction. There were many other rock'n'roll artists, a few white bluesmen, and numerous heart-throbs who could perhaps have been more successful wearing the ballad jacket into which Liberty had crammed Cochran – Ricky Nelson for one. But 'Summertime Blues' was Cochran's alone. And eventually, at last, it provided the evidence to Liberty that he should be given his head. 'Teresa', nice enough in a marshmallow way, is long forgotten, but somewhere right now a band is playing – even recording – 'Summertime Blues'.

Meanwhile, Cochran played on a Jerry Capehart record that was leased to Dot. 'I Hate Rabbits', with a Bugs Bunny impersonation from engineer Stan Ross, was a comic novelty that was neither particularly funny nor novel. With Earl Palmer and saxophonist Plas Johnson involved it has a lively feel to it, but Capehart was never going to put the Coasters out of business. The moody instrumental B side, 'Scratchin' ', is far more interesting, but it sounds more Cochran than Capehart – possibly even 100%, overdubbing everything, and good-naturedly handing over the track to his manager.

Having established a successful style with 'Summertime Blues', Cochran and Capehart came up with a song with a similar feel, 'Let's Get Together', intended as the follow-up single. Cochran went into Goldstar on 9 October, again with Palmer and Guybo, and pianist Ray Johnson. Although the song has a generic musical connection to the hit there is a vital difference in the lyric – from teenage frustration to exactly the opposite. An empty house and the parents are away, so it's party time.

When it was released after Cochran's death, in 1962, 'Let's Get Together' was revealed as an almost-perfect candidate to repeat the success of 'Summertime Blues'. With hindsight, however, we can hear that the wrong title, and therefore the wrong pay-off phrase to each verse, had been filleted from the first line of the lyric: 'Well, c'mon everybody and let's get together tonight'.

The word 'let's' forces Cochran to pause awkwardly, to interrupt the drive of the song, whereas 'C'mon' is a smooth exhortation. By changing the title to 'C'mon Everybody', Cochran and Capehart found that the title phrase was far more effective when delivered after the pause, covered by a whoop from the singer. The song was indeed now perfect. There are no other differences between the two songs – in fact, the backing track from one 'Let's Get Together' take was used for 'C'mon Everybody'. When they were satisfied, however, Waronker added a little more urgency to the song by speeding up the tape slightly, raising the key half a tone. This was a not-unfamiliar trick in the comparatively simple technology of 1950s studios.

A routine ballad, 'Don't Ever Let Me Go', first attempted in July but now revisited, was selected as the B side, and in early November the single was launched into the Christmas market, just as 'Summertime Blues' slipped down the charts. It was a respectable but surely disappointing success, peaking at No. 35 at the end of November. In the UK it fared far better, and by March 1959 it had climbed to No. 6.

During the period between the recording of 'Summertime Blues' and 'Let's Get Together' Jerry Capehart was not the only beneficiary of Cochran's expertise and enthusiasm in the studio. Particularly of note is a vigorous session in late summer 1958 for singer Troyce Key, producing two Warner Brothers singles. Palmer and Johnson were once again present but Red Callender, not Guybo, slapped the bass and they were joined by rhythm guitarist Howard Roberts and vocal group the Sharps. Troyce Key later paid tribute to his sessionman. 'I thought Eddie's guitar playing was the greatest. He was a great dude to work with.'

'Drown In My Own Tears' is a cover of a passionate Ray Charles wail, backed by Key's version of 'Baby Please Don't Go'. A second single offered 'Ain't I Cried Enough' and 'Watch Your Mouth'. Cochran played on a Silver single by John Ashley, an actor-singer managed by Capehart, strangely billed as Voice of Allah on the Johnny Burnette ballad 'Seriously (In Love)', and on the Four Dots doo-wop records 'It's Heaven' and 'Take My Hand (I'm Lonely)', before resuming his solo recording career.

A week after cutting 'C'mon Everybody' Cochran was joined at Liberty Custom Recorders by three of the current Blue Caps, Johnny Meeks, Cliff Simmons and Clyde Pennington. With Cochran adding the missing instrument, electric bass, they laid down a backing track for 'Don't Wake Up the Kids', which was overdubbed by Albert Stone and Jewel Akens of the Four Dots and released on the Freedom label. The song is a barefaced rip-off of the Coasters' 'Yakety Yak', a No. 1 hit in the summer, while Cochran's bass line suggests that he had been listening to his friend Duane Eddy, who also began his chart career that year.

Soon afterwards Cochran co-wrote and cut his next classic. He was introduced to Mario Roccuzzo, who worked at a Hollywood record store that Cochran frequented. Roccuzzo had an idea for a song, and at the home of another record-store regular, actor Corey Allen (*Night of the Hunter*, *Rebel Without a Cause* and, later, *Sweet Bird of Youth*, described in Leslie Halliwell's *The Filmgoers Companion* as 'specialising in depraved adolescents'), they built up 'Nervous Breakdown' line by line. Roccuzzo pieced together the lyrics and Cochran welded a riff behind them.

At Goldstar, Guybo and Earl Palmer added their magic. As so often, Guybo's menacing bass line melts perfectly into the mix with Cochran's precision-strummed Martin, a combination that in 1958 became the defining characteristic of a Cochran number, and Palmer emphasises the stops in the edgy rhythm, a musical metaphor for the singer's mental agitation. In 1981 Glen Glenn went as far as to say that 'Connie [Guybo] was probably a better bass man for recording than Bill Black.'

Cochran, a reluctant singer two years earlier, is now the finished article, swooping from booming bass to rocking, rasping tenor, and Roccuzzo supplies some great lines, as when the doctor pronounces: 'After giving you a physical check, I've come to the conclusion you're a total wreck.' Lyric and riff are sealed together with the elegance of a Chuck Berry song. Remarkably, Liberty decided to ignore this obvious follow-up to 'C'mon Everybody'.

Although he was now a star, out on the road exploiting his fame and partying hard every night, Cochran still worked his familiar day shift backing others in the studio – late in 1958 the beneficiaries included Sherman Scott ('How'd Ja Do?' on Freedom), old friend Bob Denton ('Pretty Little Devil' on Crest), the Four Dots (five tracks from a December session remained in the can until Rockstar unearthed them), and Al Lee Perkins (a demo of 'One Sweet Tomorrow'). Cochran also cut a demo of Sharon Sheeley's 'Hurry Up', which he passed on to Ritchie Valens for a recording session less than a month before the young Chicano's death.

Meanwhile the live work was relentless. In October, once 'C'mon Everybody' was in the can, he was booked by GAC on a package tour with a mouthwatering bill – Buddy Holly and the Crickets, Dion and the Belmonts, Jack Scott, the Olympics, Clyde McPhatter and Bobby Darin, along with Frankie Avalon, the Elegants, Connie Francis, Bobby Freeman and the Imperials. Later in the year he headlined on a trip to Canada.

Until now Cochran had not seriously considered forming a road band to accompany him – before he had hits it would not have been financially possible in any case. He relied heavily on Guybo, of course, but apart from that he would allow bookers, promoters or the agency to supply him with a drummer, a second guitarist, maybe a pianist or saxophonist.

This arrangement may have suited Chuck Berry, to whom the financial savings were always more important than the creative risk of using unrehearsed musicians, but it was becoming unsatisfactory for the musical perfectionist Cochran. For the Canadian gigs he put together his first band.

Joining Guybo was drummer Gene Riggio from the snappily titled Los Angeles group Dick D'Agostin and the Swingers, with pianist Jim Stivers and, briefly, saxophonist Jimmy Seals. Seals had played on the Champs' hit of that year, 'Tequila', and would later form a successful duo with Dash Crofts. As a nod to D'Agostin's group the band was dubbed the Hollywood Swingers, and the departure of Guybo to get married early in 1959, together with Seals, brought in other members of the Swingers including D'Agostin himself.

Many years later D'Agostin recalled his impressions of Cochran and of the scene at Goldstar. He was clearly an in-demand musician – among those he played with were Freddy Cannon, Jan and Dean, Bobby Vee, Sam Cooke, Johnny Otis, Ritchie Valens, Jack Scott, Lou Rawls and Big Jay McNeely.

'The guy I worked with most, and liked the best, was Eddie . . . part of the reason I sort of drifted off from the business was when he died

. . . I was on his recording of "Boll Weevil" – I played piano on that . . . There were numerous times when I played on a session [and] I really didn't know what they were until I heard them on the radio . . . There were a lot of us that hung around Goldstar because there was always something going on . . . All we would hear is perhaps a rhythm track or something, and we would add our part to it.

'I remember Eddie doing a western TV show. We played "Night Walk" while Eddie did a couple of Hank Williams songs. I also remember during one of our many tours that Eddie had an appointment with one of the local radio stations to do an interview. He told me he didn't want to . . . I tried to talk him out of missing it. Eddie said that if I felt that strongly about it then I should go and do it in his place, which I did. The DJ did the interview, thinking it was Eddie.

'During the show that evening the DJ arrived with two girls and was obviously telling them that he had met Eddie earlier in the day . . . On comes Eddie, and the DJ . . . just stood there with his mouth open.

'The tours in the '50s were very tiring, and also very exciting. There were always practical jokes going on . . . Eddie was the most fun to work with. I liked his intensity, but he always had a good time, did good work . . . some joke [was always] brewing. Eddie could do it all . . .'

D'Agostin, who recorded briefly for Accent, Dot and Liberty in his own right as well as working on the road and in the studio with such a huge roster of headliners, died on 19 February 1993 from hepatitis, aged 56.

Cochran spent Christmas 1958 and the New Year in New York (where he played on the Al Lee Perkins demo mentioned earlier) on an Alan Freed package. Johnnie Ray topped the bill from Christmas Day until 30 December, and was replaced by the Everly Brothers for five nights from New Year's Eve. The wonderful support cast included Bo Diddley, Chuck Berry and Jackie Wilson. As for the post-concert relaxation, Phil Everly recalled that 'Eddie could pull the prettiest girl without even talking to her'. As was to prove the case throughout their brief relationship, including the last few weeks of his life in the UK, Cochran would often forget that he was meant to be an 'item' with Sharon Sheeley, and she just had to put up with it.

Soon after playing on the Freed bill, Cochran filmed his contributions to the disc jockey's next quickie movie, *Go, Johnny, Go*, which was originally titled 'Johnny Melody' after the lead character played by Jimmy Clanton. Several of the New York package, including Berry and Wilson, were also included, and of course Berry provided the new title. Cochran's next Goldstar date after touring was on 17 January 1959, with the brief to record his *Go, Johnny, Go* contributions 'Teenage Heaven' and 'I Remember', both Cochran–Capehart compositions.

'Teenage Heaven' is another for the 'best of' compilation, a jaunty, bouncy list of adolescent demands, cheekily presented as a rewrite of 'Home on the Range'. But whereas the original singer merely wanted to be 'where the deer and the antelope play', he now demands a private phone (Daddy pays the bill, of course) and a Coupé de Ville. Cochran, only just a graduate from teenage status himself, continued to mine the 'Summertime Blues' seam with ever-greater confidence.

What is most striking, however, is that – like his great friend Buddy Holly, now heading out with Valens for his frozen and fatal sweep through the Midwest – Cochran never rested on his musical laurels. Having found that characteristic sound in Guybo's plummy electric bass and his own crystal-clear acoustic Martin, he now turned to a rasping saxophone, probably played by Plas Johnson, to bounce the song along.

Johnson was the busiest session saxophone player on the West Coast, the equivalent to King Curtis – who worked with Buddy Holly during his final New York period – in the East. Talking of Cochran, Johnson later said: 'He was just a real nice kid ... very talented and very outgoing. He was easy to work with. When we lost Eddie, we lost a great talent.'

And they repeated the magic with 'My Way'. The singer's demands focus on his girlfriend, now that he's got everything he wants out of his parents, and as a result the lyric has a bragging, even misogynist, stance. But it probably reflected how the ever-more-confident charmer Cochran was feeling at the time, always ready to put his affection for Sharon on hold if he felt it was necessary.

Two other songs were cut at this session, both excellent in their way, making this one of Cochran's most productive days in the studio. 'I Remember' is a beautiful, contemplative ballad, with Cochran adding acoustic lead lines of crystal clarity to dress up the familiar chord structure. It is let down only when one verse ends with the words 'Oh yes', which sounds like a memo to 'fill in later'. Cochran now sounds fully confident in this, his secondary, smouldering singing style. 'Rock'n'roll Blues', neither rock'n'roll nor a blues, is an engaging, mournful song with a charming hook beneath the repeated words of the title.

Both 'Teenage Heaven' and 'I Remember', teamed as the next single, were filmed for *Go, Johnny, Go* although the latter landed on the cutting-room floor. Given that Freed movies had tiny budgets and cramped shooting schedules, with straightforward plots allowing songs to be fitted in at will, this is a great pity. 'Teenage Heaven' gives Cochran a somewhat embarrassing opportunity to dance with his guitar, but the film has valuable footage of Ritchie Valens, who was dead by the time it reached the cinemas. His frantic regret for a night's drinking, 'Ooh My Head', is one of the film's highlights, along with Chuck Berry's 'Memphis Tennessee' and 'Little Queenie'. Alas, the new Cochran single bombed as mysteriously as ever, limping into the Hot Hundred at No. 99 for a week.

The tragedy of 3 February, when his friends Buddy Holly and Ritchie Valens died, would haunt Cochran for the rest of his life. It was to become an obsession, a preview of his own death, strengthening his feeling that he was above all a studio guitarist, and a potential producer – you can't crash a plane in a studio. On the British tour, although everyone was struck by his approachability and friendliness as well as his extraordinary talent, he had low moments of drunken depression when he would think broodingly about Holly. Once, when briefly off the road, staying in a rented flat in Jermyn Street, he went out and bought Holly's albums, listening to them for the first time in a year.

Johnny Rook visited Cochran at his parents' home as soon as he heard the news of the tragedy, and Cochran was already filled with foreboding. The death of his friends simply confirmed, in the starkest way possible, his own growing fear of travelling. Cochran asked Rook to promise that, if anything similar happened to him, Rook would always look after his mother Alice, whom Cochran always called by her nickname Shrimper. Cochran then went out into the yard, crying.

Two days after the crash, sounding close to tears, he was in Goldstar with a song called 'Three Stars', an instantly coined tribute to Holly, Valens and the Big Bopper written by San Bernadino disc jockey Tommy Donaldson, who pitched the song to Sylvester Cross at American Music. Indeed, Cochran was actually crying during an emotional, often-halted session.

Although there was talk of the record royalties being donated to the families of the three dead stars, Liberty could not come to an agreement that satisfied them and decided against releasing Cochran's heartfelt, sentimental tribute. Donaldson, credited as Tommy Dee, cut his own version for Cross's Crest label, billed with Carol Kay and the Teen-Aires, and it was comfortably Crest's biggest-ever hit, almost cracking the Top Ten in April. A cover version by Ruby Wright on King also crept into the Hot Hundred at No. 99 for a week, so Liberty may well have lost out for their reticence. Cochran's is comfortably the finest of the three. It was 1966 before his version surfaced, and then only in the UK. In

America it first appeared in 1972, on United Artists' handsome *Legendary Masters* double album devoted to Cochran.

Following Guybo's decision to quit the road the band was reorganised. Jim Stivers agreed to switch to bass – it was an impromptu bluff, since he could not play the instrument and did not own one – and multi-instrumentalist Dick D'Agostin replaced him on piano. D'Agostin's brother Larry on second guitar and saxophonist Paul Kaufman completed Cochran's intake from the earlier Swingers band. They were already out on the road when Stivers confessed that he had no idea how to play the bass. Cochran nursed him through one gig by pasting cribs of which note was which to the neck of a borrowed instrument, before Stivers returned to the piano stool and the versatile Dick D'Agostin moved to bass. This line-up played their way through the Midwest in the spring of 1959, but then D'Agostin received his call-up papers and more reorganisation was required.

From the pool of Los Angeles musicians another line-up was assembled – Stivers and Riggio remained and saxophonist Mike Henderson and guitarist Mike Deasy were recruited, along with bass player Don Meyer. After a summer tour back in the Midwest Meyer left and Dave Shrieber joined to complete Cochran's last working line-up, carrying him through to his departure for Britain. The band were soon renamed the Kelly Four.

Cochran's studio work continued in early 1959 during breaks between tours, and he played around with a number of instrumentals. He was well aware of the success of his friend Duane Eddy, whose long chart career began in spring 1958 with 'Movin' 'n' Groovin' ' but really took off three months later with 'Rebel Rouser', which reached No. 6 in the Hot Hundred. Cochran felt that there was mileage in non-vocal records, particularly as he continued to think of himself more as a guitarist than a pop star. Liberty Records, however, disagreed – it did not fit the way they were marketing him. One track from this period, 'Country Jam', shows another side to his guitar playing. Although the existing version is too muddy in sound to be commercially viable, his country finger-picking is quite stunning – this could be an outtake from Dylan's *Nashville Skyline* sessions, where he was backed by Nashville's finest.

On 2 April Cochran first began work on an instrumental tribute to his friend and longtime musical partner. 'Guybo', with the man himself pumping away on electric bass, is a lively if repetitive workout, and Cochran returned to these tapes in August. A version with dubbed-on drums , sometimes known as 'Drum City', appeared on Sylvester Cross's

Silver label. The flipside, also cut in August, was the reverb-heavy 'Strollin' Guitar', crisply recorded at a clip-clop tempo.

More to Liberty's taste was the spring session that produced 'Weekend', by American Music staff writers Bill and Doree Post, and 'Think Of Me'. Nevertheless, they ignored the potential of 'Weekend' until after his death. This classic Cochran track, bursting with teenage enthusiasm, is in sharp contrast to the sickly crooning of 'Think Of Me', which he can surely only have sung under orders from his record company minders.

After playing guitar behind such forgotten artists as Jay Johnston, Barry Martin and Baker Knight – and making a first attempt at 'Three Steps to Heaven' – Cochran returned to Goldstar on 23 June with a song written by Sharon Sheeley and Bob Cochran. In Eddie Cochran's hands 'Somethin' Else' is one of the greatest of all rock'n'roll songs, and in reaching No. 58 it gave him his last American hit. Not many songs in the genre exhibited such a coherently developed plot, as Cochran's pursuit of the girl turns from fantasy to reality. It was backed with a version of the traditional folk song 'Boll Weevil' by 'a guitar picker from Oklahoma City'.

In the UK, reviewer Don Nicholl picked the record as a likely hit in his *Disc* column: 'It will have the jukes rocking and the hit parade too, I think.' He was right. It reached a useful No. 22 in the charts and in *New Musical Express* in October, as reported earlier, a piece supposedly written by Cochran was headed 'Eddie's Fondest Wish Is To Visit Britain'.

Meanwhile in August, as well as working on 'Guybo' and 'Strollin' Guitar', Cochran cut a couple of blues instrumentals, similar in feel to each other. 'Eddie's Blues' is a tremolo-heavy display of virtuosity with Jim Stivers' piano bubbling nicely away beneath the guitar lines. Cochran is clearly showing off, but surely with a smile on his face. 'Chicken Shot Blues' shows just as much dexterity, but is a little less satisfying, as the stops in the arrangement are under-rehearsed. Clearly in a blue mood, Cochran also cut his wonderful version of 'Milk Cow Blues' at this time.

This Kokomo Arnold number had already been recorded by Elvis Presley, which would normally make any further attempt redundant, but Cochran's sheer blues power wins out. At this time he would often jam with B.B. King and Lowell Fulson, mighty company for a white youngster. At the end of one of these sessions Cochran played on three tracks featuring singer Darry Weaver, possibly a protégé of Jerry Capehart, but even his genius can make little out of 'Lovin' I'm Wastin' ',

'Iddy Bitty Betty' and 'Bad Baby Doll', which remained in the can. Perhaps mindful that Liberty were not interested in his blues skill, Cochran also recorded the likeable but not earthshaking 'Little Angel' and 'My Love To Remember'.

For his next recording session, still in August, Cochran changed musical direction once more, towards a sophisticated, jazzy sound. The Kelly Four had long featured their version of Ray Charles's album track 'Hallelujah, I Love Her So' in their set, and now backed Cochran on his own arrangement. There is evidence that he was interested in developing a nightclub act as an alternative to the risky road – in fact he refers to it as a *fait accompli* during a *Saturday Club* interview – and 'Hallelujah' would have been a natural candidate for inclusion in the set. As when Buddy Holly made a similar move and recorded Bobby Darin's gospel-influenced 'Early in the Morning', Cochran is confidently at ease with a song a long way from rock'n'roll . According to Sharon Sheeley, 'Hallelujah' represented 'the kind of musical direction he would have liked to pursue'.

After further work it was released in October as his next single, with 'Little Angel' on the B side, but his hit career as far as America was concerned was already over. In the UK it was the song that he was promoting during his visit, and it popped in and out of the charts, peaking at No. 22 in February.

Cochran was not happy, however, with the liberties taken by Liberty after he had arrived at a satisfactory take – the twelfth of a long night. The company's new A&R man 'Snuff' Garrett seemed keen to douse the fire of rock'n'roll with a blanket of strings, a technique that was to turn the great but uncommercial rockabilly Johnny Burnette, another picking partner of Cochran's, into a pop star. Garrett gave 'Hallelujah' the treatment – ironically it successfully highlighted the broadening of Cochran's musical base, but it was at odds with the singer's idea of small-combo swing. What it cannot subdue, however, is Cochran's crackling, perfectly achieved guitar solo – it is one of those pieces of music that, decades after the first encounter, can be played on one's mental record deck with note-for-note recall.

Tommy 'Snuff' Garrett was a Texan from Dallas, but as a teenage disc jockey out west in Lubbock he got to know Buddy Holly and the Crickets, and worked with them after Holly's death – he brought the post-Holly Crickets to Liberty and two of them, guitarist Sonny Curtis and drummer Jerry Allison, played on Cochran's last session before leaving for Britain. Garrett then discovered Bobby Vee, a Holly imitator, and in fact first tried him out at Holly's old studio run by Norman Petty in Clovis, New Mexico. He teamed Vee with the Crickets virtually as a tribute act before hitting on the double-tracked, string-backed formula that, after a couple of modest successes, hit pay dirt late in 1960 with 'Devil or Angel' and 'Rubber Ball'. He delivered many hits to Liberty during the 1960s, notably with Gary Lewis and the Playboys, before moving more into mainstream country.

A curious, undated session from around this time (Derek Glenister's discography puts it next, after the first 'Hallelujah' session) found Cochran doing his best with two songs pitched to him by Maurice McCall, the manager of nearby Biff's Restaurant. Neither 'Jelly Bean' nor 'Don't Bye, Bye Baby Me' adorns his CV and, while Rockstar has allowed us to hear them in the original form, they appeared at the time stripped of Cochran's vocals but with a harmony group added, billed as the Tigers.

Cochran then played behind the lead singers from the Four Dots, Jewel Akens and Eddie Daniels, on their Silver singles 'Opportunity' and 'Who Can I Count On', as well as serving as rhythm guitarist for the Kelly Four on 'So Fine, Be Mine' and 'Annie Has a Party', another Silver release. Cochran and the band also cut 'Have an Apple, Dearie', a Halloween novelty, and an acoustic instrumental variously called 'Jam Sand-Witch' (perpetuating the Halloween theme) and 'Jam Sandwich', released in the UK on the *My Way* album in 1964. It is a pleasant twelve-bar with a pulsing rhythm that sounds almost like a backing track to a version of the Isley Brothers' 'Money'.

Cochran's interest in instrumentals continued with a delightful parody of the zither theme to the Carol Reed–Graham Greene film *The Third Man*, played by Anton Karas. His 'Fourth Man Theme', retitled 'Song of New Orleans' (perhaps to deflect accusations of plagiarism) when released a year after his death on Crest, is a bouncy, overdubbed exercise that indelibly recalls Vienna, not New Orleans. The single was credited to the opportunistic Jerry Capehart, who may not even have been in the studio at the time.

On another break from touring Cochran laid down the basis for a lively instrumental that, with overdubbing and vocal chorus, eventually appeared as 'The Scream', and he played on sessions by Buddy Lowe and Bob Orrison, a name that came close to being an anagram of (but was not a pseudonym for) Roy Orbison. He also cut yet another instrumental, 'Hammy Blues', with a damped, pizzicato guitar sound that strolls along pleasantly but doesn't really go anywhere. The throwaway title, added later, suggests that it was seen as work in progress.

Something else that was beginning to wander aimlessly was Cochran's relationship with Jerry Capehart. As Hal Carter has said, Cochran wanted him to move to the States partly as a buffer between the two partners. In the opinion of two people close to Cochran, Si Waronker and Bob Denton, as reported by Julie Mundy and Darrel Higham, Capehart was of no particular use to Cochran. In Denton's view he held him back, and was equally ineffective later when handling Glen Campbell. Cochran was beginning to resent Capehart's claim to co-credits that were undeserved – and certainly for Capehart to put his name on 'Song of New Orleans' after Cochran's death does suggest a degree of dishonesty. It seems, however, that Cochran was simply too nice to make a decisive break, hence his later idea of using Carter as a go-between. In the view of Cochran's brother-in-law Red, married to Gloria, 'if it weren't for Ed, Capehart couldn't make a living'.

Capehart was also handling Sharon Sheeley, the Four Dots, John Ashley and, for a while, Johnny Burnette, whereas at this crucial stage of his career – with hits under his belt but with his career yet to be put on a sound, long-lasting footing – Cochran needed undivided attention. As far as record releases were concerned, he had little choice but to leave matters to Waronker and Bennett at Liberty, discreetly moonlighting to satisfy his own desire to make instrumentals as well. But there was no overall strategy, no concerted move into films, just a succession of tours and recording sessions. Cochran's reported cabaret ambitions were an attempt to break that cycle.

To be fair to Capehart, however, he did secure Cochran a tiny part in the movie *Rally 'Round the Flag, Boys* after *Untamed Youth*, and arranged a screen test with Sandra Dee, but Cochran's family – he continued to live at home as part of an extended family – felt that it was not prestigious enough for him.

Late in 1959 Cochran was booked for his second tour of Australia, playing many of the venues that had greeted the Little Richard tour so enthusiastically two years earlier. This time he shared the bill with Duane Eddy and the Rebel Rousers – who followed him over to the UK shortly afterwards – Santo and Johnny, the Diamonds, Billy 'Crash' Craddock, Johnny Restivo and Australian rocker Dig Richards.

Ten years after Cochran's death the West Coast rock'n'roll fanzine *Rollin' Rock*, whose moving spirit Ronnie Weiser also ran a record label of the same name, ran a piece by a Cochran fan, Bill Fergusson, about what is described as the last American gig. It was at the Moonlite Gardens, Wichita, Kansas, although since it is dated November it may not actually have been the very last performance.

The quotes here are taken from an edited version published in the tribute booklet *Somethin' Else*, by Eddie Muir and Tony Scott. They say, with admirable British restraint, that they included 'this rather unusual article' for its historical value, being a rare account of Cochran's stage act in America, but that 'the original article was, in a number of places, almost incomprehensible, and in order to remedy this we have changed the odd phrase here and there'.

Interestingly, the backing band was still being billed for this occasion as the Hollywood Swingers, though by this time they had settled on the Kelly Four as their trading name. 'Of all the bands I ever saw at the Gardens,' says Fergusson, 'I believe that the Hollywood Swingers was the heaviest . . . In common with most of the instrumental groups of the time they featured such classics as "Honky Tonk", "Raunchy" and "Movin' 'n' Groovin' ".'

His description of Cochran is revealing. 'My first recollection of Eddie that night was that he seemed rather short as he weaved through the crowd to the stage. Up on the stage I saw the make-up. Underneath I imagined his face a baby tangerine. Actually it was baby smooth and plump.' Many publicity shots of Cochran, as well as Adrian Owlett's memory of meeting him in a Finsbury Park café and numerous informal snaps taken backstage, show that Cochran believed that a performer should at all times be bronzed, unpimpled and often wearing eyeliner as well.

The tension on stage built up as the bass riff to 'C'mon Everybody' churned on and on, while Cochran casually tuned his guitar. Then he nodded, and the band were off. 'Everyone stood in awe,' says Fergusson, 'as one of the hardest rockers of all time laid down some really great rock'n'roll: spitting, squinting, straining – the veins in his neck seemed about to pop.'

The set that followed 'C'mon Everybody' was Leiber and Stoller's 'Kansas City', 'Twenty Flight Rock', 'Summertime Blues', 'Sittin' in the Balcony', 'Milk Cow Blues' (clearly a stubborn favourite, since Liberty persisted in showing no interest in his blues skills), 'Hallelujah, I Love Her So', 'Three Steps to Heaven' (still unfinished in recorded form, and therefore unfamiliar to the audience), 'Somethin' Else', 'Drive-In Show', Chuck Willis's 'What Am I Living For', later said by Sharon Sheeley to be their favourite song, 'Don't Ever Let Me Go', 'Cut Across Shorty' (yet to be recorded), 'Boll Weevil' and an encore of 'Summertime Blues'.

The Ray Charles number 'Hallelujah, I Love Her So' was a fixture in his set list by this stage, and 'What'd I Say' was to make a dynamic opener to many of his British gigs. Like Buddy Holly before him, who expressed an interest in recording with Charles, Cochran was bowled over by his fusion of blues, R&B and gospel, and the Charles influence indicated one direction in which his career might well have developed. Another, prompted specifically by Holly's death and hinted at in a *Saturday Club* interview in the New Year, was the development of the nightclub act demonstrating his musical versatility on such instruments as drums and piano, which would enable him to play a smaller West Coast circuit and cut down on the risks of travelling huge distances.

The last American recording session – there were to be TV and radio dates while he was in the UK, of course – was convened at Liberty Custom Recorders for 8 January 1960, with Snuff Garrett now officially named as producer, although Waronker was also present. In the studio, however, Cochran was now in charge. Although Guybo was there, instead of using the Kelly Four Cochran was reunited with Jerry Allison and the guitarist on Holly's early singles, Sonny Curtis, now a Cricket. What an ironic situation, given that Cochran's own death was just weeks away. Curtis was struck not just by Cochran's all-round expertise, but by how good a bass player Guybo was. It was a friendly, creative evening, in spite of the potential conflict of having at least three 'producers' in the room.

Nearly forty years on, Allison remembered the occasion. 'The Crickets were about to be signed to Liberty Records,' he explained. 'We'd known Snuffy Garrett . . . since way back in Texas . . . I remember Si Waronker directing us on "Cut Across Shorty", trying to keep it together with the time change and everything . . . It was great fun because Eddie was always a fun guy to be around . . . Worked out well.'

Cochran returned to 'Three Steps to Heaven', first attempted the previous June, and both stereo and mono masters resulted. He had juggled with the lyrics a little and with sensitive help from the others built an affecting little tale around the chunky chords from his Martin. He then recorded Sheeley's 'Cherished Memories', with Allison giving the song a crisp military air as the singer prepares to leave his girl behind for service overseas, which was indeed true. Finally there was the amusing country-rocker 'Cut Across Shorty', which was tweaked up half a tone for the original release. Garrett later recalled that Cochran left the studio and went directly to the airport for his flight to Britain. This was confirmed by Curtis: 'Eddie was really under the gun for time because his plane was leaving for London at midnight.'

Cochran had achieved so much in such a short time that it is necessary to remind oneself that, when he wasn't being screamed at on stage or adding so much mature class to the records of his friends, he was just a teenager who never moved out of his parents' home. 'I don't think his bed was ever made,' said Glen Glenn. 'Eddie just never kept things neat. He had records all over the place, dubs and stuff . . .'

Ironically, Johnny Rook recalls that for once Cochran was really looking forward to a tour, relishing the prospect of being one of the first rock'n'roll artists to visit the UK.

5. EDDIE COCHRAN: EPILOGUE

'Eddie Cochran isn't dead. He's away on a long tour and it won't be long before I see him again.' So said Sharon Sheeley to Mike Hellicar in *New Musical Express* five weeks after his death. In *Disc* Jack Good's piece immediately after the accident was headed 'Cochran Was Living On Borrowed Time', a reference to the fatalistic attitude that developed after Buddy Holly's death.

At this time the idea that Cochran was intended to be on the plane with Holly was still being rumoured. A jumbo jet rather than a three-passenger charter plane would be needed to accommodate everyone to whom this story has been attached at one time or another – in fact the lucky survivors were Holly's musicians, guitarist Tommy Allsup and bass player Waylon Jennings. Nevertheless, Cochran did brood on his feeling, during that last year of his life, that he had 'bought Buddy's ticket'.

In June 1961 Good wrote about Cochran once more. 'Although [he] has already slipped into oblivion as far as the American kids are concerned, I have a feeling it will be a long, long time till we forget him over here.'

During his time in the UK Cochran, his sense of humour struck by all things British, developed a Holmes–Watson routine with Good. 'He had made up his mind,' recalled Good, 'that when he flew back to New York he would walk off the plane dressed in a bowler, pinstripe trousers and carrying an umbrella. If he were asked whether England had affected him, he had practised his reply in clipped Oxford English. "Good Lord, no. Not a bit, not a bit." '

Cochran was indeed an accomplished impressionist – the cartoon Kingfisher character, for example, who says, 'Holy Mackerel, there, what is all this?' in 'Weekend'. During the Freeman J. Hover interview he uses a very silly voice indeed at one point, and he could do cockney just a little bit better than Dick Van Dyke.

Jack Good moved to America to introduce it to his style of TV rock'n'roll show with *Shindig*. Later he turned to painting and became something of a recluse, resurfacing only when he felt like it. In 1977 he returned to London to launch his musical *Elvis – A Tribute to the Artist*, one of the earliest 'compilation' shows in which three singer-actors represented Presley as the young rockabilly, the huge pop star and the sequinned Las Vegas doughnut. The show proved that Good had lost none of his touch for noisy, garish and exciting spectacle. In the 1990s the tables were turned and the musical *Good Rockin' Tonight* took Good's own life as its theme.

After Cochran's death Sharon Sheeley returned to Los Angeles, but the excitement of the music business had died with Eddie, for the time being at least. She had enough published titles to keep ticking over, after all. However, almost a year after the tragedy she was introduced to singer-songwriter Jackie DeShannon by local disc jockey Jimmy O'Neil.

They began to work together, beginning with DeShannon's next single 'Baby (When Ya Kiss Me)'. Although this was not a hit, they did far better with a song for the Fleetwoods, who had scored seven times in the charts to date, notably with their No. 1 'Mr Blue'. Perpetuating their liking for brackets, Sheeley and DeShannon wrote '(He's) The Great Pretender' for the harmony group, and it reached No. 30.

Even more fruitful was their relationship with Brenda Lee. 'Dum Dum' went to No. 4 (No. 22 in the UK). 'So Deep', the B side to the top-ten hit 'Break It To Me Gently', made No. 52 in its own right, and 'Heart in Hand' reached No. 15. Another B side, 'He's So Heavenly', charted at No. 73 on the flip of the top-ten hit 'Losing You'.

As a singer DeShannon, after modest hits with 'Faded Love' and 'Needles and Pins' in 1963 and 'When You Walk in the Room' the following January, reached the Top Ten in 1965 with 'What the World Needs Now is Love', and she continued to enjoy hits into the 1970s. In the UK the Liverpool band the Searchers picked up on her material ('Needles and Pins', 'When You Walk in the Room') and the Sheeley–DeShannon partnership supplied them with 'Can't Help Forgiving You', 'Each Time' and 'Till You Say You'll Be Mine'. When original Searchers drummer Chris Curtis tired of life on the road and left the band, he wrote 'Night Time' with Sheeley, recorded by Paul and Barry Ryan.

Sheeley married Jimmy O'Neil, who moved into television as presenter of Jack Good's *Shindig*, although they divorced five years later. Such later covers as the Sex Pistols' version of 'Somethin' Else', which reached No. 3 in the UK, kept the royalty cheques coming in, and there were some later songs like her collaboration with Del Shannon, 'Runnin' On Back', but in 2002 Sheeley was involved in a serious car accident. She died on 17 May 2002 in a Los Angeles hospital, of complications following an aneurism.

Jerry Capehart managed Glen Campbell for a while after Cochran's death and remained active both as a manager and songwriter. Although he never repeated the success of the classic 'Summertime Blues', which was also a hit over the years for Blue Cheer, the Who and Alan Jackson and kept the royalty and PRS cheques flowing in, there were other hits like 'Turn Around, Look at Me' for the Vogues, which reached No. 7 in 1968.

In 2001, on the 'findadeath' website, Warren Beath recalled tracking down Capehart in 1986 in Noel, Missouri. 'He was very strange, a Bible-toting right-wing Christian fundamentalist,' says Beath, '[a] Curtis Lemay CIA conspiracy theorist . . . who believed he had been recruited to kill Martin Luther King.' In 1988 Capehart was diagnosed as suffering from brain cancer, and he died just two weeks later, on Sunday 7 June.

In retrospect rock'n'roll history will no doubt judge Capehart's positive input into Cochran's career as outweighing the bullshit and the exaggerated claims to authorship of some of the songs. There was, of course, nothing he could teach his young partner about musicianship, singing, record production or stagecraft, but he must surely have opened some doors that the diffident Cochran would not even have knocked on.

Hal Carter was left in the lurch by Cochran's death, as they had formed a close working relationship. 'Ed and I had got on really well and he offered me a job travelling with him, looking after him, and dealing with Jerry Capehart, being a middleman between them.' This would seem to be confirmation that Cochran was cooling in his attitude towards Capehart, even if he could not bring himself to make a complete break.

'So when he died I thought that was that. But in the meantime it seems that Norm Riley had been speaking to the Shrimp, Ed's mum, and suggested that he brought me over to work with him. In those days you needed a sponsor, a job and somewhere to live before you could get a green card to move there. Norm gave me the job and Eddie's mum sponsored me and gave me a room – Eddie's room. So I was a tour manager for Norm. Because of what Ed had promised me, he took me on.'

But then Norm Riley, agent for both Cochran and Vincent, mysteriously disappeared. 'I think Norm must have had some connection [to organised crime],' says Carter. 'I don't mean that he was a crook himself, because I don't believe for a moment that he was, but the tours might have been financed by the boyos. He lost so much money, though, that I believe they simply took him out. Those tours never seemed to make money.

'I had moved to Hollywood, near the office on Sunset Strip. I wanted to be able to take girls home, whatever, and I couldn't do that at the Cochrans' house. I still went over and stayed at weekends and so on. So I had this bedsit. I did tours for Riley with Brenda Lee, Bobby Vee,

Dorsey Burnette. One day I went over to the office and it was closed. I decided I'd go back the next day – still closed. Third day I rang up and spoke to Norm's wife and she said he hadn't been home. From that point on I've never seen or heard of him, and as far as I know he never came back. He had four lovely kids, he was only about forty. I don't know what happened but I'm surmising that they sorted him out for losing their money. He just went missing. It would have been January or February 1961, because I had spent Christmas at his house and it was just after that. Unless he left to escape, of course, disappeared deliberately.'

Ronnie Hawkins, another Riley artist, has a different but equally bizarre version. 'Later on he [Riley] got himself checked into a mental institution and said he couldn't remember where the money was. We never got our money, so he got away with it.'

In 1971 Vincent, somewhat incoherently, backed up the Hawkins version. 'We had a man called Norm Riley. Now we had picked up almost a quarter of a million dollars on our tours, me and Eddie, and we were leaving for Bristol that night. And Riley he ... now, how do you go about stealing a quarter of a million dollars? Can I tell you how? He booked himself into a mental hospital, got out and collected the money and booked himself back in. Now you can't touch him. Who are you going to get? The police?' And so the mystery remains – was Riley fitted out with a concrete overcoat or did he do a Reggie Perrin, running away from his debts?

'So I was out of a job,' continues Carter. 'I ended up joining AMB, Artists Management Bureau in Hollywood. They gave me an agent's ticket so that I could work. I did that for a while, booking stuff in Hollywood. But I was only there less than a year. I was a small fish in a big pond. I came back and struggled for a while. Then I met Jess Conrad. He wanted me to go on tour with him. He offered me seventy pounds a week or something.

'Then Mr Wycherley [Billy Fury's father] rang my mum and left a message. He needed me to go back with Bill. I said I couldn't work for that kind of money any more, a tenner a week. I couldn't live on that. But he said he could get me the money I wanted. Parnes would have to pay, because Bill was falling apart. He needed to be guided, pushed, and Mr Wycherley asked me to see him. I went up to Newcastle, made out I was just passing, and Bill also asked me to go back. So I agreed as long as I got a decent wage.

'Parnes said £18 a week. But the deal was that he paid me £13 and a fiver went into a bank account with both our names on it. Then he added a fiver to that. So it was £23 altogether. But if I left in the first year I got nothing. I would have to stay two years to get all of the first year's money from the account. And so on. So any time I wanted to leave it would cost me at least £500. But I agreed, because I needed the money. I can't remember how it finished, but that's how I got back together with Bill. I could motivate him. So in 1961 he had "Halfway to Paradise" and from then onwards it rolled.'

Jack Good, meanwhile, built a new career in America. He had been quite correct in predicting that Britain would remain true to Cochran's memory. As with Buddy Holly there were no posthumous hits in America, but in the UK the appetite for both stars continued for many years. 'Three Steps to Heaven', helped no doubt by the poignancy of the title (just as Holly's final statement had been 'It Doesn't Matter Anymore'), entered the charts on 12 May and just kept climbing, reaching No. 1 and remaining in the list for almost four months.

Decca, who were then releasing Liberty product on their catch-all imprint for licensed American records, London, were prompted to start trawling the back catalogue. The lively and engaging 'Sweetie Pie' was the next release, reaching No. 38 in October, immediately followed into the chart by its B side, 'Lonely', which appeared for a week at No. 41. The following June, at long last, the potential of 'Weekend' was recognised – Good's second piece about Cochran, quoted above, was written to tie in with its release. With 'Cherished Memories' on the flip it reached as high as No. 15 and lingered in the charts until October, one of Cochran's biggest successes.

As soon as 'Weekend' dropped from sight London turned back to 'Jeannie, Jeannie, Jeannie', which peaked at No. 31. In 1963 'My Way' spent ten weeks in the charts, reaching No. 23. Former Tornado bass player Heinz went solo that year, and in Joe Meek's Holloway Road studio recorded his tribute 'Just Like Eddie', a late-summer hit that reached No. 5.

In 1968 Cochran's original 'Summertime Blues' was reissued and climbed to No. 34. In 1970 the Who owned up to one of the mainsprings of their music, which so often expressed the inarticulate frustrations of youth, and recorded their cover version of the song. It could almost have been their theme song, a 'My Generation' for a *different* generation. It reached No. 38, and for many years was their chosen closing number.

Move on a further generation, and it was the Sex Pistols who continued the Cochran legacy. In 1979 they had hits with 'Somethin' Else' (No. 3, sensitively coupled with 'Friggin' in the Riggin'') and

'C'mon Everybody' (also No. 3). In February 1988 the original 'C'mon Everybody' began another long run of success, reaching No. 14. Sid Vicious, meanwhile, murdered 'My Way', but fortunately it was the Frank Sinatra song.

In the 28 October 1960 issue of *New Musical Express,* readers (960 of them) voted Gene Vincent the 13th most popular male singer, even though his controversial departure from the country was still fresh in the memory. Cochran came 21st with 549 votes. Elvis Presley came top, with almost three times the votes of second-placed Cliff Richard.

A year after Cochran's death the *NME* ran a tribute piece suggesting that, in spite of his continuing popularity in the UK, Decca had no great plans for releasing the more obscure material. 'Time and again the question crops up: What other discs can we expect from Decca? Surely there is a stockpile of unissued Cochran material? Although it was at first anticipated by Liberty recording executives that Eddie had recorded a great deal of material, it was later found that many of the tapes were purely experimental, and were unsuitable for release . . . Liberty revealed recently that they have some of Cochran's purely instrumental recordings . . . As they could not have known about Cochran's recording plans, it's unlikely that they attached much importance to the finding of the instrumental tapes, for he always preferred to listen to guitar playing rather than singing, and often experimented with his guitar in Liberty's Hollywood studios.'

'We are trying to meet a tremendous demand for Cochran records,' said a spokesman for London Records in July 1961. '[But] we are scraping the bottom of the barrel.' Such reticence prompted the later emergence of the Rockstar catalogue, and then to a strange alliance between the 'official' label and the upstart. Two years on, with 'My Way' climbing the UK charts, Liberty were saying that 'as long as the demand is there, there will be no shortage of Cochran material for some time'.

Recycled material, presumably, because the sleeve notes to the *My Way* album claimed that the vaults were bare. This persuaded Tony Barrett, who had just joined the new Memorial Society, to begin the detective work that led eventually to his founding Rockstar. 'I started to try and find things out. I knew he had recorded for Crest and so on. But it was slow going. About 1975 Rob Finnis, Derek Glenister and I got together with the idea of producing *The Many Sides of Eddie Cochran* for the fan club. We thought that must have covered most stuff that hadn't been available.

'Then in 1978 I got in touch with Jerry Capehart. He said he had some unreleased material but he didn't come up with anything. I then went to the States with my brother-in-law, who financed the company, but unfortunately he got involved with Capehart's wife! That didn't help. Capehart went after us, EMI, everyone. It took up all my savings just fighting it.

'So I just carried on Rockstar by myself, building it up as and when I could afford it. I was dealing with Chuck Foreman for seventeen years, trying to find out if he had access to anything. This at long last resulted in the CD *Rockin' It Country Style*, which featured tracks cut by Eddie when he was thirteen to fifteen years old, Bell Gardens stuff from before the Cochran Brothers. Prior to that I researched the original recordings of *Boy Meets Girls* and *Saturday Club*, and I put out "What'd I Say", which he never recorded commercially, even though it was such a highlight of his act. The CD *Rock'n'roll Memories* includes *Boy Meets Girls* and *Saturday Club* material by both Cochran and Gene Vincent, together with rare interviews.

'This is a hobby, really, a quest [Barrett is a school groundsman in "real life"]. And I'm still searching. I'm still hoping for stuff he did with country artists around 1954, '55. And there's some Billy Fury stuff with Eddie on guitar. Rockstar is really an extension of the fan club. It's all part of the same thing. You've got the Connection, an annual Albert Lea event which attracts three to four thousand people, some events in Europe, and this year [2004] it's the Tenth Chippenham Festival. We are hoping to get as many of the acts who have appeared over the years back to celebrate.

'Is there any more? Well, you never know. Liberty were saying forty years ago there wasn't. Every day I expect more tapes, though. "My Babe", with Billy Fury, Eddie and Gene, that exists somewhere. There are always new developments. A few years ago when I did the boxed set I said I wanted the original mono tapes. The engineer Bob Jones told me that "Three Steps to Heaven" was in stereo. And then we discovered some twenty stereo tracks. So *Portrait of a Legend* presented the stereo material. I'm doing a collectors' CD now, which will have "Hallelujah, I Love Her So" without the sweetening, unreleased outtakes of "Teenage Cutie", rare items. With Gene Vincent I found four hours of unreleased material. There's still stuff to turn up. We're not at the end of the line yet . . .'

But this is leaping ahead in time. Back in May 1963, proving that the enthusiasm for Cochran still burned, *Hit Parade* magazine published a 'fact file' on him. It gave his height as 5'9", displaying a couple of inches of generosity, and recorded his love of guns and hunting. Duane Eddy and Joe Brown were named as his 'favourite instrumentalists' and

Vincent, Holly and Vince Eager as his best friends. His ambitions were reportedly to be as versatile as Sammy Davis Jr and to land a non-singing role in a film. Culled from existing sources, some of them no doubt press releases with a somewhat cavalier approach to the truth, the profile nonetheless presents a real and rounded young man whose potential can only be imagined.

Four years after Cochran's death, in 1964, The Eddie Cochran Memorial Society was founded by Tom Law in Leicester. It was this that set Tony Barrett out on the long Rockstar trail. The club was taken over by Andy O'Neill in Northumberland in 1966 before passing to Peter Morgan in Bristol. In 1973 the presidency was taken up by Mick Mirams in Ramsgate. At the time, Mirams gave me an insight into the struggle to keep Cochran's name alive. While enthusiasts were busy tracking down examples of his prodigious teenage session work, they seemed perpetually at loggerheads with Cochran's official representative on earth, United Artists, who had acquired the Liberty catalogue.

'Our primary aim is to make sure that all this Cochran stuff that's available is released, and to see what else can be discovered,' said Mirams. To a degree the society had to be run like a conventional fan club, he said, with the glaring handicap that Cochran was dead. And so to maintain interest, it was constantly necessary to make new discoveries, to make new Cochran connections.

'There's a company called Union Pacific, run by Ian Sippen. Or it was – he was recently reported as missing, presumed drowned, off Morocco. He released an album called *A Legend In Our Time*, and he was sorting out a second Cochran album. Alan Warner at United Artists has accused Union Pacific of being bootleggers. But take that *Legendary Eddie Cochran* album that Warner has put out. Various tracks on that were given to him by Jerry Capehart, who's suddenly reappeared after all these years and realises there's a bit of money still to be made out of Cochran.

'But those tracks originally belonged to Ekko, Crest and Silver, owned by Sylvester Cross. They didn't belong to Liberty. When Cross died those tracks would have become the property of his family.' The implication is clear – that in Mirams' view the legal owner of Cochran's Liberty material had, inadvertently or not, also become a bootlegger by issuing material from other sources. Since then Barrett has dealt openly with the family, and he unravels the rights to material before he puts it out.

The admitted bootleg *A Legend In Our Time* contained six tracks from Ekko, the early country material by Cochran, together with four instrumentals originally released on Silver and credited to the Kelly

Four. The album also included the original takes of 'Skinny Jim' and 'Half Loved', and the version of 'Cotton Picker' from *Untamed Youth*.

Mirams gave an example of the detective work needed to build up an ever more complete picture of Cochran's prolific teenage work. 'Say someone goes to a rock'n'roll auction and sees a record by Ray Stanley on Zephyr. They think the name rings a bell for some reason, so they buy the record. The guitar sound seems familiar, so they go through all their old interviews and they find one where Gene Vincent mentions Stanley when he's talking about Eddie. So they check through composer credits on Cochran's albums. And see Stanley's name on one of the tracks. They play the single again, and by this time there's no doubt it's by Cochran.'

Mirams also revealed that devious means are sometimes needed to winkle out evidence of Cochran's involvement on these records that were released in California and usually died the death. 'Eddie Bond cut tracks for Ekko at the same time that Cochran was sessioning for the label, so I got in touch with him. I wrote and asked him about four tracks – did Cochran back him on them? He wrote back and didn't answer my question. He said that these two singles were incredibly hard to come by. So I thought I'd try and bluff him. I said we had these tracks, and wanted to know if Cochran was on them because it sounded like him. He confirmed that it was Cochran, and could we let him have a couple of copies, as even he couldn't get hold of them. I had to do the dirty on him and tell him that we didn't have them. But if I hadn't done it I wouldn't have found out anything.'

The old fan club did not always run smoothly, as a rather testy letter from Mirams to *Record Mirror* proves. 'One or two things regarding the Eddie Cochran Memorial Society. A couple of items recently, the Society has been mentioned in *RM*, with the address still being at Bristol and the Society still being run by Peter Morgan. In fact this is not so. Morgan handed the Society over to me at the beginning of the year, after failing to turn up at our all-important social in November last . . .'

In spite of Mirams' purist reservations about the manner in which Liberty/United Artists in the UK approached the Cochran catalogue, the company cannot be accused of ignoring it. In September 1960 came the excellent *Memorial Album*, which packaged the hits Cochran had scored while still alive with a representation of his lesser-known material, and in November 1962 *Cherished Memories* included a lot of material that until then we had had no access to, notably 'Nervous Breakdown' and 'Pink Pegged Slacks'. *Singin' To My Baby* was re-released in September 1963, and a year later came *My Way*, which for the first time stressed

Cochran's blues expertise with such items as 'Eddie's Blues' and 'Milk Cow Blues'. In 1968 all Cochran's existing albums were reissued at a 'budget' price.

In April 1970 came the *Tenth Anniversary Album*, a 'best of' repackage – it includes 'Three Stars' – and in November of the same year came a cheap reissue of familiar material, *C'mon Everybody*. It is perhaps at this point that the patience of the hard-core fans was beginning to shred somewhat – 'C'mon Everybody' had now appeared on four of the posthumous UK albums. But in June 1971 United Artists did attempt to make amends – the double album *The Legendary Eddie Cochran*, for the first time, acknowledged what were then the lesser-known aspects of his career, with early material like 'Latch On', instrumentals ('Drum City', 'Strollin' Guitar', 'The Scream' and 'Fourth Man Theme') and examples of his session work like the Kelly Four's 'Annie Has a Party'.

In April 1972 the most comprehensive collection so far was put out, the thirty-track compilation in the *Legendary Masters* series alongside Ricky Nelson and Fats Domino, and now the grumbles were growing louder – the die-hard completist was required to buy yet another copy of 'C'mon Everybody' and the other familiar cuts, maybe just to catch up with one or two new tracks. In the following September *On the Air* offered something different, with interviews and material from the British tour, while April 1975's *15th Anniversary Album* was, predictably, predictable.

After various permutations over the next decade United Artists did Cochran proud for the fiftieth anniversary of his birth with the handsome *Eddie Cochran Box Set*, containing six albums, Rob Finnis's excellent notes, plenty of pictures and Derek Glenister's massive discography. Meanwhile, however, Rockstar had entered the market.

Their first release, *The Many Sides of Eddie Cochran* in May 1979, was a revelation. However quaint much of the material sounded – there were no unsuspected rock'n'roll masterpieces here – it had a similar impact to hearing Buddy Holly's taped adolescent doodlings for the first time. Behind Hank Cochran's defiant 'squareness' and Jerry Capehart's lack of any discernible vocal spark was the teenage prodigy, fully revealed for the first time.

Another comparison could be made with the early Aristocrat releases put out by Leonard and Phil Chess into an uncharted market. They clearly had no idea what might be a hit and so tried a bit of everything, until Muddy Waters started selling strongly and pointed the way. It is just the same here – Sylvester Cross had no clue either. As described earlier, we hear artists in search of a style, and in the case of Hank and

Eddie they are artists who would soon agree to disagree. Nasal hillbilly harmonies, back-porch picking, supposedly comic novelties, moody instrumentals – the uniting element, of course, is the fiercely burning musical intelligence and inventiveness of a young genius.

In December 1981 Rockstar teamed Cochran with Vincent for a *Rock'n'roll Heroes* tribute, drawing on material from the UK tour, and had the satisfaction of licensing it to EMI for wider release. Cochran performs 'Somethin' Else', 'Hallelujah, I Love Her So', his familiar set-opener 'What'd I Say', 'Milk Cow Blues' and 'Twenty Flight Rock', backed by Wildcats Big Jim Sullivan, Brian Locking and Brian Bennett.

A few months later more tracks were unearthed, including that wobbly but stunning 'Country Jam', together with interview snippets including Buddy Holly. In September 1982 *The Young Eddie Cochran* filled in a few more gaps and in 1986 *Hollywood Sessions* revealed what such mysterious titles as 'Don't Bye, Bye Baby Me' sounded like. This completist material was in contrast to the intervening Rockstar release, *Portrait of a Legend*, which contained the familiar titles. At the very least, Rockstar proved to be a useful irritant to United Artists, with David ensuring that Goliath could not neglect their stewardship of Cochran's music, culminating in the 1988 box set which represents the finest collection drawn from his entire career. In the previous year he had been inducted into the Rock'n'roll Hall of Fame in Cleveland, Ohio.

Also in 1988, Levi's launched a television campaign for their 501 jeans by looking back thirty years to the start of the romance between Cochran and Sheeley. Having failed to attract his attention wearing party frocks, Sheeley at lasts succeeds when she turns up wearing a pair of Levi's. The target market had probably never heard of Cochran, and certainly not of Sheeley, but the legend was enough.

On 3 April 1995 the formation of a new Eddie Cochran Appreciation Society, operating from Chippenham, was announced, with a former mayor of the town, Angela Powell, as chairman. On 18 April an inaugural meeting was held. The most notable result was the setting up of an annual Eddie Cochran Weekend in late summer, around the time of his birth, which has attracted such artists as the Crickets and Cochran's nephew Bobby, who first appeared in 1997 with Big Jim Sullivan in his band together with pianist Freddie 'Fingers' Lee and former Pirates Frank Farley on drums and Brian Gregg on bass. As Tony Barrett pointed out above, the 2004 event will be the tenth.

From teenage prodigy to smouldering rock'n'roll star, Cochran burned briefly but so brightly. His transient pop-star fame in America during his lifetime has given way to a deeper recognition that he stands, with Vincent, in the first rank of 1950s icons, and such great musicians as Bobby Cochran and Darrel Higham are still keeping his spirit alive. The finest of British country-rock guitarists, Albert Lee (a spooky echo of Cochran's birthplace Albert Lea), plays in that spirit, as do countless others.

As Bobby Cochran himself has put it: 'Embraced by rockers of every stripe . . . Cochran represents the unifying, youth-empowering and universal might of raw rock'n'roll.' He worked in an industry that was considered to be transient even by those who ran it, and most recordings of the late 1950s understandably leave today's teenagers cold. Not so 'Summertime Blues', 'Somethin' Else' or 'C'mon Everybody'.

Somehow Cochran's genius enabled him to instil into these crystal-clear expressions of his art, at the dawn of the modern recording age, a spark of recognition that has reached out over successive decades. The most blasé, truculent, 21st-century 15-year-old *knows* what Cochran was on about. And those of us who were around at the time will never cease to be thrilled as Cochran and Guybo grind into one of those fat, growling, reverberating intros.

He could perhaps be the only artist whose finest, most distinctive work can instantly span a fifty-year age gap, without patronisation or qualification, with no need to explain, speaking to child and ageing rocker alike, and at once. He did not go gentle into that good night in a ridiculous Las Vegas jump suit, or fade away in some small-town cabaret. He went out with fist raised, shouting, 'I'm a gonna make a fuss, I'm a gonna make a holler.' And he played the sweetest guitar we'd ever heard.

6. GENE VINCENT: EPILOGUE

Vincent could not afford to lie low for too long, and if it could not be proved that he had sent the telegram about the death of his daughter, Melody, he could rely on the sympathy, rather than the anger, of the fans. Back in the UK the president of his British fan club, Mike Bartlett, said: 'Since Gene went back to America we have not had any reason to think [his] popularity has decreased. In fact we are still getting plenty of letters asking for details of how to join the club. The general feeling . . . is that the whole story has yet to be told, and until it is no one should be condemned.'

Even Cliff Richard rallied to Vincent's defence. 'I hope this hoax telegram affair does not mean Gene is finished over here,' he said. 'It would be a great shame, for he is a gifted artist and I know a lot of people are still very interested in him.'

While Vincent remained in hiding in Oregon with Darlene, Capitol could take comfort that his controversial flight from the UK had not yet harmed his commercial appeal. Perhaps borne along on a tide of sympathy, the Cochran-arranged 'Pistol Packin' Mama' entered the charts on 16 June and reached No. 15 in July.

In September he had a new American release, 'Anna-Annabelle', from the final Blue Caps session on 17 October 1958, with 'Pistol Packin' Mama' on the B side. In November it came out in the UK, backed by 'Accentuate the Positive' from a Jerry Merritt session on 3 August 1959, but it failed to make the charts on either side of the Atlantic.

To coincide with his new US single Norm Riley had Vincent back on the road, up in Alaska for ten days and then for a ballroom sweep in the States. For some gigs he could call on the Fendermen as his backing group – they had reached No. 5 with their version of 'Mule Skinner Blues' in early summer, and so helped to augment the crowd – and on other occasions he relied on local groups. By November, lively photographs of a performance at the Prom Ballroom in St Paul, Minnesota suggest that he was back on form. He had retained the leather trousers but now wore an embroidered white jerkin.

He shared this bill with Wanda Jackson, a fellow Capitol artist, who had just hit the charts with her storming version of 'Let's Have a Party'. Before discovering country music and God, Jackson had hinted with this wonderful record, driven along by a stunning Capitol session band, that she could have kept the rock'n'roll flag flying. Vincent must have gone down well, because he returned to the St Paul venue just after Christmas, this time with the Fendermen.

1961

In January Vincent was back in the Capitol Tower studio with a new producer, Karl Engerman, along with the Jimmy Haskell Orchestra. This did not augur well, and it was clearly the label's intention to steer him away from the raw power of his best early sides towards something more cosy and '60s-friendly. Fortunately Haskell's guitarist Scotty Turner, who was A&R man at the session, did his best to make Vincent relevant to the new musical mood with some sympathetic song selections.

In the course of two days he cut 'Crazy Beat', 'I'm Gonna Catch Me a Rat', 'It's Been Nice', 'That's the Trouble with Love', 'Good Lovin'', 'Mr Loneliness', 'Teardrops' and 'If You Want My Lovin''. The standard was reasonably high overall, but the sweetening added by a cautious record company took giant strides away from rock'n'roll.

Vincent and Darlene rented a house in Niles, on the San Francisco Bay, and he returned to the UK. He was greeted with a 'new' single release – 'Jezebel' from 1956 and 'Maybe', cut in 1958. The follow-up was equally backwards looking: 'Brand New Beat' (1957) and 'Unchained Melody' (1956).

Don Arden took over Vincent's management in the UK and fixed him up with a new backing band, the Echoes, sending him out on tour with Johnny Kidd and the Pirates and Johnny Duncan and the Blue Grass Boys. This was an excellent bill – Kidd, one of the most convincing of British rockers, had reached the top of the charts the previous summer with 'Shakin' All Over', following it up with 'Restless' and a cover of Ray Sharpe's 'Linda Lu'. Expat American Duncan had not had a hit for three years, when 'Footprints in the Snow' reached the Top Thirty, but his energetic brand of folk-blues and bluegrass remained popular.

Arden, comic and compere turned manager, was what is now politely referred to as a 'colourful' character. As his website testifies, he revels in his reputation as a heavy, with a physical approach to the complexities of business. Whether or not he was financially scrupulous in his dealings with Vincent – and he was certainly harrying him towards the end of his life – both the singer's English wife Margie and his friend Adrian Owlett have some charitable recollections of him.

Says Margie: 'Don Arden was always quite reasonable to me. He had no scruples, of course, but when you look at modern business practices, so what? He found us a house and helped us set up home. He bought the pram for Sherri. So privately he was always very kind and supportive. He sent me money until he eventually got tired of it.' Protective as he is of his bad reputation, this may not be the kind of endorsement that Arden wants. At the same time, Margie says: 'When I was living with Gene, Don Arden was just paying him a flat weekly wage. I don't know what happened to the rest, but I began to see some of the suspect ways that money was being handled.'

Owlett adds: 'Arden made Gene Vincent the most popular solo artist in the country for a while. He kept him working and the last thing you wanted was to have Gene with nothing to do. He was as tough as old boots but he got the work for Gene and provided a structure for his career. Don't forget that the options in the States were effectively over as far as he was concerned.'

Capitol came up to date for a spring record release with two of the January cuts, 'Mr Loneliness' and 'If You Want My Lovin' '', but a hit remained elusive. In April Vincent returned home briefly, filming a segment for the Pat Boone movie *State Fair* that landed on the cutting-room floor, but when he got to Niles he found that Darlene had left him. 'I'd just had enough,' she said. 'I wanted a real marriage.' Vincent tried to persuade her, during a series of tense meetings, to change her mind, but it had been made up. She knew that his only life was out on the road, and probably not at home in the US where his star was on the wane, and that was not enough for her.

Back in the UK, Henry Henroid (his real name was Henriod, but people kept getting it wrong so he bowed to the inevitable) had moved from working in the Two I's coffee bar to a job with a boxing promoter, and in 1960 he joined Don Arden's management company as a road manager. One of his early jobs was to find him a backing band for Vincent. He came across Sounds Incorporated, playing a Saturday night residency at, of all places, Leyton Baths in east London.

The band were formed early in 1961 in north Kent, a six-piece consisting of drummer Tony Newman, bass player Dick Thomas, guitarist John Gillard, brass and woodwind players Dave Glyde and Alan Holmes, and Baz Elmes, who commuted between baritone sax and keyboards and also wrote their arrangements. 'As I understood it the word was out around London that there was this band who were a bit different,' says Thomas. 'We had saxophones and so on, playing full-tilt Little Richard stuff rather than the usual guitar, bass and drums. I seem to remember he offered us the job that night.'

'We were playing semi-pro at the Baths,' says Holmes. 'This bloke came round after we'd finished a show and asked if we'd be interested in being Gene Vincent's backing group. A bit of a surprise, out of the blue.'

'We met Gene in a little drinking club off St Martin's Lane,' recalls Thomas. 'We had a little rehearsal and he gave us the nod. So we had to buy transport – it was an old ambulance – and we went on the road in May. The first gig was a dance hall in Bradford. People were baking cakes and stuff for us as if we were going to the end of the world.'

'Gene was very polite to us, a very nice man – when he was sober,' says Holmes. 'He soon took to riding in the van with us. He said that Henry's job was to keep him away from the drink. When we were in Hamburg later on a fan gave him a gun. And behind the bar they had gas pistols in case of trouble. He managed to get hold of one and let it off.

'He seemed to be affected by the full moon, you know. He'd go off his head. He had a knife at Dave Glyde's throat once, and he threatened Tony Newman with a gun. "You've been sleeping with Margie." '

One story about Vincent's use of his knife, which he called Henry, is told by both Joe Brown and Hal Carter, but with a different victim – in Brown's case it is Carter, in the latter case an unnamed member of the backing group.

'We used to go on the tour coach,' says Brown. 'Gene would sit up front next to the driver with this knife . . . You didn't go near him. I actually saw him cutting a bloke's suit off once without hurting him. Hal Carter. He looked round and said, "Hal, I'm going to cut you fourteen times." Swish, swish, swish. Suit in ribbons.'

Thomas's reaction to Vincent was similar to that of Holmes. 'My first impression is that I was scared of him. Staring eyes, the black leather, the way he posed with the mike. He was probably the worse for Johnnie Walker. It was a shame, because when he was sober he was very, very good, but when he was drunk he couldn't handle it. Not like, say, P.J. Proby. He could be waiting in the wings drunk but as soon as he got on stage he straightened up. Gene wasn't like that.'

At a gig in Torquay Vincent was not only too drunk to sing but also to stand up, and he collapsed on stage. 'When he was drunk,' says Thomas, 'it was more unfortunate for the audience than for us. All we could do was stand there and listen to the dissent coming at us from the hall.'

'He would drink bottles of Scotch every day,' continues Holmes, 'but he never seemed to eat anything. That's what killed him. That and the aspirin. And sometimes he nearly killed us. He didn't take any notice of where we were – it was as if he couldn't see us. When he swung the microphone stand around you just had to get out of the way – we'd be playing on our knees!'

'For a couple of months we worked every little dance hall in the country, it seemed like,' says Thomas. 'And we'd also do weeks on variety bills, at the Hippodromes, with comics and speciality acts.' One of those Hippodromes was at Bristol, scene of Cochran's last gig. Chillingly, the group ambulance was involved in a crash on the way home. 'We all became mates,' says Thomas. 'He would travel in the band bus. He was in it when it got written off – the brakes went. But it wasn't going very fast and it just banged into the back of a truck. It must have shaken him up, though.'

In June Vincent, accompanied by Henry Henroid, returned briefly to America to renew his passport. In Portland he made a desperate attempt to see Darlene and the children, turning up at a police station in the middle of the night. Later she grudgingly kept an appointment with him, but her attitude towards him had not softened.

Back in London Vincent rejoined Sounds Incorporated and went back on the road. In July he and the band went into Abbey Road Studios and recorded the wonderful 'I'm Going Home' together with 'Spaceship to Mars'. He also cut two ballads with the Norrie Paramor Orchestra, 'Love of a Man', a tribute to Cochran, and 'There I Go Again'.

'I'm Going Home', backed by 'Love of a Man', was released in the UK but not in America. The A side was one of his finest 1960s recordings, singer and band rocking as one, and it proved to be Vincent's last hit record, reaching No. 36 in August – it was followed up by 'Brand New Beat'. The disappointing novelty 'Spaceship to Mars' was Vincent's contribution to Dick Lester's feature-film debut *It's Trad, Dad*, which also starred Craig Douglas, Helen Shapiro, the Brook Brothers and John Leyton.

Henry Henroid also managed other Arden tours, included the one topped by Little Richard and Sam Cooke, who were both backed by Sounds Incorporated. He subsequently moved to Germany and managed the Star Club, famous as the place where the Beatles served their overseas apprenticeship. In this capacity he was responsible for several albums, including *Jerry Lee Lewis Live at the Star Club*, with the Nashville Teens as his backing band.

Margie had little time for him. 'Some people, like Henry Henroid, had their own agenda, their own way of controlling Gene. Like they'd say they were trying to keep him off the drink but they'd supply it, to keep him under their thumb. Henry was a particularly spiteful person. A lot of Gene's jealousies and fantasies were encouraged.'

Back in Hollywood in October Vincent cut two tracks, produced by Nick Venet, that were to make his next single early in 1962 –

'Lucky Star' and 'Baby Don't Believe Him'. Both were later sweetened with a string section.

1962

In the spring Vincent returned to the UK for a tour with Brenda Lee, 'The King and Queen of Rock', and both artists were backed by Sounds Incorporated. The itinerary included a live television performance on the top-rated variety show *Sunday Night at the London Palladium*. It was on this tour, after a gig at the Tooting Granada – scene of his first-ever British appearance – that Vincent met Margie, Margaret Russell, for the first time.

Margie feels angry at the suggestion published elsewhere that she had to beg for an invitation to go backstage. 'I didn't have to try to get invited to parties in those days. I was working as an actress and a dancer. I had worked with Joan Littlewood in *Fings Ain't What They Used To Be*, and I had film work as well. When I met Gene I was doing a stint at a cabaret club. In fact, I broke my contract when he said he wanted me to go on the road with him.

'I went with a crowd to see the show and then we went backstage. Gene pursued me relentlessly. I was doing the cabaret show the next night and he was up north, but he phoned the stage door. When he came back to London he was staying in a hotel just off Gower Street. He invited me to lunch with him and he gave me a gold bracelet. I don't know if he bought it for me in the first place! Anyway, that was the start of it.'

Margie had previously been out with Terry Dene. 'I grew up with him. Living opposite us was Brian Gregg, who later became the bass player with Johnny Kidd and the Pirates. I got friendly with him, and Terry Williams – as he was then – was his best mate. We set up a skiffle group together, and started to go down the Two I's coffee bar.'

Vincent's tour ended in Slough and instead of returning immediately to America as he had planned, Vincent stayed with Margie for a week, and even managed to impress her parents with his shyness and courtesy. 'He was due back in America and he told me all about Darlene,' says Margie, 'but he said it was all over. Gave me a load of old bollocks – sorting out all his property, selling his boat and so on – and he said it would take about a month. But ten days later I got a telegram saying he was arriving at Heathrow, and would I meet him.

'He arrived with one suitcase and when we got to the hotel I saw that he had a couple of T-shirts, some underwear, some socks and a Scalextric toy car. And a few bits of paper, contracts and so on. That was it. I said, where's everything else? Oh, it's coming. Of course, it never did. The idea that he could start a new life with some socks and a toy car!' While Arden hurriedly sorted out a new work permit, he packed Vincent off to the Star Club. 'I had a flat at Park West near Marble Arch,' says Margie. 'That's where we went when we decided to stay together.'

Back in the UK he went into Abbey Road Studios to cut 'King of Fools', 'You're Still In My Heart', 'Held For Questioning' and 'Be Bop a Lula', the latter a pale and pointless reflection of the great original. This was to prove his last session for Capitol, ironically ending the relationship with the same song as he started it, and within a few months he was out of contract.

'Britain is to be the new home of Gene Vincent,' announced *Hit Parade* magazine. 'At present Gene has a flat in London, but his working permit only allows him to play restricted periods during each stay, so he has had to go out of the country in order to return and work. Gene remains one of the few consistent box-office draws to emerge from the early rock'n'roll era . . . His stage act has always been reminiscent of his way of living. He has never cared about himself or his property but always about the performance he is giving . . . Only recently the manager of one theatre approached him after the show complaining, "Gene, you've wrecked three of our mikes." To which Gene replied, "Mister, you bought my act." '

In July Vincent went back to Europe. 'We went to Italy with him in 1962,' says Holmes, 'with this team of Italian dancers, playing beach clubs. We toured down one coast and up the other. I remember that our coach driver, Bruno, would steer with one hand and be holding a jug of grappa with the other, round all these hairpin bends. Money was always a problem – Henry had to follow the promoter around like a dog.'

'Yes, Italian promoters were notoriously dodgy,' agrees Thomas. 'Henry wouldn't let us get off the coach until he had got the money. And they booked him into some real upmarket resorts.' These included The Lido in Venice, a hangout for the rich and pampered. 'Sometimes they just didn't want to know. I broke his leg on that tour – I hit him. He had Margie with him. They were at the front of the coach having one helluva drunken argument. He had a go at me and I retaliated. I've still got a scar on my thumb. Next day he had a new cast on and he was right as rain, as if it had never happened.'

It seems that when Thomas punched Vincent, his bad leg got trapped in the coach seat as he fell. By the evening it had swollen badly, and the coach was diverted to a hospital for emergency treatment. In spite of being warned to keep the plaster cast dry, the next morning Vincent and Margie were out in the bay on a pedalo. 'I considered pushing him overboard,' says Thomas, darkly.

In Henry Henroid's opinion: 'I'd say Gene was a schizophrenic. He could be so kind and yet so hateful . . . But on stage he was an athlete . . . [He] would never do the same thing twice.' As for life on the road with Vincent, 'It was like a living lunatic asylum.'

Tornados drummer Clem Cattini had similar recollections of Vincent's mood swings to those of Holmes and Thomas. 'Gene was a great entertainer on stage but a very weird person. One night he went berserk and attacked Johnny Kidd with a knife. He would down two bottles of whisky each day of his tour.' In spite of this Kidd remained friendly with Vincent, and just before his death in a car crash in 1966 he proposed that they should tour together.

From Italy it was on to Frankfurt and then Vincent returned to Hamburg, performing at the Star Club at the same time as the Beatles. Legend has it that Sounds Incorporated followed him to Germany by train and did not arrive in time for his first gig, and so the Beatles stepped in to assist one of their heroes. 'I was pregnant at the time he was at the Star Club with the Beatles,' says Margie. 'He was overjoyed at the fact that I was expecting a baby.'

It was on this trip that Vincent brandished the gas pistols referred to earlier, and began to accuse various members of his entourage of sleeping with Margie. Adrian Owlett recalls: 'The first time he met Cliff Bennett, in the dressing room at the Star Club, the very first thing Gene said was, "Have you been fucking Margie?"' Vincent confronted both Henry Henroid and Tony Newman about it, and though it seems that his suspicions were misplaced, his musicians at this time do hint that there was some justification for his jealousy.

Margie vehemently denies the rumours. 'From the day I met Gene to the day I left him I was entirely faithful. After all, until he took up with Jackie Frisco he was with me all the time. The idea that I had an affair in Germany, which I've seen in print, is ludicrous. I was expected to be there, where he could see me. If I went to the loo he wanted to know where I was! It was some of the people around him, feeding his jealousy.'

Back in England, Vincent and Margie moved into a three-bedroomed house in Welling, Kent, rented by Arden and close to where members of Sounds Incorporated lived. There was another single release to follow 'Lucky Star', 'King of Fools', with the lacklustre revival of 'Be Bop a Lula' on the B side. Vincent's next overseas trip was to Israel, but the tour was aborted after less than a week due to riotous behaviour. By October, his tempestuous relationship with Margie not helping his demeanour, Vincent was getting close to the edge. A working trip to Paris was marred by brawling, more accusations of infidelity, fighting with Margie and drunkenness. A restaurant aquarium was reputedly smashed in one bottle-throwing tantrum.

It was as Christmas 1962 approached that Margie realised that she was pregnant. 'It began snowing on Boxing Day and didn't stop until March,' she recalls of one of the most severe British winters of modern times. Just before New Year, Vincent entered St George's Hospital in London for more surgery on his deteriorating leg.

When Henroid left the UK, his job with Arden was taken by Peter Grant, later to manage Led Zeppelin, who at the time was working with his brother as cab drivers retained by Arden. The Grant brothers' job description sometimes went beyond chauffeur duties, however – they were heavies themselves, working for the man who pioneered the muscular approach to rock management.

1963

After a brief tour early in the New Year Vincent and Margie obtained a special licence and, with Henroid as witness, they married at Dartford Registry Office on 23 January. Then it was on to France and back to the Star Club yet again. Marriage had not lessened the tempestuous nature of the relationship, and there was one incident in which he threw her possessions out of the window on to the snow-covered garden and locked her out of the house, before the police insisted that he let her back in.

In between tours with Sounds Incorporated, Vincent worked briefly with Mike Berry's backing band the Outlaws, who included pianist Chas Hodges. Hodges teamed up with bass player Dave Peacock and drummer Mick Burt in the mid-'70s as the highly successful Chas & Dave, but he was a veteran of numerous 1960s bands. 'I always got the feeling that Gene would sooner have been one of the boys than a star,' he later recalled. 'He couldn't really handle stardom . . . We bunged everything into a Thames van, the whole lot of us . . . Gene helped as well to carry amplifiers in and set microphones up . . . He wasn't a sex symbol – there weren't many girls that would come to see him . . . He didn't want to be a star . . . When stardom is pushed on anyone who doesn't really want to be a star, then the pressures get to him – I think they got to Gene in the end.'

Ian Dury talked about Vincent at the same time. 'Gene Vincent . . . in case you didn't know, was one of the greatest singers who ever lived.' He then gave a concise summary of the music business. 'Lawyers, accountants, managers, image-fakers, journalists, record companies, promoters, agents, overpriced studios and lots of other greedy people usurp the talents and skills of the artist, however unbewildered, and erect an insurmountable barrier around which somebody as ill-equipped as Gene Vincent could never hope to crawl.'

Dury also confirmed the effect that Vincent had had on him – not the voice, which he admitted was inimitable, but the image. 'When I was a boy of fifteen or sixteen he used to be my real hero. He looked naughty and he looked skinny. Black hair. Bit dodgy but he had a voice like an angel . . . Very early Elvis Presley and very early Gene Vincent are the most beautiful two male voices of the [twentieth] century.'

Vincent agreed to an attempt to treat his alcoholism, without conviction. He was put to sleep and fed intravenously for several days. On discharge from the clinic he returned to drinking, boasting that he had hoodwinked the doctors. In April he was ordered to rest, and the couple went to Majorca for a brief holiday before visiting Paris on the way home. Sherri Ann was born on 29 May 1963. The Beatles were at No. 1 for the first time with their third chart entry, 'From Me To You', a symbolic indication that the days of the unreconstituted rock'n'rollers were on the wane.

'We were in the house in Welling until Sherri was born,' says Margie. 'I went into labour virtually as we were leaving there. We bought a flat in Streatham [south London], Leigham Court Road, but it was bought off plan and still wasn't ready. So we borrowed Adam Faith's house in Wyndham Mews in Marylebone – Adam was away. Sherri's birth was registered at that address.'

Late in the summer Vincent moved out of the Marylebone address but was soon back again. In September he was performing in Ireland. He broke his contract and came home early, drunk and somehow armed. Margie noticed that blood was sometimes seeping from his mouth. Police were called to their flat – he and Margie were now living in Lansdowne Road, Holland Park, still waiting for the Streatham flat to be ready for occupation (they finally moved there in November). Margie reported that Vincent had threatened her with a revolver, prompted by jealous anger at yet another alleged affair. 'Just like any other jealous husband' is how he described his action.

When he appeared on crutches at Marylebone Magistrates Court he was fined £20 for possession of two guns and ammunition without a licence, and conditionally discharged on a count of assault. The guns were confiscated. Quoted in the *Daily Mail*, magistrate Walter Frampton warned him: 'You had five cartridges in the magazine of this Luger, which is a pretty easy weapon to discharge. If you had lost your head and gone on to press the trigger you might have found yourself facing a more serious charge.' Except that it would presumably have been Margie who lost her head.

'I hope my fans remember my name is Gene Vincent and not Gene Autry,' he told the *Daily Express*. He denied that he and Margie were splitting up, and said contritely: 'The trouble was I listened to some of my alleged friends while I was on tour in Germany. There wasn't a word of truth in what they said.' Whether or not he believed this, he seemed to be trying at this stage to keep the year-long marriage on the road.

'When I was in the US Navy I was a crack marksman,' Vincent fantasised. 'I have a collection of guns at home in New Mexico and the guns in this case were given to me by friends in Germany for that collection. I guess I just brandished one in a moment of temper.'

'But I could never have pulled the trigger,' he told the *Daily Mirror*. 'I could never have murdered her. I love her too much. I did it just to scare her.'

In October Vincent undertook a strenuous trawl through France and Belgium backed by French band Les Sunlights, involving 25 dates in 4 weeks. Back in London he submitted to psychiatric treatment in Harley Street, but it was no more successful than the cure for his alcoholism. It was now Margie's turn to leave home and return, and to celebrate Christmas Vincent pulled a knife on Don Arden and assaulted Margie with one of his crutches. At the end of what was supposed to be a reconciliatory holiday on the Isle of Wight Vincent threw a five-pound note on the bed and stormed out.

Vincent had signed with Columbia, an arm of EMI in the UK, in the summer and the first result was a change of style in 'Where Have You Been All My Life', a pounding pop-rock ballad with a strong hook, but a mile away from Vincent's familiar style. He took to the change of direction with ease, however, and the track is a convincing example of its type. It's just not Vincent, though. With his marriage deteriorating he was still vulnerable to the assault charge, which had remained on the books, and he offered to pay Margie £20 per week to drop the action. She agreed, but the payments lasted only until he next left the country.

Vincent's life, not just marriage, was now falling apart. An incident when Henroid, glancing into his shaving mirror, saw Vincent coming at him armed with a chair convinced the road manager to seek a quieter life at the Star Club. And now Sounds Incorporated had their own contract with Columbia, which would reward them with two 1964 hits in 'The Spartans' and 'Spanish Harlem', both of which made the Top Forty.

They had been one of the most in-demand backing bands in the country, working first for Arden and then for Brian Epstein. 'The reason we were sought after,' explains Thomas, 'is that we'd take the trouble to get a running list of songs before an American artist came over. Baz would work out arrangements that suited our instrumentation and also suited the record. We'd go to a little pub in Woolwich and rehearse endlessly. So when the artist turned up he'd be bowled over – we'd have the songs at the right length, in the right key, and they didn't have to do a thing. We also helped by being one of the first bands to assemble our own travelling public-address system, so that we had control over the quality of the sound regardless of the venue and what they'd come up with.

'So we played with Little Richard, including a live television show on Granada, Jerry Lee Lewis, Ben E. King, Gene Pitney, all of them. When Richard arrived he handed us these parts but they were all gospel songs. We reckoned he was going to die if he went out there and did that stuff. But he kept us working on them, then there'd suddenly be a glint in his eye and he'd go into "Good Golly Miss Molly". And of course we'd be ready for him. Then Epstein took us on to back Cilla Black, because her style needed a fuller backing than his band, the Remo Four, could supply.'

And so as Sound Incorporated graduated to becoming headliners in their own right, there was an inevitable but amicable split with Vincent. 'He was a magical performer on his day,' says Thomas. 'Today you can manufacture anything, put it on television and have a hit. But in those days you needed something special, and he had it.'

In December Columbia released 'Where Have You Been All My Life' and 'Temptation Baby', and Vincent filmed a cameo performance miming to the latter title for a forgettable film called *Live It Up*.

1964

With the Rolling Stones joining the Beatles in the charts, the 'British invasion' gained momentum early in 1964. It was a countrywide phenomenon, with successful groups springing up in every city and hundreds of others playing in the clubs every night. There was Liverpool, of course (the Searchers, Gerry and the Pacemakers, Billy J. Kramer and the Dakotas, the Merseybeats, the Swinging Blue Jeans, the

Fourmost and many more), London (Manfred Mann, the Dave Clark Five, Georgie Fame and the Blue Flames, the Kinks), Belfast (Them), Newcastle (the Animals), Sheffield (Dave Berry and the Cruisers), Birmingham (the Spencer Davis Group) and Manchester (John Mayall and the Bluesbreakers, Herman's Hermits).

If late 1963 represented the heights of Vincent's emotional turmoil and irrational behaviour, the New Year brought a fresh professional challenge as the old order of rock gave way to noisy, chirpy Britishers. Vincent's reaction was to hire a Liverpool band, the Shouts, and to go back to his trademark black leather.

Although Vincent had always been able to use his extraordinarily expressive voice to good effect on some unlikely material, notably his masterly 'Over the Rainbow', the attempts by various producers of the late 1950s and early '60s to turn him into a straight pop singer, with strings and backing chorus, had not been a success. His chart career in America never revived, and after that first UK tour his three further UK hits were all rockers – 'Pistol Packin' Mama', 'She She Little Sheila' and 'I'm Going Home'.

Whether they realised this, or were merely desperate, Columbia allowed him and the Shouts to record a rock'n'roll album, *Shakin' Up a Storm*. Along with rock classics like Little Richard's 'Long Tall Sally' and Dale Hawkins's 'Suzie Q' he revisited 'Baby Blue', and unlike his later returns to 'Be Bop a Lula' the result was a dynamic re-reading of one of his strongest numbers.

All the time, the condition of his left leg was getting worse – the original accident, the Cochran crash, Vincent's stubborn refusal to follow medical advice, his wild stage act when sheer adrenaline proved a powerful painkiller, and the frequent fractures, each weakening the bone – all these were leading to the gradual development of osteomyelitis within the bone itself, which had he lived would inevitably have led to amputation.

One of the drummers he worked with in the mid-'60s, as the bone disease took hold, was Terry Noon, who vividly contrasted the onstage athlete with the backstage cripple, writing in the *Gene Vincent Fan Club Magazine*. 'Not many people realised after seeing him going from one end of the stage to another with just the microphone as an aid, that off stage he could hardly walk without the aid of two crutches. He would take codeine tablets to relieve the pain and the daily consumption of these obviously increased.'

The crutches came in handy one night when a taunting crowd in the car park proved too daunting even for Peter Grant, who had now succeeded Henry Henroid as Vincent's road manager. Like Arden, Grant was to become one of the legends of the business for his strong-arm tactics, particularly when protecting the interests of his most celebrated charges, Led Zeppelin. But on this occasion even he wanted to summon police assistance, so Vincent waded in, crutch swirling around his head, and dispersed his tormentors.

Vincent's private life took a turn for the better, as far as he was concerned, when he began to see Jackie Fusco, stage name Frisco, a South African singer whom he had first met when touring her country in 1961. She was the sister-in-law of singer and later record producer Mickie Most, and she now turned up in London to get reacquainted with Vincent. One charming photograph in the possession of the Craddock family, reprinted in Britt Hagarty's biography, shows them arm in arm in Trafalgar Square, feeding the pigeons like young lovers do. Jekyll and Hyde? Schizoid? It is impossible to detect the mad, violent, crippled, drunken Vincent in this tousle-haired, carefree tourist.

But, of course, he was still married to Margie, and had abandoned her and Sherri. 'I was just left in Streatham,' she says. 'And he went off touring with Jackie Frisco. I knew that she had always had a soft spot for him, and as soon as I was out of the way it started up.'

One of the tours was *The Big Beat Show* of 1964, six weeks on the road performing two shows a night. As well as Vincent and the Shouts, the bill consisted of Preston band the Puppets, the Beat Merchants, Daryl Quist, the Applejacks, Lulu and the Luvvers, Millie, and the Honeycombs. Vincent was clearly impressed by the Puppets, because they were to become his next backing band.

Late in 1964 Vincent and Jackie went to South Africa, and thence to the USA and down to New Mexico where his parents were then living. On 29 December 1964 Vincent applied for a divorce from Margie, in the court at Albuquerque, New Mexico, citing mental cruelty, adultery and the fact that she had left the family home. He stated that he was a resident of Albuquerque – his parents were then living there. He did not inform Margie of this action. This divorce did not stand scrutiny in the UK, but he went ahead and married Jackie.

'I didn't know for some time that he'd gone down to New Mexico and applied for a divorce,' says Margie. 'He said I'd deserted him and that I'd agreed to a divorce, which simply wasn't true.' The divorce was finally granted on 27 August 1965, with the agreement that Sherri would remain with Margie and that Vincent would pay child maintenance.

'He was coming backwards and forwards,' says Margie. 'He got a letter from my solicitors. He said that we weren't married any more but in the eyes of the British authorities we were. The Mexican divorce was ruled to be invalid because there had been no attempt to contact me. So I was granted the divorce, on the grounds of cruelty. It seems that after that he married Jackie in Las Vegas. You know, it is very ironic, but she was in the process of filing for divorce when he died. She had served papers on him three times but he had just ignored them, he hadn't responded. She was about to go to court. So when he died she was still married and got the estate, but she might have had no claim. She ignored Sherri's existence even though she knew of her.

'When I finally left him I went to a hotel in Bayswater with Sherri. I took all my furniture and curtains and so on and put them in storage. I think Don Arden arranged the hotel. I couldn't work and the idea of going on social security seemed very alien – I'd always worked. The idea of saying that you hadn't got any money, when you were married to a rock'n'roll star, it would have been hard to believe. But the thing is that as far as Gene was concerned when something ended, it ended. Just like that.'

Adrian Owlett agrees. 'He was totally compartmentalised. He just moved on, and the past was dead.'

1965

On returning to Britain early in the year, Vincent asked if he could have the Puppets as his backing band. They were managed by Joe Meek and recorded for him for most of the 1960s. They also became one of the house bands for the major booking agency the George Cooper Organisation, backing such visitors as Brenda Lee and the Ronettes. The band consisted of Des O'Reilly on drums and vocals, Dave Millen on guitar and Jim Whittle on bass. A year after they started they were augmented on Hammond organ by Don Parfitt. After rehearsals, and dates in Britain, France and Germany, they settled in for a summer season at the Rainbow Theatre in Blackpool, and reckon that they did up to 200 shows with Vincent.

O'Reilly recalls the visit to Germany, which inevitably included a return to the Star Club. 'We discovered just how big a star Gene was there. He was huge . . . Gene, having been to Hamburg before, took us to a bar where it turned out all the "waitresses" were actually blokes. When one of the band members tried to hit on one of these "waitresses" Gene thought it was hilarious!

'He asked us if we'd like to share a house together for the season when we got to Blackpool. He also said that he would pay the first £10 of the rent, provided that he could have a room of his own. We ended up getting a large, multi-bedroom property on the North Shore, and it cost only £12 a week.'

Also on the Blackpool scene that summer was another Preston band led by David Smith – David John and the Mood. John recalls: 'Once Vincent showed me a dog-eared black-and-white snapshot he carried with him all the time. It was of Eddie Cochran, backstage on the UK tour, talking to two girls in a corridor. The light had cast a shape on the crown of Eddie's head in the shape of a crucifix. Of course it was just a trick of the light, but Gene treated that photograph with such reverence. It was an indication to me of how important Eddie had been to him.

'On another occasion I visited the house where Gene was staying with the Puppets. He was reading a newspaper. He suddenly said, "It's gonna rain." He said it again. I assumed he was looking at the weather forecast. He said, "No. My leg's leaking. When it leaks, it rains." Within about twelve minutes, totally without warning, it started to rain. Not a storm or anything. Just a cloud passing over.

'Gene could be frightening, with his mood changes. He had a bullwhip, maybe twelve or fifteen feet long. When he got morose and bad-tempered with all the drink and the medication he'd get it out and start cracking it. You knew that he was a man in pain, both physical and emotional. But at other times he was such a gentle and genuine guy that I found it easy to forgive.

'Because he could be very kind. One time I was upstairs at the house and my band had a record out, produced by Joe Meek. It was a cover of Bo Diddley's "Bring It To Jerome". One of the guys said, "Come downstairs. Your record's on Radio Caroline." I said it was on a lot at the time. "No, no. Gene's listening to it." He was sober, standing in the kitchen, concentrating on the record. He said, "I know what makes a good record, and that's a good record." Well, it couldn't have been more flattering if Elvis had said it.

'One day the band invited me to the show. I watched Gene and Jackie leave the house. As he walked down the path he looked so old and worn that I wasn't sure I wanted to go. I expected a travesty of the old Gene Vincent. Well, I've worked alongside a lot of big names but he was simply fantastic. The performance, the physical presence, they commanded attention, but it was the voice that drew you in. The apprehension I'd felt just washed away. I felt so grateful to have seen him perform that night. It was a privilege.

'That voice just took the breath away. I was stunned by its beauty. Years later I was asked to front a Gene Vincent tribute band but I couldn't do it, unfortunately, because of ill health. But I did get round to writing a song about him, called "Rollin' Danny". "Remember the man sweet Gene, Vincent and his Blue Caps mean, Way back forty or fifty years ago, His dirty beat was the music on the boppin' floor, So one more time now just for you, Rollin' Danny gonna play Mr Vincent's blues." '

The Blackpool stint, with Jackie, his new band, a settled routine, a short set and the sea air was a rare – and inevitably short-lived – period of calm in Vincent's turbulent life. Late in the summer, things began to close in. As Adrian Owlett has put it: 'I think that Don Arden was starting to get heavy. Margie was also getting heavy. Don Arden's business methods were very suspect. Things weren't going that good. The world started shrinking in on Gene. His creditors and would-be creditors were getting ready to pounce. He'd had a very successful season and if anyone was getting ready to pounce, then now was the time.'

In September it became too much for Vincent, and he suddenly upped and left Britain for South Africa, with Jackie in tow, cursing Don Arden and all his tormentors. With her contacts and the lingering charisma of his name he found work there for a while before heading back to America. He went into a period of withdrawal and retirement, staying with his parents in Albuquerque over Christmas as he had done a year earlier, and remaining there into the New Year.

1966

Vincent's leg now needed further attention, and he checked into the Veterans' Administration Hospital in Albuquerque where, as an ex-serviceman injured while on navy duty, he was still entitled to treatment. The specialists eventually decided on amputation as the only satisfactory option and, although he may now have begun to realise that this would soon be inevitable, he took fright, and escaped in a cab.

It was soon time to go back to work. He made contact with one of his former musicians, guitarist and ex-Champ Dave Burgess, now an executive at Challenge Records in Los Angeles. Burgess was happy to cut a session with him, and it resulted in 'Bird Doggin'' and 'Ain't That Too Much'. Vincent and Jackie, optimistic that a new chapter was beginning, moved back to Los Angeles. Jerry Lee Merritt provided his old partner with two new songs, 'Hurtin' For You Baby' and 'Born To Be a Rolling Stone', the latter a poignant slice of biography tailored for Vincent. Released as a single, 'Bird Doggin'' did little, and so did the Challenge follow-up 'Lonely Street' and 'I've Got My Eyes on You'. Apart from his

Challenge sessions Vincent did little, nursing his leg and convalescing. Other tracks recorded for Challenge at various sessions from June 1966 were 'I'm a Lonesome Fugitive', 'Hi Lili Hi Lo', 'Poor Man's Prison', 'Words and Music', 'Love is a Bird' and 'Am I That Easy to Forget'. They eventually appeared on a UK album, *Gene Vincent*.

1967

In January Vincent was briefly reunited with Jerry Lee Merritt and they returned to Japan. Although the hysteria of eight years earlier was more muted, he was still welcome in this outpost of rock'n'roll.

In the summer Challenge released an album, *Gene Vincent*, while in the UK EMI put together *The Best of Gene Vincent*, the first such compilation of his best material. On 11 September he and Jackie arrived in Paris for another French tour. After rehearsals with a French band called Le Rock'n'roll Gang the tour began in Rennes, where he was enthusiastically welcomed. As he moved around France it was clear that he was still regarded, as one banner proclaimed, as 'The Rock'n'roll King', and he was on great form. He was equally well received during a brief diversion into Switzerland.

There were, of course, the usual problems with promoters regarding money, and occasional fights with Jackie. However Adrian Owlett, who rode his motorbike down to join Vincent on the tour, confirms that it was, in general, a successful return to Europe.

In the autumn Vincent began working once more with Oregon-based promoter Pat Mason, who had briefly managed and booked him in 1959. Mason reported that Vincent seemed in good shape. 'Gene looked fine. [He] always drank a lot, ever since I can remember him. But he seemed to have a good relationship with Jackie and she was taking care of him.'

1968

Mason booked Vincent into gigs around the Northwest, and in the spring sent him out on a lengthy tour of the Midwest. A projected return to the UK was put on hold due to illness, but at the end of the month Vincent was back in the studio in Los Angeles to record 'Story of the Rockers', written by local disc jockey Jim Pewter, and 'Pickin' Poppies', written by Vincent with Jackie. The former is a roll call of the greats, plus Bobby Rydell, while the Vincent–Frisco cut would seem to be an anti-drug anthem. They were released on Pewter's own label, Playground, and did nothing.

In September Vincent and Jackie moved to Simi Valley, just outside Los Angeles, and their address – significantly or not – was on Cochran

Street. The 1961 recording 'Lucky Star' was put out by Capitol, and his contract with Challenge ran out, not to be renewed. Vincent had hit another quiet period.

1969

Although Vincent had no record label, he had the satisfaction of knowing that EMI in the UK valued his Capitol back catalogue enough to put out a second *Best of . . .* volume in February. In early summer he cut four songs at his own expense at G&M Studios in Hollywood, 'Rainy Day Sunshine', 'Green Grass', 'Mr Love' and 'Roll Over Beethoven'. Finding no interest in America, he sent an acetate to Adrian Owlett in London. 'I've still got it,' says Owlett, who contacted Radio 1 disc jockey John Peel, an avowed Vincent fan.

Peel was at the time co-owner of the Dandelion label with Clive Selwood, and he later recalled in his *Radio Times* column: 'I only met Gene Vincent once, although he did make a rather disappointing album for a company with which I was associated. He asked me, I remember, if I knew where there was a phone he could use. I did and was able to tell the lithe rocker so. He smiled and thanked me.'

Apart from Gene Vincent, Dandelion's best-known act was Principal Edward's Magic Theatre, hardly a household name, and the label ran out of steam and folded in 1972. The one-off Dandelion deal with Vincent produced the album *I'm Back and I'm Proud*. Selwood put Vincent into a Los Angeles studio with the eccentric Kim Fowley as producer and bass player Skip Battin as musical director. As half of Skip and Flip, Battin had enjoyed three hits a decade earlier, notably 'Cherry Pie', and was now a member of the Byrds.

Selwood recalls: 'Kim advanced across the room and said, "Hey, grease me some of that teenage dogshit!" . . . Gene was a bit odd and Kim Fowley was considerably odder.'

'Gene was a difficult artist in some ways,' says Battin. 'He was a bit of a perfectionist and Kim likes to move pretty quickly. Gene tried very hard, but he was pretty sick at the time. His leg was bothering him and he was in constant pain.'

Surprisingly, perhaps, Vincent was not drinking at all during the weeklong sessions. Perhaps he should have been, because the results are disappointing. He revives Bobby Day's chirpy 1958 hit 'Rockin' Robin', Hank Ballard's 'Sexy Ways', the Big Bopper's 'White Lightnin'' (which in 1960 he had taped for the BBC with Cochran), another 'Be Bop a Lula' and a revival of 'Lotta Lovin'', together with two country songs, 'Rainbow at Midnight' and 'In the Pines'. The other tracks were 'Black

Letter', 'Ruby Baby', 'Circle Never Broken', 'I Heard That Lonesome Whistle' and 'Scarlet Ribbons'. Even Battin was lukewarm. 'I was familiar with his Capitol records with the Blue Caps and I kind of preferred them.'

Battin had assembled an impressive list of musicians, however. Red Rhodes played pedal steel and dobro, Mars Bonfire was on rhythm guitar, Jim Gordon on drums, Grant Johnson on piano and Battin himself on bass, and the icing on the cake was that Johnny Meeks came in to play lead guitar, replacing the originally hired Jim Fonseca. Vincent may have faded commercially in America, but he was still a legend in the business – among those who dropped by the sessions were Jim Morrison, Linda Ronstadt, John Sebastian and Michael Jackson.

There was tension between Vincent and Fowley, and Vincent would regularly call Adrian Owlett complaining that his songs were being ruined. When Don Arden heard about the sessions he threatened Selwood, claiming to have a contract that covered all Vincent's activities, but after some ritual blustering he failed to provide the paperwork in evidence of his claim. The record failed to do much, though it was reissued in the UK by Magnum Force in 1981 as *The Bop They Couldn't Stop*.

In September Vincent was at the Varsity Stadium in Toronto to take part in what was originally billed as a rock'n'roll festival, until John Lennon chose it as the occasion to launch his new Plastic Ono Band, featuring a shrieking Yoko Ono and a bemused Eric Clapton. The event was filmed by the 'rockumentary' pioneer D.A. Pennebaker, director of such classic rock movies as Bob Dylan's *Don't Look Back* and the festival film *Monterey Pop*. The film, originally titled *Sweet Toronto*, went through various edits and eventually emerged as a straight rock'n'roll movie, *Keep On Rockin'*, starring Little Richard, Jerry Lee Lewis, Bo Diddley and Chuck Berry.

Vincent's tearful, drunken performance did not even survive the first cut. He went on after Alice Cooper and was backed by Cooper's band, picking his way through the chicken feathers and other detritus of Cooper's act. He had been drinking all day in excessive heat, and did not take to the stage until early evening. But there was to be some positive news from Capitol in America before the year was out – at long last they put out a 'Best of . . .' compilation, *Gene Vincent's Greatest*.

In October Vincent was in France for a short and disastrous tour. Vincent's luggage failed to arrive in Paris, mislaid by the airline. At Lyon his backing band failed to turn up and the last-minute replacements were clearly unfamiliar with the material. The same misfortune occurred at Grenoble and the deputising band was even worse. Promoters disappeared when it was time to pay up, and Vincent and Rob Finnis, who was acting as road manager, were mugged in their hotel room. Anything that could go wrong did.

On the morning of 5 November Vincent arrived at Heathrow from Paris for yet another UK tour, this time trailed by a BBC camera crew for a documentary directed by Tony Wheeler, to be called *The Rock'n'roll Singer*. There was a glimpse of Peter Noone of Herman's Hermits also arriving, probably wondering how he had gained so many fans with greased-back hair and drape jackets. In welcoming Vincent, disc jockey Emperor Rosko probed fearlessly, asking him for his loves and hates. 'I love my wife and my dog,' Vincent replied. 'My hate is French groups, because they never turn up. They'd book a place and I'd go to the place a couple of hours before the show – and no group.'

Alas, his bad experiences in France were to continue, in the country that allegedly held Vincent in greater affection than any other – although these days Holland might challenge that assumption. He said that the reason for his visit was to promote his new single and album under the deal with Dandelion – the remake of 'Be Bop a Lula' and *I'm Back and I'm Proud*, produced in Hollywood by Kim Fowley – but he forgot to mention the name of either.

The BBC film, even without the hindsight that Vincent was within two years of his death, is darkly poignant. He limped badly, was short of breath – late in his life asthma was added to his list of problems – and he seemed decidedly unwell. Although those famous cheekbones had long been clothed in a softening layer of flesh, there was still a strange and peaceful beauty in his face. Even when he was the shortest member of the group, which was often, he stood out – and not just because he was Gene Vincent, and therefore the centre of attention. He still had charisma.

In fact he was often not centre stage, but a forlorn and abandoned figure resignedly watching the wheels fall off his faltering career. What came over most strongly in this badly lit film – undoubtedly in the interests of naturalism and spontaneity, it should be said – was his fatalistic dignity. He was almost unfailingly polite and, while there was no humour to be gained from his physical condition, the grey English weather, the cramped rehearsal facilities, the modest venues and the invariably missing cash, he seemed to want to find reasons to smile.

We all know that Vincent was a deeply flawed character, but it is impossible not to feel both pity and admiration for him, watching this bleak procession. At one point he sat down 'before I fall down', but he said it with a weary smile. The self-pity that people such as Sharon Sheeley found so off-putting no longer seemed to exist. It was almost as if he was quietly preparing for death.

He accepted a last-minute invitation to sing on Thames Television's early evening magazine programme *The Today Show*, hosted by Eamonn Andrews, because 'we've got no choice'. But of course the party arrived at the studio too late, delayed by a flurry of transport, equipment and costume problems.

However, the invitation was repeated and he ripped into 'Be Bop a Lula' in front of a handful of press-ganged jivers hauled in by rock'n'roll publicist Waxie Maxie, a hilarious contrast with Andrews' previous item, a solemn list of the meat-and-veg prices to be expected in the weekend markets. His demeanour in the wings and after the song, waiting until he was sure he was no longer in shot, was utterly disciplined. Afterwards, Vincent was ushered into Andrews' presence and was graciously, modestly deferential, the rock'n'roll legend enjoying a joke with Seamus Android. It was almost unbearably sad.

Vincent displayed strange fixations. 'Hitler ran the Gestapo and the CIA run the President. That's the difference. The President don't know who runs the CIA. Nobody knows. It's a secret.' This might have seemed to be an admirable summary of America's clandestine foreign policy in the dark days of Nixon and Kissinger, were it not combined with a passing dig at 'students', in other words troublemakers. It suddenly seemed possible that he voted for Nixon, if he could have been bothered, and that he was actually expressing sympathy for the corrupt politician.

Later he waxed enthusiastically about Japanese ingenuity. He had reason to admire the Japanese, because audiences there hero-worshipped him, and he no doubt recalled the ecstatic reaction to him on his 1959 tour with Jerry Lee Merritt. There was, he insisted, a needle so fine you could hardly see it with the naked eye, sent round the world on exhibition. 'The Japanese cut it in half, drilled it out, put another needle inside and sent it back.' If he had not been in a Transit van at the time you would surely have edged away from him, before he got on to Scientology or Tarot cards.

There were earnest discussions about getting money up front – 'I hate to do it that way' – but they were invariably thwarted, in spite of the best efforts of his helpers like Rob Finnis and Adrian Owlett. As he sat dejectedly backstage he said, with a deep sigh: 'This is the hard part. Waiting to rehearse. Waiting to get on.' Just living was getting to be the hard part, for a man who had only ever really come alive when on stage.

The one piece of comic relief showed Vincent having his hair washed before his television spot, reluctantly being eased into a hairnet before sitting under the dryer 'like a girl'. What is striking watching it today is that the woman humouring and mothering him had a cut-glass accent nowadays only heard at polo grounds or in radio comedies written by Simon Brett. At what stage, one wonders, did Essex girl take over the entire hairdressing and make-up industry?

On the chilly Isle of Wight Vincent fought to preserve his fragile equanimity. 'The procedure is, after I finish the show the manager is supposed to bring me my money, the receipts and so on,' he explained patiently. 'He's supposed to sign them and leave. I take the money, sign the receipts, pay my hotel bill and leave. Which is not gonna happen . . .'

In the most touching scene of all he stripped off his sweaty shirt – revealing a paunch, but nothing too startling for such a devoted drinker – and said: 'Tell that man I want my money or else there's gonna be trouble.' He said it in a tired, resigned voice, knowing that his fighting days were over and so, it seemed, was his influence over such essential matters as getting paid. Then came the killer. 'What's in my pocket? Ninepence. Even you [the television crew] bought the sandwiches, you know? It's embarrassing . . .'

'A lot of stuff was too frightening to put in the film,' said Wheeler. 'We felt that Henry Henroid was in league with Don Arden.'

And yet, assisted by a dynamite band in the Wild Angels, Vincent was transformed on stage, a seasoned professional doing the only thing he knew. Late in 1969, he still had it. Yes, the waiting was indeed the hard part, because once he was on stage his existence was justified, and he did indeed come alive, even though the stages were now cramped and tatty, the dressing rooms rudimentary, and his fee had gone walkabout.

The Wild Angels were by this time established as the UK's top rock'n'roll revival band. They were formed in 1967 and 'Wild' Bill Kingston joined as pianist in the following year, when they supported Bill Haley and Duane Eddy. In 1969 they released their version of Cochran's 'Nervous Breakdown' as their debut single (and when original bass player Mitch Mitchell left, it was to form a group called Somethin' Else). Kingston says: 'Our first album sold one and a quarter million worldwide. We got about £620. The record company went bust to avoid paying us.

'When the film was shown, for some reason they pretended it covered the first four days of the tour, but they were with us for two weeks,' says Kingston. The crew developed a protective attitude towards

Vincent, seeing the plight he found himself in, and stayed on longer than they had been booked for. 'We got on with Gene really well,' continues Kingston. 'There's a lot of misinformation about him – there were no problems at all between us and him. His only problem was with Don Arden, getting the money out of him, although *we* got paid. If Arden had wanted to argue with us he'd have been picking on the wrong people. But Gene always reckoned it was a problem. Yes, I reckon he was conned.

'But Arden was the sort of guy who would set people up when they got here – house, car, gigs, whatever. One day he's going to call that money back. I'm prepared to believe he took back more than he should have, but in the end somebody's got to pay the bills. That's why so many of the rockers insisted on the money up front. As Chuck Berry said, you don't let a dog bite you twice.

'I remember when we were playing Belfast, we'd only done four or five numbers when they stopped the show because of a bomb scare, so Gene didn't even get on the stage. Then we had to drive across the border to Dublin. The police were after Gene because he wasn't paying his alimony, and he was convinced that there'd be armed border guards waiting to arrest him. So we smuggled him across, disguised as an armchair! I sat him down on a box and draped a blanket over him. Made it look good.

'Although he was drinking all the time he was still a very good performer. In fact I never saw him drunk – he seemed to get acclimatised to it. Sometimes he seemed a bit distracted, maybe thinking about being ripped off, but on form he was magnificent. The voice was still there – take "Over the Rainbow". No other rocker could sing that. Gene was very laid back. He didn't walk around thinking he was a genius. In fact he was humble. He thought he was lucky to get the chance. I shall always remember him as being very good to work with.'

Adrian Owlett, with whom Vincent stayed in Walton-on-Thames during this visit, agrees with Kingston regarding Vincent's drinking. 'His threshold was far greater than most and it did not affect him too much.' However, he was on his best behaviour while the film crew were tagging along. 'That tour saw Gene in probably his least-drunk state,' recalls Owlett. 'Certainly during the BBC filming period he drank only infrequently, as he was well aware that he needed to keep cool. He was being pursued by Don Arden.

'He was also in great pain during the tour. My own doctor attended him and prescribed injections of morphine and morphine-based tablets to be taken daily. When he mixed these with drink it did have an adverse effect on occasions. My view is that Gene held it together very well on that visit, though – much better than he did on the final tour, when drink was a serious problem. So my impression is that in relation to Gene's capacity the drinking was in check.'

In Owlett's recollection, therefore, the film's editor had no need to be diplomatic in making sure that any drinking was cut out, because Vincent was aware of the potential problem. On the ferry heading for the Isle of Wight he was filmed taking two pills, but these could well have been the prescribed morphine, and there was only one glimpse of a bottle – Vincent's now chosen tipple, red Martini. And it is Owlett who is carrying it!

The tour continued in disastrous fashion, with bookings cancelled, cheques bouncing and various parties in pursuit of the hapless Vincent. Owlett says: 'There was the Inland Revenue, Margie seeking child support and agents for Don Arden, who claimed he had exclusive management on Vincent in perpetuity, and was after a slice of the action.'

Arden's beef was that Henry Henroid had suddenly reappeared on the scene and was promoting the tour independently of his former employer. According to Adrian Owlett, Henroid – who died in 1998 – paid himself 30% of the take plus expenses!

Owlett recalls that at the first gig, the Royal York Hotel in Ryde, on the Isle of Wight, there was an Arden 'representative' there called Wilf Pine. 'Wilf and some of his chums did their best to damage Gene by giving him Mickey Finns, but we managed to ensure that they were unsuccessful. The object was to make Gene incapable, cop the dough that had been paid up front and leave us high and dry. As it was, Gene was stone-cold sober and did a great show – but we still did not get paid. There was something of a battle between Henry Henroid and Wilf but the net result was that we left the Isle of Wight without a fee being paid to Gene. The BBC had to buy our breakfast. Henry's reasoning was that there were "people who had to be paid" – end of story!

'We also got wind that Margie was after him. When I took Gene to London airport on the Sunday night as he was leaving for Ireland, I was approached by a process server who asked if I was Gene Vincent! In all honesty I could assure him that I wasn't and with that he wandered off, failing to notice Gene limping along beside me, presumably looking just a bit more like a rock'n'roller than I did!

'Then I received a letter from the Inland Revenue, who were claiming back tax – unpaid, it said, for most of the time that Gene had been resident in the UK during the early '60s. I was able to keep them on the back burner but they made it clear that although Gene was out of their jurisdiction they would deal with him when he returned to the country. In fact on his next tour, at the Coronation Hall in Kingston, where he was playing with the Houseshakers, the Inland Revenue did indeed serve him with a demand. As events panned out, of course, they never did get their money.'

After the disastrous experience on the Isle of Wight, however, there were some high points on the tour. One was a gig at the nightclub that was the favourite hang-out for musicians at the time, the Speakeasy. 'Gene went on and slayed the audience,' remembers Owlett. 'Nearly through the set, Georgie Fame took over on piano . . . Gene broke all house box-office records and the audience included many stars such as John and Yoko, George Harrison, some of the Who . . . In the end there were dozens of people who came to congratulate Gene.' Another prestigious and successful gig was at the London Palladium, perhaps the most celebrated variety theatre in the country.

1970

The *I'm Back and I'm Proud* album was released in January, and in March the leading rock paper *Rolling Stone* ran a complimentary piece on Vincent. At this time he acquired a new manager, Tom Ayres, who had been Johnny Burnette's bass player at the time the Blue Caps started. He also managed Texan band the Sir Douglas Quintet, led by Doug Sahm, and he put Vincent and the band, without Sahm, together at the Sound Factory in Los Angeles.

The resulting album, *Gene Vincent* (called *If Only You Could See Me Today* in the UK), was another failure, although Vincent gave a good reading of Bobby Bare's wistful 1963 hit '500 Miles'. Like similar attempts by Chess Records at this time to 'update' the sound of such 1950s legends as Howlin' Wolf and Bo Diddley, the album by and large simply proved that late-1960s guitar gadgets and rock'n'roll do not mix.

In March Vincent played a rock'n'roll revival show in Madison Square Gardens, New York, alongside Little Richard and Bo Diddley, put on by promoter Richard Nader, and then returned to California for a San Francisco gig with country-rock band Commander Cody and the Lost Planet Airmen, on a bill headlined by Merle Haggard. At this time he was briefly reunited with his children by Darlene, Vince and Melody.

In June Vincent was back in Paris for yet another tour, this time backed by another British rock'n'roll band, the Houseshakers. Graham Fenton was their regular singer, and performed the warm-up set with the band. 'I first saw Gene in 1964,' he says, 'when he was touring with the Shouts, at Hounslow Baths. In winter they'd board over the pool and put on shows. It sent shivers down my spine – he was the first rock'n'roll star I'd ever seen live, and it was bedlam. When he came on and started swinging the microphone the crowd went absolutely wild.

'Then I saw him again in 1969 when he was with the Wild Angels. He became my mentor, really, my biggest influence. That haunting voice never left him. When I got to work with him I saw both the hero and the tormented man. The pain in his leg was constant. I was learning the trade and he was very helpful to me.

'But there were two Genes. When he was sober he was a polite, quiet, Southern gentleman. When he was drunk he gave everyone a hard time. He was like a coiled spring, he could snap at any time. But with all the dodgy promoters and the endless travelling and the pain he was in, I can sympathise somewhat.'

Fenton recalled one story that Vincent told him about Cochran. 'Well, you know Eddie was a practical joker – pulling the communication cord on the train and all that. Gene said that if you knocked on his hotel door he would sometimes answer it with no clothes on, with no idea who was on the other side.'

Later Fenton became lead singer with Matchbox, one of the pioneer 'rockabilly revival' bands of the late 1970s and the most successful commercially. They had eight hits between 1979 and 1982, including a medley of 'Over the Rainbow', Vincent style, and 'You Belong to Me', the 1962 harmony hit by the Duprees. They made the Top Ten with 'When You Ask About Love'.

'Later on,' says Fenton, 'I was privileged to sing with the Blue Caps, over in America and across Europe. Johnny Meeks, Bubba Facenda, Dickie Harrell. We went from Hollywood up to San Diego. We also played Clear Lake, Iowa, at a big Buddy Holly memorial festival. Bubba said it was just like the old days. He said that in spite of all the problems it was fun touring with Gene. Any bad feelings were soon forgotten.'

Terry Clemson was guitarist with the Houseshakers. As Terry Gibson he had been in 1960s band Downliners Sect, club heroes who stubbornly refused to make the charts, though they came very close with their revival of the Coasters' 'Little Egypt'. After working with Vincent on the 1970 tour of France and again in 1971, he then backed both Bo Diddley and Chuck Berry at the 1972 Wembley Rock'n'roll Festival, before forming another rock'n'roll outfit, the Hellraisers. In the early 1980s he spent two years touring with Johnny and the Hurricanes before forming his current band, the TTs. The Houseshakers were completed by saxophonist John Earl, bass player Jimmy Walls and drummer Billy Williams.

Clemson remembers Vincent fondly. 'He never shouted at anyone. There's a story in one book that he bawled me out at a gig in Norwich because my guitar was out of tune. He didn't. I noticed that I had slipped a bit out of tune and wondered what the hell I should do. I was nervous of stopping Gene in mid-number, to say the least, so I was really sweating. But it didn't matter, because he just turned to me and said, "You're a little bit out of tune there." That was it. I tuned up while he waited, and we carried on. He certainly didn't lose his temper.'

Clemson came to play with his hero because 'Earl Sheridan was managing the Houseshakers and he had contact with Gene, and also with Adrian Owlett. He arranged the French tour. I remember that until we were on the boat I never thought it would actually happen. We first met up with him in Paris.

'The first gig was in the open air [at Saint-Gobert], and we had about half an hour to rehearse beforehand. Everything was so loose and disorganised – that first day we were meant to do a double, somewhere else in the evening. But we didn't realise how far it was. We just didn't get there in time. Gene had travelled on by car and he had to go on with one of the other bands backing him, while we followed on in our old beat-up van. That's how badly organised it was – the gigs were simply too far apart.'

Sheridan, perhaps not surprisingly, remembers it differently. In a review posted on the Internet he says that, after the open-air performance: 'No sooner had the last note disappeared before the artists had boarded the band wagon and were on their way to the second show of the evening . . . where the Vincent show played to a capacity audience of nearly 2,000 people. The first day had been very tiring but very successful.'

'It was a nightmare really,' Clemson continues, 'and gigs were being cancelled. In the promoter's home town we didn't get on because he wouldn't come up with the money.' Here, Sheridan agrees. 'Due to very bad organisation and non-payment to artistes, the French fans were deprived of seeing Gene Vincent perform this night and [they] spent the entire evening showing their disapproval.'

'Everyone said that if Gene was still big anywhere it was in France,' says Clemson. 'But you wouldn't have known it from the organisation. The gigs were well attended, sure, but they were fairly small. It was such a shame – I felt sorry for him, because it was all out of his control. None of this happened because of his waywardness, and he just put up with it. But at least we could say that we had toured with the great Gene Vincent. And he was always easy to get on with – he was on his own, making the best of it.'

Vincent was back in America at the end of June, and a new single, 'Sunshine', was released. In October he returned to the studio, and it was a more successful venture than the previous few sessions had been. He cut a meditative original, 'The Day the World Turned Blue', Mickey Newbury's 'How I Love Them Old Songs', Carl Perkins's 'Boppin' the Blues', Gene Allison's 1957 soul hit 'You Can Make It If You Try', Brook Benton's 'Looking Back' and Big Jay McNeely's 'There Is Something On Your Mind'. Other tracks included 'High On Life', 'North Carolina Line', 'Looking Back' and 'Oh, Lonesome Me'. The session ended with 'The Woman In Black', another Vincent original. Perhaps the most telling song, however, is 'Our Souls'. As Vincent repeats the title phrase it clearly becomes 'Arseholes', and just to make his intention clear he says, 'How's that, Mr Arden?'

Towards the end of the year Rob Finnis stayed with Vincent and Jackie Frisco in Los Angeles. Although he had reputedly been 'dry' during that recording session, he was now back on the bottle with a vengeance. 'Gene used to sneak down to the garage in the basement,' says Finnis. 'One time Jackie came up from the basement with about twenty empty bottles and screamed at him, "You said you were going to stop drinking!" Sometimes he would be pissed before eleven o'clock. One time he was drunk, his whole face almost purple, crawling on his knees in the kitchen . . .' This image, of course, is a chilling foretaste of the way he died.

1971

Vincent's marriage to Jackie was effectively over, but he was not alone for long. He met a woman called Marcia Avron in Waldorf, Maryland, and she became his last significant partner. *The Day the World Turned Blue* was released in January on Kama Sutra, and at long last represented a return to form. Not the form of 1957, of course, but so much better than the standard of most of his late-1960s recordings.

Graham Fenton met Vincent and Marcia at Heathrow in his 1959 Chevrolet, and on the way back into London he deliberately drove past the rocker and biker hangout the Ace Café on the North Circular Road, pointing it out to Vincent as a place where his music had never died.

Vincent was supported on this tour by Lee Tracey and the Tributes, and the first gigs of this latest visit were at Liverpool Polytechnic, Bangor University and a coffee bar in Norwich, where Clemson's guitar slipped out of tune. Adrian Owlett drove Vincent up to Liverpool to start the tour. 'I have to admit I found Gene a bit flaky,' says Clemson. 'He didn't seem to have much of a sense of humour. You could hardly blame him,

I suppose. He'd been used to better things. These tours were shabby. And of course he was in fairly constant pain. He'd have these strange ideas that he'd suddenly come out with. He said that in Japan they had wristwatch TVs, but they couldn't be exported because they would ruin the world economy!

'He used to carry a briefcase everywhere. Inside there were three bottles of red Martini, and he'd drink his way through them during the day. I guess his ulcers were getting worse – I never saw him drinking scotch, and maybe he thought that Martini was less harmful. I heard that he coughed up blood once on the tour, and at Swansea he was in so much pain from his leg that they had to bring in a couch so that he could lie down. He came alive once he was on stage, though.

'That second tour wasn't well organised, either. He claimed he was being ripped off. I know that Graham Fenton put up the money to fly him over, and presumably Marcia as well, and maybe Sheridan took that money out to repay Graham, so Gene would have got less than he expected. Again gigs were being cancelled or rearranged, and again I felt sorry for him. Here was my idol getting very poor gigs, probably not much money, and just one rehearsal at the King's Head in Colliers Wood.

'Yet he still never really lost his temper. Even the last gig, at the Seagull in Northolt, when he was demanding his money, he was annoyed but he wasn't bursting any blood vessels. He was just resigned. He started having a go at Sheridan about his money. I remember that he sent Marcia out of the room. I've always been sorry that this was my last memory of Gene.

'We did a session for B&C Records, "Say Mama" and "I'm Movin' On". For a compilation album, it turned out. This was an indication of his desperation to earn a little money. I think he was paid a flat fee of around £200. His voice was totally shot that evening, but he didn't seem to care. It was just a case of go in, do the business, collect the money and get out.'

After the recording the musicians, together with publicists Roger St Pierre and Waxie Maxie, repaired to a Soho pub. 'Vincent felt that he had missed out somewhere along the line,' remembers St Pierre. 'He thought that with the right management he could have been as big as Elvis. He was still living the part of the wild rocker, though. Leather trousers and all that. Sadly, I think that the thing I remember most about him was that his leg smelled bad. It was literally rotting away.' Indeed, by this time Vincent's lower left leg had shrunk to little more than blackened skin and bone.

Back on the road, and the legendary jazz and blues pub on Green Lanes in Wood Green, north London, the Fishmongers. It was here that Vincent was served with a court order for non-payment of child maintenance owed to Margie. The caravan moved on to Swansea, to Kingston in Surrey where the demand for back tax greeted him, and so to Chelmsford.

'The gig was at the Magnet, a kind of youth centre out of town,' says Clemson. 'It was an all-dayer. Screaming Lord Sutch was on the bill. After Gene had done his set the promoter asked what time he'd be doing his second show. But Gene only ever did one set, he was exhausted after it. This was explained to the promoter, but he was adamant. "All the artists that play here do two sets." In the end Gene went on again and we just repeated the first set. He did it without arguing, just to make sure he got paid.

'And so the desperation angle comes into it once again. Once upon a time Gene might have told the promoter where to stick his second set, but I guess work was drying up for him in most places and he couldn't pick and choose any more. He just wanted to sing and earn what he could. Countless times I am sure he could really have lost his temper, but he didn't. He just made the best of it. And maybe with Marcia around he was a little embarrassed that things weren't going as well as he would have liked.

'I felt that Marcia didn't really like the band. Maybe she thought he was too good for all this, too big a star. But he wasn't, unfortunately. She thought he was worthy of better things. Well, so did we, of course, but to her we were just part of this badly organised mess.' By the time they reached Northolt it had clearly dawned on Vincent that this tour had not exactly been a money-spinner, and he left from Heathrow on 10 February.

In Graham Fenton's recollection the money worries referred to by Clemson actually spilled out on to the stage at that last gig. 'Between the songs he made nasty comments about being ripped off. He'd had a bit too much to drink and said something nasty about Sheridan. Then a scuffle broke out in the wings because some bouncer wanted to get Gene off stage.'

This accords with Adrian Owlett's recollections. 'That last date was a total mess, and Gene was wrong to take the argument on to the stage. It was a sad end to the tour.'

'The bottom line is that I loved and worshipped the man,' says Clemson. 'I always felt that I wanted things to be better for him, and a better experience for me to look back on. And when he was good, he was *great*. He still had it. It was obvious that he still loved doing it but you could tell – you could see that it was kind of slipping away . . .'

Indeed, Vincent's health now seemed to be in free fall – not just vomiting, but vomiting blood from his complaining and painful ulcer. The drink he absorbed to dull the pain of his withered leg, and the irritant painkillers he was sluicing down as part of his strict Martini diet, had wrecked his gut.

In March Vincent was interviewed by the underground magazine *International Times*. He credited Carl Perkins with being the first ever rockabilly artist, and embroidered a tale about how he missed his opportunity to appear on the all-powerful *Ed Sullivan Show* when he first started out. 'Perkins was on his way to do the *Ed Sullivan Show* when he hit a tractor and wrecked his back. So they said to themselves: who can we get to take his place? Well, they said that there was this boy Elvis Presley and there's one called Gene Vincent. But I was in the hospital at the time and Presley did it.'

Fifteen years on, this idea that he had missed his big break clearly still rankled, even though he denied it. Asked if he ever wondered what might have happened if he had been on the show, he said: 'No, not really. I'm a singer. Listen, I never meant to make money. I never wanted it . . . But all of a sudden I was getting $1500 a night. And you take a nineteen-year-old boy and put him in those circumstances – I had a Cadillac and all. It was a bad scene. It shouldn't have happened on that first record.'

But money was indeed on his mind. 'Hey, everybody was making money 'cept me. When I was 28 I got a letter from the Government saying I was a millionaire. I wish to hell they would have told somebody else about it – like me, I never knew about it. I never had that money . . . But I don't care. I just don't care.'

He then embarked on another fantasy. 'Before I went to England in 1960 I played in Europe. [This is almost true so far – after his UK debut at the Tooting Granada he did play Paris and American bases in Germany, but the story then lurches further from reality]. I went to Hamburg and met a group there. I was very impressed with them. We met and talked a lot – that was at the Star Club. They were really good. Now they're called John Lennon and the Beatles. They didn't have a record out or nothing. God, I could have picked them up so cheaply – which was so foolish of me. But, like I said, I'm a singer, not a bloody businessman.' John Lennon did indeed meet his hero in Hamburg, and as we know the Beatles did back him once, but there was never any suggestion that the summit of the Beatles' ambition was to be Vincent's backing band. And, anyway, the incident happened on a later visit.

Vincent returned to Marcia, her children and Simi Valley, gigging locally and drinking copiously with another hero-worshipper, Jim Morrison of the Doors. Then Kama Sutra, having got to hear about the cash-in-hand B&C recording in London, threw him off the label.

Just before departing for the UK for his last tour, Vincent was tracked down by Ronnie Weiser, of Rollin' Rock Records. He agreed to record four vocal tracks, and sang them into Weiser's portable tape recorder. They were Buddy Knox's 'Party Doll', his own 'The Rose of Love', Sam Cooke's 'Bring It On Home To Me' and Little Richard's 'Hey Hey Hey Hey'.

So in September he was back in the UK. 'He was in a very confused state,' remembers Adrian Owlett. 'He referred to those Rollin' Rock tracks but said they were for Capitol, who had cancelled his contract years before. He looked dreadful.'

Vincent had travelled with his new road manager and guitarist Richard Cole, and rehearsed with Birmingham-based band Kansas Hook – keyboard player Dave Bailey, bassist Charlie Harrison and drummer Bob Moore. But he was in no shape to work. The first week, in a club at Leigh in Lancashire, was quickly cancelled when his voice went, as was the second booking, at the Wookey Hole Club in Liverpool.

Vincent returned to London and on 1 October went into the BBC's Maida Vale studio with Kansas Hook to tape a contribution to Johnnie Walker's Radio 1 show. They recorded 'Be Bop a Lula', 'Say Mama', 'Roll Over Beethoven', 'Whole Lotta Shakin' Goin' On' and, at Vincent's last-minute insistence, Jim Reeves's 1966 hit 'Distant Drums'. 'We actually recorded it as we rehearsed it,' says Bailey. 'As we did the run-through so they taped it, so we only ever played that song once.'

The song was, in fact, omitted from Walker's programme, but three of the cuts, 'Be Bop a Lula', 'Say Mama' and 'Roll Over Beethoven' were chosen to be BEEB1, the first release on the new BBC record label launched three years later.

Meanwhile, Margie was still chasing the maintenance payments she was due. 'A pop singer's ex-wife "living on bread line"' reported the London *Evening Standard*. 'A bench warrant for the arrest of American pop singer Gene Vincent was issued by a High Court judge today after his ex-wife, Margaret, had complained that he owed £605 maintenance arrears for herself and her eight-year-old daughter Sherri.'

Margie's counsel James Townend, painting a picture of a high-earning entertainer and a woman on state benefits, also referred to a judgement six years earlier that had awarded her £925, which had not been paid. This first amount was awarded following their separation. Vincent was served with the summons when he arrived at London Airport on 15 September 1971 but he was not in court, hence the application for him to be arrested. But he did eventually turn up brandishing a note from an official at Manchester Airport confirming that his flight to London had been delayed by fog.

Since she had been separated from him when she was still a baby, Sherri Ann had no early memories of her father. But during this last tour, while he was staying in London, Vincent expressed a wish to see her. Her recollections of that day remain vivid.

'My one and only memory of seeing my father was when I met him two weeks before he died. My mother and father had earlier met in the High Court in London regarding the non-payment of child maintenance and he asked to see me. I came home from school and my mother said, "Your father's in England and he'd like to meet you – would you like to see him?" I of course said yes, and remember asking my mother if I could wear my favourite party dress, as this was a special occasion, to which she agreed. So, wearing my best dress, a new pair of socks and black patent shoes, my mother and I took a taxi to see my father, who was staying at the Carnarvon Hotel on Ealing Broadway. I remember being so excited about the whole thing – the fact that we got a taxi was unusual in itself, as we were at the time living on welfare benefit and therefore had very little money.

'When we arrived at the hotel, we were met by a man who I now know was Richard Cole, although I didn't know who he was at the time. He was a Bohemian, hippie-looking guy. I instinctively knew that he wasn't my father, though, and yet didn't really know what my father looked like, so I wasn't sure what I expected to find.

'Richard Cole led my mother and me into a private lounge of the hotel, where I first saw my father, who was standing before a very large fireplace, and upon seeing him I immediately knew it was him. We hugged each other and said hello. There was a conversation between him and my mother which I can't really recall, after which he asked me if I'd like to take a walk around the garden with him. We went through the French doors of the lounge into what was a rose garden.

'We walked around the garden with him holding my hand and he asked me questions about my childhood, school, friends and so on, and then he sat down on a wooden bench and sat me on his lap. He told me how sorry and sad he was to not have been a part of my life – I still get upset when I think about it – and how he hoped that as of that day, we would get to know each other and begin to build a relationship. We both cried and cuddled each other and made a promise to each other to stay in touch.

'He said he would keep in contact by telephone and would arrange for my mother and me to travel to the States. I think the overriding memory I have, which is heightened by time and perspective, is the responsibility I felt for maintaining a relationship with my father and the personal undertaking I made to keep in touch with him. I told him, "I'll make sure that Mummy lets me phone you." He said that he loved me and had always loved me. It was really a conversation about past regret. And of what the future could or might hold. He told me he was returning to America in the next few days but that we would renew our relationship from that day on.

'We returned to the hotel lounge where my mother and Richard Cole were waiting, and then he asked me if I would like to go out to dinner. I said yes and he asked, "Would you like to go with me alone or would you like Mummy to come?" I remember feeling immediately anxious at the thought of being separated from my mother and being with him alone, fearful that he would not return me to her, so I said, "No, I want Mummy to come with me." He said that was fine, and so the four of us got a taxi to Chiswick High Road and we went to a Wimpy Bar. I remember ordering a Knickerbocker Glory – a big ice-cream sundae – because that was something we could never afford. We'd go shopping down the High Road on a Saturday and I would always ask my mother if I could have a Knickerbocker Glory, and the answer was always that we couldn't afford it. But my father said I could have anything I wanted. In my excitement I only ate the cherry and a couple of spoonfuls of ice cream.

'In the Wimpy Bar my father gave me a photograph of himself, which he signed: "To Sherri, I love you. I hope to see you one day again soon. Love, Gene Vincent." And then at the bottom he wrote: "Love, Daddy Gene." Then he put us into a taxi and my mother and I returned home, two or three miles up the road, and that was the last I saw of him. I had all these hopes and dreams of having found my father, and that we would have this relationship, but ten days later I woke up to be told by my mother that he had died in America.

'I remember feeling devastated, thinking that's the end of that then, after all these promises we'd made to each other. My mother asked me if I wanted to go to school and I said that I did. I didn't cry until it was playtime and as I was going out of the classroom, my teacher, Mrs O'Donald, said: "What's wrong with you, Sherri? You've not been yourself." I burst into tears, and told her that my father had died that morning. She put her arms around me and said she was sorry and explained that we all have to die sometime, accepting that it was nevertheless all very sad. As she comforted me, I remember feeling a fraud. How could I cry for someone I didn't know?

'I'd never met death until then and within ten days of my father's death, I learned that my teacher had died as well. She had gone off sick with flu. We were all sent home with a letter addressed to our parents and one of the kids I was walking home with opened their letter, which told of how our teacher had died unexpectedly of pneumonia. It was a very powerful and significant experience for me, as I was faced for the first time with the death of my father, with all the hope and promise of our last meeting together, and then my teacher who had been so supportive in those first hours of learning my father had died.

'When my father arrived in England, my mother took him to court for the non-payment of maintenance, and the judge ordered him to pay £600 within two weeks or go to jail. My mother and him had a sort of peacemaking after the court hearing – they went for a drink and that's when he had said: "I'd like to see Sherri."

'In court he said he was penniless and he was, basically. And so my mother never believed there was any money to claim after his death and she certainly couldn't afford to instruct a lawyer in America. She worked on the assumption that if there was an estate to be shared then she'd hear about it in due course. I have subsequently learned that Jackie Fusco had applied for the administration of his estate a year after my father's death, but in her application she failed to declare that he had any children. However, it seems that Darlene, the mother of my father's first two children, Melody and Vince – Darlene and Gene were never married – learned of the probate and entered her children in the probate proceedings. Jackie Fusco was asked by the Californian Court whether there were any other beneficiaries outside the United States and she categorically replied "No", although she undoubtedly knew of my existence.

'As a consequence the estate was shared out between Jackie, Melody and Vince, a third each. My mother only discovered this in 1980, after she obtained legal advice. The only reason she was able to access advice at the time was because she was a student undertaking a placement within a law centre as part of her training to become a Youth and Community Worker. She had been talking to a solicitor about my father and his estate and he had offered to make some enquiries on her behalf free of charge. That was the first time, 1980, when we had sight of how the estate was distributed. There it was in black-and-white, that the three of them were in receipt of the probate.

'There had been about $50,000 in capital or cash. It has since been suggested that when he died he owned two – possibly as many as five

– properties, which she [Jackie] may have sold before the probate. The long and short of it is that for the past 32 years the three of them have benefited, a third each, from my father's estate. They have between them, over the years, received a substantial income from the royalties, and yet never done anything to promote his life and music. Essentially, they have taken the money and yet neglected to manage the estate in any positive sense.

'I've made repeated attempts over the years to get myself recognised as the rightful heir to my father's estate, but due to the geographical distance and a lack of money, I had until now been unsuccessful. I went to see a solicitor in 1990 and gave him all the documentation I had in my possession that evidenced my legitimacy and heirship. At that time I had just qualified as a social worker and for the first time I had a little money of my own. I was advised that I certainly had a case but due to the statute of limitations I would need to instruct a lawyer who specialised in Californian state law. And so once again, I didn't really have the wherewithal to pursue a claim at the time. I was left feeling that I needed to get on with my own life, believing that my destiny was to make my own way in the world. I tried to let it go, believing perhaps any money from my father's estate was not intended to bring happiness.

'Then about two years ago I got familiar with the Internet and discovered a number of Gene Vincent websites. One night I was sitting at home exploring the Internet when I came across a web page, which featured a piece written by my father's younger sister, Donna – also known as Piper – and I managed to get hold of her email address. This was a very exciting time for me because it was the first time ever that I was about to get in touch with a member of my family. I sent Donna an email and within ten minutes I had a reply. She immediately recognised who I was. "You're Margaret's daughter," and half an hour later we were talking on the phone.

'She happily acknowledged me as her niece, and then she told me about Melody and Vince, which was not particularly positive. However, I was not put off and said that they were still my brother and sister and I was keen to get in touch with them. Donna gave me Melody's phone number, although she hadn't spoken to her for a long time, and it was evident from this conversation that there was incredible dysfunction, conflict and paranoia within the whole family, so I wondered what I was getting myself into.

'I contacted Melody out of the blue in October 2001 and I said: "Hi, this is your sister Sherri, your half-sister in England." We got talking and at no time did she challenge my claim to being my father's daughter.

In the course of the conversation I asked her what she did for a living and she said: "God, nothing, I've never had a job, I live off the inheritance of my father."

'I was more than surprised to learn of this as I had understood there was little or no money, and particularly all these years later. I said: "Really? Well, forgive me for asking, but how much is it, as I am sure you know that I don't receive a penny?" I explained to Melody that while I didn't resent her and Vince as beneficiaries, I did more than resent Jackie for knowingly excluding me from the probate proceedings.

'Melody told me she was receiving in the region of $30,000 a year. I told her that in view of what she had said I might look again as to whether I could make a claim on my father's estate. Her response was one of encouragement, suggesting I should get a lawyer. It was following my conversation with Melody that I started trawling the Internet looking for a Californian lawyer. I contacted three lawyers and one actually went to the Superior Court of California and pulled the probate file, but he wasn't familiar with the music business and didn't appear to quite understand the nuances of the case.

'At that point my mother read an article in the *Observer* about the estate of Jimi Hendrix, and it quoted a lawyer who had represented the Hendrix estate. So I got in touch with him by email and after lengthy negotiations I convinced him to take on my case. Upon receiving the documentary evidence I had in my possession, I was told I had a strong case, but that the statute of limitation could be a difficulty. He suggested a phased approach, and that it would cost me five thousand dollars to start with.

'I said I just couldn't do it. What money I did have, I'd worked bloody hard for and I couldn't throw it away on something that might not even exist. I asked about a "no win, no fee" arrangement. He said this would only be considered where there was sufficient evidence they would win. Well, I thought we could win, and the more documentation I sent, the more they were convinced of my case.

'Within twelve months the lawyers had got me into the Superior Court and Federal Court of California. We then had to find Jackie. Melody was suddenly evasive. For all she had said, when it came to the crunch she wasn't into giving anything away. Vince was served with my petition – he was in jail at the time. Lawyers came over to see me in July 2003, and they took a deposition from my mother's British divorce lawyer. I was strongly advised to attend a settlement conference in Los Angeles, and with 24 hours notice I left for Los Angeles. My lawyers were of the view that if anyone could argue my case effectively, it was me. I arrived in LA late in the evening on 17 July and the following morning I was sat before Jackie and Vince and their respective lawyers. Melody participated by telephone link. We sat for eleven hours in the mediation conference trying to achieve a settlement.

'A consent judgement was made by the Superior Court of California on 29 September 2003, in which I was declared the daughter and offspring and lawful heir of Gene Vincent. I have many plans for the future management of my father's estate and in realising these I hope to bring positive meaning to his life and music. Historically, the Gene Vincent estate has been left in a state of neglect, but that is all about to change – and I intend to tell my own story in the days to come, which I hope will serve to set the record straight.'

Dogged by terminally failing health and the British courts, Vincent was now in his final decline. He left London in disarray and despair, which deepened when he arrived home to find that Marcia had left him. 'Momma,' he said in a phone call to his parents' home, 'she took everything I had, even my record player.'

His parents were driven to Simi Valley and found him in terrible shape. They pleaded with him to check into hospital but he refused. The next day he was drunk and tearful. 'If I get through this I'll be a better man,' he famously promised. Kie and Louise took him to their trailer on Hacienda Mobile Home Court in Saugus, California, and as soon as he arrived he tripped and fell to his knees. As his mother cradled him he vomited blood, and his last words were, 'Momma, you can phone the ambulance now.' He died within the hour.

Three days later he was buried at the Eternal Valley Memorial Park. The funeral ceremony was chaotic and emotional. 'Typical Gene,' thought Johnny Meeks, who was a pallbearer. 'He can't even die right.' On the gravestone his death is recorded as being on 12 October 1971, and his name as Vincent Eugene Craddock. History records him as Eugene Vincent, however. In 2003 Sherri visited the grave, and found that it was just yards from a busy highway.

After Vincent's death the *People* rated the story of married life with him highly enough to run it over three weeks, beginning on Sunday 28 November 1971. 'Heaven and Hell!' was the first headline, with the strap: 'My violent life with a pop idol, by the cabaret girl who married Gene Vincent'.

The confessional style of ghosted tabloid memoirs has not changed much over the years. Margie was made to say: 'I've always had a weakness for a good-looking bloke with a smooth line in chat. Nothing unusual in that. But if only I had known the trouble it would land me in!' She referred to the 'tempestuous rock singer and marathon drinker' as someone who had died without ever really growing up. They had parted seven years earlier after 'fifteen catastrophic months'. Margie described their first meeting, in 1962, with Vincent 'already drunk', although she stressed his gentlemanly behaviour and how he courteously walked her home. 'I went to bed alone,' she says.

Their romance developed at the end of Vincent's tour, in spite of his nightly habit of sitting up late with friends and a bottle. Margie said that she went to Hamburg and on around Europe with Vincent, who she recalled was being paid £1,500 a week, an indication of his continuing box-office power. It was in Hamburg that his violent side first became apparent to her. They were drinking in a club after his performance when he staggered off into the night. She searched for him but when she returned to their hotel he was waiting, 'drunk and vicious'. 'He grabbed me, held both my wrists with one hand and slapped me around the face with the other.'

Vincent was contrite, a pattern that was to become familiar, and they moved on to a month-long sweep around Italy with Sounds Incorporated. He was always complaining about not being paid – also familiar. At this time, though, Margie insisted that he was indeed being paid but that he immediately spent it, too drunk to remember. There are echoes here of W.C. Fields in *The Bank Dick*, asking the barman in the Black Pussy Cat Café if he'd been in there the previous night with a ten-dollar bill. Assured that he had been he is hugely relieved, because he'd been afraid that he might have lost it.

At this point in her *People* story Margie referred to the two ways in which Vincent exploited his bad leg – he could wriggle out of potentially dangerous situations provoked by his bad behaviour by pointing out that he was a cripple, and he sometimes boasted that it was a war wound heroically sustained in Korea. The teaser for Part Two of the story was: 'Our baby is born, but the rows become a way of life. I call the police after Gene produced a gun.'

On the following Sunday the headline screamed, 'The Night He Threatened To Kill Us All'. After their marriage, Margie said, they celebrated in familiar Vincent style by going to the nearest pub. Then it was back to Hamburg. Vincent beat her up, Margie returned to Welling – and the Lewisham Hospital, fearful of a miscarriage – and Vincent apologised. Whereas Jack Good had referred to his 'Jekyll and Hyde' character as being the contrast between the softly spoken man off stage and the wild rocker on stage, it had a more sinister meaning for Margie.

When Sherri was born they took a holiday in Majorca, and Margie observed: 'I suppose I was so used to the pressures and turmoil of the entertainment business that I was prepared to accept the bizarre as the norm.'

In Paris, always a temple of Vincent worship, she was struck by the welcome of thousands of fans. On their return they bought the Streatham flat, but Vincent's cycle of drinking, violent rage and subsequent contrition was escalating. Margie noted that this had now been going on long enough to alienate promoters, and that his nightly rate of pay was dropping. She told the familiar story that he had taken to drinking from flat half-bottles of whisky, easily concealed and willingly bought by hangers-on, who would be given a five-pound note and told to keep the change.

Margie related the story of him returning early from Ireland and assaulting her, and said that when she persuaded him to see a psychiatrist he apparently convinced the shrink that it was *she* who was deranged. As the teaser for the third instalment says: 'Gene agrees to go into a nursing home for psychiatric treatment . . . and I agree to give our marriage a final chance.'

'The final heartbreak of Gene Vincent's ex-wife' began with his violent, drunken behaviour on that Christmas Day. The psychiatric treatment failed, and on a conciliatory holiday in the Isle of Wight Vincent stormed out of the hotel and threw her a five-pound note. 'That's the last cent you'll get from me.'

The marriage was now over, and Vincent offered Margie £20 a week in return for dropping the summons for assault. She agreed to the deal but the payments stopped when he next left the country. On the following trip to the UK she discovered that he was booked into his hotel with a 'Mrs Vincent', and he refused to give her any more money, the basis for the court summons seeking arrears of maintenance.

Of the Wimpy Bar visit Margie said that 'the change in him was shattering . . . He was fatter and looked debauched.' She noted that when he signed the photo for Sherri he first wrote 'Gene Vincent' – 'just as if she were any teenage fan', although as we know he did also sign it 'Daddy Gene'.

IN MEMORIAM
In 1998 Vincent was inducted into the Rock'n'roll Hall of Fame in Cleveland, Ohio. John Fogerty, a lifelong fan of Vincent and the Blue Caps, sang a verse of 'Be Bop a Lula' a cappella and said: 'It doesn't get much better than that – I do believe that this record is probably one of the greatest ever made.'

In 1999 former Blue Caps Grady Owen and Willie Williams died. Williams, then aged 63, met his death in a tragic accident. He and a friend were preparing to go to a shooting range when he reached into his car for the bag containing his gun, a .38 revolver. Somehow it went off, the bullet hit him and he died on the way to hospital. Then in 2000 Vincent's sister Evelyn, married name Butler, died of lung disease in New Mexico. In 2001, after years of heart trouble, Jerry Lee Merritt died aged 67.

Guitar legend Jeff Beck is still in awe of his hero. 'I didn't get into Presley much,' he says, 'because he was too perfect. But Gene wasn't. There was an ugliness about him, and he played ugly rock'n'roll, that's what I liked. He was pure rebellion, the first punk. And the Blue Caps just twisted my head, what Gallup could do on guitar. I first saw him at the Kingston Granada. It was scary, like watching a murder on stage. The album pictures just didn't prepare us for what he was like. I felt that any minute I might get a bullet in my head. And I didn't care!'

It is the unique collision of image and voice that keeps Vincent in the pantheon of the greats more than thirty years after his death and closer to half a century after he did his finest work. It is the negatives that are more easily put aside – the often shoddy recordings of the 1960s, the forgettable pap that caution sometimes forced on him even at his peak, the graceless behaviour towards so many people, even those with his best interests at heart, the morose and paranoid drunkenness, the violence.

What lives on and rises above all this is the dramatic, razor-cheeked face framed in the upturned collar, the charismatic, demonic stage persona that no one could dare to follow, the soaring voice and maybe a double-album's-worth of some of the most exciting music ever recorded. That is a mighty epitaph.

And if anyone suggests that Vincent's music has passed its sell-by date, nobody told the hundreds of faithful fans who jammed into the Ace Café in north London on Saturday 7 February 2004 for the third Gene Vincent Tribute Evening. Giant motorbikes and lovingly polished rocker cars covered the tarmac outside, Jeff Beck held court at the bar, flying the flag for his hero, the Wild Wax Show disco belted out Vincent classics – more on vinyl than CD, of course – Steve Aynsley talked about perhaps reviving his Gene Vincent magazine, maybe via the Internet, and Sherri Vincent was greeting everyone.

Pint in hand, Adrian Owlett insisted that the finest reincarnation of Vincent was the French group Ervin Travis and the Virginians, and as a veteran of over a hundred gigs by the great original his opinion carries weight. But I stayed faithful to the stars of the musical *Race with the Devil*, the Blue Cats Carlo and Steff Edwards, who were at the Ace that night, with Paul C. Maitland as the living embodiment of Gene. 'When Gene left my house for the last time,' Owlett reminisced, 'he left behind a spare leg brace and a hand gun!'

Later on Graham Fenton's band turned in a storming Vincent set. The guitarist Harvey Hinsley is best known for a string of hits with pop-soul group Hot Chocolate, but that night he was pure Cliff Gallup – with perhaps just a touch of Johnny Meeks. Maybe some of the quiffs in the crowd were now dusted with grey, and some of the bopping a touch sedate, but there were plenty of youngsters in the room and they were clearly not just there on sufferance.

'When you listen to the rubbish in the charts today you realise how great Gene Vincent was,' said one. 'How about Eddie Cochran?' I prompted. 'He's my other favourite,' said the lad, right on cue. Rock on, Gene and Eddie.

BIBLIOGRAPHY

Clark, Alan, *Rock and Roll Legends, Number One,* Leap Frog, 1981.

Clarke, Donald (Ed.), *The Penguin Encyclopedia of Popular Music, Second Edition*, Penguin Books, 1998.

Clayson, Alan, *Beat Merchants,* Blandford, 1995.

Collis, John, *Eddie Cochran,* Wise Publications, 1981.

Colman, Stuart, booklet accompanying *The Eddie Cochran 20th Anniversary Album,* 1980.

Colman, Stuart, *They Kept On Rockin',* Blandford, 1982.

Cochran, Bobby with Van Hecke, Susan, *Three Steps to Heaven: The Eddie Cochran Story*, Hal Leonard, 2003.

Encyclopaedia Britannica.

Finnis, Rob and Dunham, Bob, *Gene Vincent and the Blue Caps,* published privately, 1974.

Finnis, Rob, *The Eddie Cochran Story,* Liberty booklet, 1988.

Frame, Pete, *Rock Family Trees,* Omnibus, 1980.

Gambaccini, Paul, Rice, Tim and Rice, Jonathan, *British Hit Albums, Fourth Edition,* Guinness Publishing, 1990.

Gambaccini, Paul, Rice, Tim and Rice, Jonathan, *British Hit Singles, Ninth Edition,* Guinness Publishing, 1993.

Hagarty, Britt, *The Day the World Turned Blue,* Blandford Press, 1984.

Jackson, John A., *Big Beat Heat: Alan Freed and the Early Years of Rock'n'roll,* Schirmer, 1991.

Kaye, Lenny, *Eddie Cochran,* United Artists booklet, 1971.

Larkin, Colin (Ed.), *The Guinness Who's Who of Fifties Music,* Guinness Publishing, 1993.

Leigh, Spencer, *Baby, That Is Rock and Roll: American Pop, 1954–1963,* Finbarr International, 2001.

Mandich, Steven, *Sweet Gene Vincent: The Bitter End,* Orange Syringe Publications, 2002.

May, Chris and Phillips, Tim, *British Beat,* Socion, 1974.

McAleer, Dave, *Encyclopedia of Hits – the 1950s,* Blandford, 1997.

Miller, Jim (Ed.), *The Rolling Stone Illustrated History of Rock'n'roll,* Rolling Stone Press, 1976.

Muir, Eddie and Scott, Tony (Eds.), *Somethin' Else: A Tribute to Eddie Cochran,* Vintage Rock'n'roll Appreciation Society, 1979.

Mundy, Julie and Higham, Darrel, *Don't Forget Me: The Eddie Cochran Story*, Mainstream, 2000.

Rogan, Johnny, *Starmakers and Svengalis: the History of British Pop Management,* Queen Anne Press, 1998.

Van Hecke, Susan, *Race with the Devil: Gene Vincent's Life in the Fast Lane,* St Martin's Press, 2000.

Whitburn, Joel (Compiler), *Top Country & Western Records 1949–1971,* Record Research, 1972.

Whitburn, Joel (Compiler), *Top Rhythm & Blues Records 1949–1971,* Record Research, 1973.

Whitburn, Joel (Compiler), *Top Pop Records 1955–1972,* Record Research, 1973.

NEWSPAPERS, MAGAZINES AND OTHER MEDIA

Sunday People (November–December 1971)

Melody Maker (various)

New Musical Express (various)

Disc (various)

Hit Parade (various)

Now Dig This (various)

Git It! (various)

Gene Vincent and his Blue Caps International Fan Club Magazine (various)

Guitar Player (December 1983)

Sh-Boom (1990)

1960 (Parkfield Pathe video, 1990)

Gene Vincent in Britain (BBC TV video, 1969)

Gene Vincent: Race with the Devil (Radio 2, 7 March 1998)

SOURCES

INTRODUCTION
'There has always been a rock'n'roll scene . . .' (Terry Clemson interviewed by author)

ON THE ROAD
'Payola Probe Sensation . . .' and subsequent quotes (*Melody Maker* as identified)

'His powerful rocking style . . .' (*New Musical Express*)

'I intend to settle down . . .' (*Disc*, 30 May 1959)

'We went down to Heathrow . . .' (Joe Brown on Radio 2's *Gene Vincent: Race with the Devil*, 7 March 1998)

'When I first came face to face . . .' (*Git It!* magazine, 1990)

'He was a quiet, thin, wan fellow . . .' (Jack Good quoted by Spencer Leigh in *Baby, That Is Rock and Roll*)

'I wore . . .' (Joe Brown on Radio 2's *Gene Vincent: Race with the Devil*, 7 March 1998)

'That was some welcome . . .' (interview with Vincent in *NME*)

'I backed him at the Granada . . .' (Hagarty)

'He looked scared . . .' (Jack Good in *Disc and Music Echo*)

'Gene and I . . .' (Marty Wilde quoted by Spencer Leigh)

'I'd been delighted to see . . .' (David Lands interviewed by author)

'I was going into the West End . . .' (Marty Wilde as above)

'I was very impressed . . .' (interview in *Hit Parade*, January 1960)

'I started as a band boy . . .' (Hal Carter interviewed by author)

'Larry Parnes was a very shrewd cookie . . .' (Hal Carter as above)

'It was a very communistic set-up . . .' (Hal Carter as above)

'Eighty per cent of our customers . . .' (Norm Riley interviewed in *Disc*, 27 February 1960)

'A friend called . . .' (Adrian Owlett interviewed by author)

'He looks a very good thing . . .' (Jack Good in *MM*)

'ABC-TV is dropping . . .' (*NME*)

'This is the first . . .' (Jack Good in *NME*)

'I remember one night . . .' (Adrian Owlett interviewed by author)

'There used to be an agent . . .' (Hal Carter interviewed by author)

'There was a pool of . . .' (Georgie Fame quoted in *The Eddie Cochran Connection*)

'The weeklong dates . . .' (Hal Carter interviewed by author)

'When Eddie came over . . .' (Vince Eager in *The Eddie Cochran Connection*)

'When he finished his act . . .' (Marge Miller in *The Eddie Cochran Connection*, issue 7)

'We saw you on TV last night . . .' (uncredited interview on *The Legendary Eddie Cochran* album)

'He taught me a lot . . .' (Brian Bennett quoted by Spencer Leigh)

'The train journeys were horrendous . . .' (Hal Carter interviewed by author)

'Eddie was a genuine guy . . .' (Johnny Gentle quoted by Spencer Leigh)

'He was not demonstrative . . .' (Adrian Owlett as above)

'He had a very strong visual sense . . .' (Jack Good quoted by Spencer Leigh)

'There were no frantic scenes . . .' (unidentified cutting)

'The lasting memory for me . . .' (Alan Sinnett in *The Eddie Cochran Connection*, issue 7)

'When Eddie first came on stage . . .' (Marilyn Guyatt in *The Eddie Cochran Connection*, issue 7)

'Eddie thought Jack was a genius . . .' (Sharon Sheeley interviewed by *NME*, 1960)

'Gene was going down a bomb . . .' (Terry McGill in *The Eddie Cochran Connection*, issue 7)

'Gene was good . . .' (Mike Priestley in *The Eddie Cochran Connection*, issue 7)

'We did sometimes have a bit of fun . . .' (Hal Carter interviewed by author)

'I will not make any comments on Gene Vincent . . .' (Billy Raymond in *The Eddie Cochran Connection*, issue 7)

'I shall always remember meeting . . .' (Carole Commander in Eddie Cochran Weekend brochure)

'His guitar playing was superb . . .' (Mick Jackson in *The Eddie Cochran Connection*, issue 7)

'The show was the best I've ever seen . . .' (John Green in *The Eddie Cochran Connection*)

'probably the only NCO . . .' (Charlie Wills in *The Eddie Cochran Connection*)

'Taunton in February 1960 . . .' (Barry Holley in *The Eddie Cochran Connection*)

'We did a session . . .' (Brian Mathew quoted by Spencer Leigh)

'We were on the train . . .' (Hal Carter interviewed by author)

'Eddie Cochran brought the house down . . .' (John Williams in *The Eddie Cochran Connection*, issue 7)

'We were dancing in the aisles . . .' (James Clark in *The Eddie Cochran Connection*, issue 7)

'Gene Vincent, who was then a well-established performer . . .' (Charlie Robbins in *The Eddie Cochran Connection*, issue 7)

'I cannot recall the support acts . . .' (Paul Barrett in *The Eddie Cochran Connection*, issue 7)

'The only time Eddie was incapable . . .' (Hal Carter interviewed by author)

'Eddie and Gene used to drink . . .' (Big Jim Sullivan quoted by Spencer Leigh)

'I don't think that Eddie . . .' (Mundy and Higham)

'When he first got there . . .' (Mundy and Higham)

'He moved around the stage . . .' (Billy Walker in *The Eddie Cochran Connection*, issue 7)

'We stopped at the traffic lights . . .' (Joe Brown on Radio 2's *Gene Vincent: Race with the Devil*, 7 March 1998)

'Gene was always moaning . . .' (Hal Carter interviewed by author)

'We went into the front room . . .' (Rita Peachey in *The Eddie Cochran Connection*, issue 7)

'The crash had taken quite a toll . . .' (Keith Powell in *The Eddie Cochran Connection*, issue 7)

'The curtains opened on a darkened stage . . .' (Jim Newcombe writing in fanzine *The Rock*, October 1971, reprinted in *Somethin' Else* by Eddie Muir and Tony Scott)

'Eddie was great . . .' (John Peel on Radio 2's *Gene Vincent: Race with the Devil*, 7 March 1998)

'Joe Brown was near the beginning . . .' (Ann Matthews in *The Eddie Cochran Connection*, issue 11)

'I have never known . . .' and subsequent quotes (Jack Good in *Disc*)

'Cochran was obsessed . . .' (Arnold Burlin in *The Eddie Cochran Connection*, issue unknown)

'Only Eddie and I . . .' (Joe Brown quoted by Spencer Leigh)

'You can't keep poking it . . .' (Joe Brown on Radio 2's *Gene Vincent: Race with the Devil*, 7 March 1998)

'I never saw Eddie . . .' (Jack Good quoted by Spencer Leigh)

'When I get to work . . .' (Gene Vincent in *MM*)

'I was with . . .' (Adrian Owlett, as above)

'When we got back from the club . . .' (Sharon Sheeley interviewed in *NME*, 1960)

'overnight I changed my hairstyle . . .' (Keith Woods in *The Eddie Cochran Connection*)

'Vincent took my breath away . . .' (David Lands interviewed by author)

'He had a piece . . .' (Joe Brown quoted by Spencer Leigh)

'We actually saw Eddie . . .' (Jerry Allison interviewed by Barry Holley for BBC Radio York, 12 April 1997)

'The stage was dark . . .' (Edward John Penny in *The Eddie Cochran Connection*, issue 7)

'I remember him talking . . .' (Terry Clemson interviewed by author)

'Sharon was besotted . . .' (Hal Carter interviewed by author)

'Eddie asked me . . .' (Johnny Gentle quoted by Spencer Leigh)

'I finished the Vincent–Cochran tour . . .' (Hal Carter interviewed by author)

'We were all packing up . . .' (Billy Raymond in *The Eddie Cochran Connection*, issue 7)

'After the show was over . . .' (Pete Purnell in *The Eddie Cochran Connection*, issue 7)

'It was Eddie . . .' (Pete Williams in *The Eddie Cochran Connection*, issue 7)

'They were meant to go . . .' (Hal Carter interviewed by author)

'I was supposed to pick up some suits . . .' (Gene Vincent interview clip on Radio 2's *Gene Vincent: Race with the Devil*, 7 March 1998)

'When the three of us travelled together . . .' (source unknown)

'Usually I got in first . . .' (Vincent interviewed in *International Times*, March 1971)

'The doctor told me . . .' (Vince Eager in *The Eddie Cochran Connection*, issue unknown)

'I suppose I was in a daze . . .' (unidentified cutting)

'I knew he would die . . .' (Sharon Sheeley interviewed in *NME*, 1960)

'Eddie had a fabulous stage act . . .' (Marty Wilde quoted by Spencer Leigh)

'I rate Eddie Cochran very highly . . .' (Joe Brown quoted by Spencer Leigh)

'He was a guitarist . . .' (Big Jim Sullivan in sleeve note to Rockstar's *Rock 'n' Roll Memories*)

'The thing about Eddie . . .' (Vince Eager, as above)

'Eddie was a wonderful guitarist . . .' (Georgie Fame quoted by Spencer Leigh)

'The original tour was tiring . . .' (Billy Raymond in *The Eddie Cochran Connection*, issue 3)

'I am thinking now . . .' (Gene Vincent in *MM*)

'It's just the sort of stunt . . .' (Sherri Vincent interviewed by author)

'It was him . . .' (Adrian Owlett interviewed by author)

'I honestly don't know . . .' (Norm Riley in *MM*)
'I am not taking . . .' (Larry Parnes in *MM*)
'When he received . . .' (Billy Raymond in *MM*)

GENE VINCENT: PROLOGUE

'My teacher in high school . . .' (interview in *Disc*, 30 May 1959)
'I still use the old guitar . . .' (as above)
'We started a [talent] show . . .' (Bill Davis talking to Steve Aynsley in *Git It!* magazine)
'I was in the control room . . .' (Gene Vincent website)
'I was in the Naval Hospital . . .' (Vincent interviewed in *International Times*, March 1971)
'I put on a record . . .' (Bill Davis as above)
'I went down to the station . . .' (Dickie Harrell on Radio 2's *Gene Vincent: Race with the Devil*, 7 March 1998)
'They said, "Shit, we'll do it . . ."' (Bill Davis as above)
'Gene was very likeable . . .' (Hagarty)
'All the chicks . . .' (Hagarty)
'He had something special . . .' (Hagarty)
'I put on a record . . .' (Aynsley)
'What was the one . . .' (Aynsley)
'I think [Gene] found it . . .' (Finnis and Dunham)
'There was tragic mishandling . . .' (Finnis and Dunham)
'I never meant to make money . . .' (Hagarty)
'He seemed pretty serious . . .' (Hagarty)
'I was looking at a picture . . .' (Hagarty)
'He was easy to work with . . .' (Finnis and Dunham)
'Get me into this . . .' (Bill Mack interviewed by the Norfolk *Morning Star*, 1998)
'When you go to a lounge show . . .' (Dickie Harrell on Radio 2's *Gene Vincent: Race with the Devil*, 7 March 1998)
'Elvis had the Jordanaires . . .' (Tommy 'Bubba' Facenda on Radio 2's *Gene Vincent: Race with the Devil*, 7 March 1998)
'At the bridge . . .' (Bubba Facenda quoted by Spencer Leigh)
'I wasn't sore at all . . .' (Hagerty)
'I think Sanford Clark . . .' (Finnis and Dunham)
'One week we might be . . .' (Finnis and Dunham)
'We were on a school-type bus . . .' (Hagarty)
'I was able to learn to fake it . . .' (Finnis and Dunham)
'The Hollywood studio . . .' (Finnis and Dunham)
'We all loved Vincent . . .' (Finnis and Dunham)

'I decided . . .' (Finnis and Dunham)

'I missed it . . .' (Finnis and Dunham)

'I had worked with [Gene] . . .' (Jerry Lee Merritt in Radio 2's *Gene Vincent: Race with the Devil*, 7 March 1998)

'Gene would say . . .' (Interview by Bob Erskine)

'If I can carry on making a go of it . . .' (*Hit Parade*, January 1960)

EDDIE COCHRAN: PROLOGUE

'Eddie was an extraordinarily fast draw . . .' (Phil Everly quoted in *The Eddie Cochran Connection*)

'I grew up in the wonderful natural scenery . . .' (unidentified cutting)

'Eddie just mainly played guitar . . .' (Glen Glenn interviewed by Alan Clark in *Rock and Roll Heroes*)

'I was born . . .' (Jerry Capehart interviewed by Tony Barrett)

'The first time I met Eddie . . .' (Don Deal in *The Eddie Cochran Connection*, issue 9)

'When Eddie died . . .' (Glen Glenn interviewed by Alan Clark in *Rock and Roll Heroes*)

'This stuff is simple . . .' (Eddie Cochran quoted in *Guitar Player*)

'Eddie really thought of himself . . .' (Sharon Sheeley as above)

'Eddie was able to mix it . . .' (Phil Everly as above)

'get his wrist . . .' (Mike Deasy as above)

'Eddie was one of the few guys . . .' (Dave Shrieber as above)

'He was not a performer . . .' (Mundy and Higham)

'The Cochrans performed . . .' (Jerry Capehart interviewed by Tony Barrett)

'Nothing against rock'n'roll . . .' (Mundy and Higham)

'To get the Liberty contract . . .' (Jerry Capehart interviewed by Tony Barrett)

'Si Waronker . . .' (Jerry Capehart as above)

'Bobby Troup and Julie London . . .' (Nelda Fairchild in *The Eddie Cochran Connection*, issue 10)

'He was several inches shorter than me . . .' (John Rook website)

'It was a hit . . .' (Jerry Capehart interviewed by Tony Barrett)

'Eddie and I seemed to hit it off . . .' (Charlie Gracie quoted in *The Eddie Cochran Connection*)

'Waronker's perception of Eddie . . .' (Rob Finnis's notes to *The Eddie Cochran Story*)

'We got a lot of "bus time" . . .' (Jerry Allison interviewed by Trevor Cajaio for *Now Dig This*, October 1998)

'I had driven the three hundred miles to Denver . . .' (Freeman B Hover interviewed by George Nettleton in *Rockin' 50s*, 2001, reprinted in *The Eddie Cochran Connection*, issue 11)

' "Summertime Blues" . . .' (Jerry Capehart interviewed by Tony Barrett)

'I didn't really care for the song . . .' (Ricky Nelson quoted in the booklet accompanying the 2000 box set *Legacy*)

'I thought Eddie's guitar playing . . .' (Troyce Key quoted by Alan Clark)

'Connie was probably . . .' (Glen Glenn interviewed by Alan Clark in *Rock and Roll Legends*)

'The guy I worked with . . .' (Dick D'Agostin in *The Eddie Cochran Connection*, issue 8)

'Eddie could pull . . .' (Munday and Higham)

'He was just a real nice kid . . .' (Plas Johnson quoted by Alan Clark)

'the kind of musical direction . . .' (Sharon Sheeley quoted in *Guitar Player*, October 1983)

'if it weren't for Ed . . .' (Bobby Cochran and Susan Van Hecke)

'The Crickets were about to be signed . . .' (Jerry Allison interviewed by Trevor Cajaio for *Now Dig This*, October 1998)

'Eddie was really under the gun . . .' (Mundy and Higham)

'I don't think his bed . . .' (Glen Glenn interviewed by Alan Clark in *Rock and Roll Legends*)

EDDIE COCHRAN: EPILOGUE

'He had made up his mind . . .' (Jack Good quoted by Spencer Leigh)

'Later on he got himself . . .' (Ronnie Hawkins quoted by Spencer Leigh)

'We had a man . . .' (Vincent interviewed in *International Times*, March 1971)

'We are trying to meet a tremendous demand . . .' (*Disc*, 8 July 1961)

GENE VINCENT: EPILOGUE

'Since Gene went back to America . . .' (interview with Mike Bartlett in *Hit Parade*)

'I hope this hoax telegram affair . . .' (Cliff Richard quoted in *Hit Parade*)

'Don Arden was quite reasonable . . .' (Margie interviewed by author)

'Arden made Gene Vincent . . .' (Adrian Owlett interviewed by author)

'I'd just had enough . . .' (Hagarty)

'As I understood it . . .' (Dick Thomas interviewed by author)

'We were playing semi-pro . . .' (Alan Holmes interviewed by author)

'We met Gene . . .' (Dick Thomas interviewed by author)

'Gene was very polite to us . . .' (Alan Holmes interviewed by author)

'We used to go . . .' (Joe Brown on Radio 2's *Gene Vincent: Race with the Devil*, 7 March 1998)

'My first impression . . .' (Dick Thomas interviewed by author)

'When he was drunk . . .' (Dick Thomas as above)

'He would drink bottles of Scotch . . .' (Alan Holmes interviewed by author)

'For a couple of months . . .' (Dick Thomas interviewed by author)

'Some people, like Henry Henroid . . .' (Margie, interviewed by author)

'I didn't have to try . . .' (as above)

'I grew up with him . . .' (as above)

'He was due back in America . . .' (as above)

'We went to Italy with him . . .' (Alan Holmes interviewed by author)

'Yes, Italian promoters . . .' (Dick Thomas interviewed by author)

'I'd say Gene was a schizophrenic . . .' (Hagarty)

'Gene was a great entertainer . . .' (Clem Cattini quoted in *Thunderbolt*, the magazine of the Joe Meek Appreciation Society, No. 36, 2002)

'I was pregnant . . .' (Margie interviewed by author)

'The first time he met Cliff Bennett . . .' (Adrian Owlett interviewed by author)

'From the day I met Gene . . .' (Margie interviewed by author)

'It began snowing . . .' (as above)

'I always got the feeling . . .' (Chas Hodges on Vincent 50th birthday tribute edition of Channel 4's *The Tube*)

'Gene Vincent . . . in case you didn't know . . .' (Ian Dury, as above)

'We were in the house . . .' (Margie interviewed by author)

'The reason we were sought after . . .' (Dick Thomas interviewed by author)

'He was a magical performer . . .' (Dick Thomas as above)

'"I was just left in Streatham . . .' (Margie interviewed by author)

'I didn't know for some time . . .' (as above)

'He was totally compartmentalised . . .' (Adrian Owlett interviewed by author)

'We discovered just how big a star . . .' (Des O'Reilly website)

'I think that Don Arden . . .' (Hagarty)

'Kim advanced . . .' (Mandich)

'Gene was a difficult artist . . .' (Hagarty)

'I was familiar with . . .' (as above)

'A lot of stuff . . .' (Mandich)

'When the film was shown . . .' (Bill Kingston interviewed by author)

'His threshold was far greater . . .' (Adrian Owlett interviewed by author)

'There was the Inland Revenue . . .' (as above)

'Wilf and some of his chums . . .' (as above)

'Gene went on . . .' (Hagarty)

'I first saw Gene in 1964 . . .' (Graham Fenton interviewed by author)

'Later on . . .' (as above)

'He never shouted at anyone ...' (Terry Clemson interviewed by the author)

'It was a nightmare ...' (as above)

'Everyone said that ...' (as above)

'Gene used to sneak down ...' (Hagarty)

'I have to admit ...' (Terry Clemson interviewed by author)

'Vincent felt that he had missed out ...' (Roger St Pierre interviewed by author)

'The gig was at the Magnet ...' (Terry Clemson interviewed by author)

'Between the songs he made nasty comments ...' (Hagarty)

'That last date ...' (Adrian Owlett interviewed by author)

'The bottom line is ...' (Terry Clemson interviewed by author)

'He was in a very confused state ...' (Adrian Owlett interviewed by author)

'We actually recorded it ...' (Dave Bailey on liner notes of *The Last Session*)

'Typical Gene ...' (Hagarty)

'I didn't get into Presley much ...' (Jeff Beck interviewed by author)

INDEX